50% OFF
SSAT Upper Level Prep Course!

By Mometrix

Dear Customer,

We consider it an honor and a privilege that you chose our SSAT Upper Level Study Guide. As a way of showing our appreciation and to help us better serve you, we are offering **50% off our online SSAT Upper Level Test Prep Course.** Many SSAT courses are needlessly expensive and don't deliver enough value. With our course, you get access to the best SSAT test prep material, and **you only pay half price.**

We have structured our online course to perfectly complement your printed study guide. The SSAT Upper Level Online Course contains **in-depth lessons** that cover all the most important topics, **150+ video reviews** that explain difficult concepts, over **750 practice questions** to ensure you feel prepared, and more than **200 flashcards** for studying on the go.

Online SSAT Upper Level Test Prep Course

Topics Include:

- Quantitative
  - Arithmetic
  - Algebra
  - Geometry
  - Statistics
- Reading Comprehension
  - Writing Devices
  - Building a Vocabulary
  - Literature
  - Figurative Language
- Verbal
  - Synonyms
  - Analogies

Course Features:

- SSAT Upper Level Study Guide
  - Get content that complements our best-selling study guide.
- Full-Length Practice Tests
  - With over 750 practice questions, you can test yourself again and again.
- Mobile Friendly
  - If you need to study on the go, the course is easily accessible from your mobile device.
- SSAT Flashcards
  - Our course includes a flashcard mode consisting of over 200 content cards to help you study.

To receive this discount, visit our website at <u>mometrix.com/university/ssatu</u> or simply scan this QR code with your smartphone. At the checkout page, enter the discount code: **ssatu50off**

If you have any questions or concerns, please contact us at <u>support@mometrix.com</u>.

FREE Study Skills Videos/DVD Offer

Dear Customer,

Thank you for your purchase from Mometrix! We consider it an honor and a privilege that you have purchased our product and we want to ensure your satisfaction.

As part of our ongoing effort to meet the needs of test takers, we have developed a set of Study Skills Videos that we would like to give you for <u>FREE</u>. These videos cover our *best practices* for getting ready for your exam, from how to use our study materials to how to best prepare for the day of the test.

All that we ask is that you email us with feedback that would describe your experience so far with our product. Good, bad, or indifferent, we want to know what you think!

To get your FREE Study Skills Videos, you can use the **QR code** below, or send us an **email** at <u>studyvideos@mometrix.com</u> with *FREE VIDEOS* in the subject line and the following information in the body of the email:

- The name of the product you purchased.
- Your product rating on a scale of 1-5, with 5 being the highest rating.
- Your feedback. It can be long, short, or anything in between. We just want to know your impressions and experience so far with our product. (Good feedback might include how our study material met your needs and ways we might be able to make it even better. You could highlight features that you found helpful or features that you think we should add.)

If you have any questions or concerns, please don't hesitate to contact me directly.

Thanks again!

Sincerely,

Jay Willis
Vice President
<u>jay.willis@mometrix.com</u>
1-800-673-8175

SSAT
Upper Level
Prep Book
2022 and 2023

3 Full-Length Practice Tests

Secrets Study Guide with Step-by-Step
Review Video Tutorials

5th Edition

Written and edited by Mometrix Test Prep

Printed in the United States of America

This paper meets the requirements of ANSI/NISO Z39.48-1992 (Permanence of Paper).

Mometrix offers volume discount pricing to institutions. For more information or a price quote, please contact our sales department at sales@mometrix.com or 888-248-1219.

ISBN 13: 978-1-5167-2090-3
ISBN 10: 1-5167-2090-3

DEAR FUTURE EXAM SUCCESS STORY

First of all, **THANK YOU** for purchasing Mometrix study materials!

Second, congratulations! You are one of the few determined test-takers who are committed to doing whatever it takes to excel on your exam. **You have come to the right place.** We developed these study materials with one goal in mind: to deliver you the information you need in a format that's concise and easy to use.

In addition to optimizing your guide for the content of the test, we've outlined our recommended steps for breaking down the preparation process into small, attainable goals so you can make sure you stay on track.

We've also analyzed the entire test-taking process, identifying the most common pitfalls and showing how you can overcome them and be ready for any curveball the test throws you.

Standardized testing is one of the biggest obstacles on your road to success, which only increases the importance of doing well in the high-pressure, high-stakes environment of test day. Your results on this test could have a significant impact on your future, and this guide provides the information and practical advice to help you achieve your full potential on test day.

Your success is our success

We would love to hear from you! If you would like to share the story of your exam success or if you have any questions or comments in regard to our products, please contact us at **800-673-8175** or **support@mometrix.com**.

Thanks again for your business and we wish you continued success!

Sincerely,
The Mometrix Test Preparation Team

Need more help? Check out our flashcards at:
http://mometrixflashcards.com/SSAT

TABLE OF CONTENTS

Introduction

Thank you for purchasing this resource! You have made the choice to prepare yourself for a test that could have a huge impact on your future, and this guide is designed to help you be fully ready for test day. Obviously, it's important to have a solid understanding of the test material, but you also need to be prepared for the unique environment and stressors of the test, so that you can perform to the best of your abilities.

For this purpose, the first section that appears in this guide is the **Secret Keys**. We've devoted countless hours to meticulously researching what works and what doesn't, and we've boiled down our findings to the five most impactful steps you can take to improve your performance on the test. We start at the beginning with study planning and move through the preparation process, all the way to the testing strategies that will help you get the most out of what you know when you're finally sitting in front of the test.

We recommend that you start preparing for your test as far in advance as possible. However, if you've bought this guide as a last-minute study resource and only have a few days before your test, we recommend that you skip over the first two Secret Keys since they address a long-term study plan.

If you struggle with **test anxiety**, we strongly encourage you to check out our recommendations for how you can overcome it. Test anxiety is a formidable foe, but it can be beaten, and we want to make sure you have the tools you need to defeat it.

1

Secret Key #1 – Plan Big, Study Small

There's a lot riding on your performance. If you want to ace this test, you're going to need to keep your skills sharp and the material fresh in your mind. You need a plan that lets you review everything you need to know while still fitting in your schedule. We'll break this strategy down into three categories.

Information Organization

Start with the information you already have: the official test outline. From this, you can make a complete list of all the concepts you need to cover before the test. Organize these concepts into groups that can be studied together, and create a list of any related vocabulary you need to learn so you can brush up on any difficult terms. You'll want to keep this vocabulary list handy once you actually start studying since you may need to add to it along the way.

Time Management

Once you have your set of study concepts, decide how to spread them out over the time you have left before the test. Break your study plan into small, clear goals so you have a manageable task for each day and know exactly what you're doing. Then just focus on one small step at a time. When you manage your time this way, you don't need to spend hours at a time studying. Studying a small block of content for a short period each day helps you retain information better and avoid stressing over how much you have left to do. You can relax knowing that you have a plan to cover everything in time. In order for this strategy to be effective though, you have to start studying early and stick to your schedule. Avoid the exhaustion and futility that comes from last-minute cramming!

Study Environment

The environment you study in has a big impact on your learning. Studying in a coffee shop, while probably more enjoyable, is not likely to be as fruitful as studying in a quiet room. It's important to keep distractions to a minimum. You're only planning to study for a short block of time, so make the most of it. Don't pause to check your phone or get up to find a snack. It's also important to **avoid multitasking**. Research has consistently shown that multitasking will make your studying dramatically less effective. Your study area should also be comfortable and well-lit so you don't have the distraction of straining your eyes or sitting on an uncomfortable chair.

 The time of day you study is also important. You want to be rested and alert. Don't wait until just before bedtime. Study when you'll be most likely to comprehend and remember. Even better, if you know what time of day your test will be, set that time aside for study. That way your brain will be used to working on that subject at that specific time and you'll have a better chance of recalling information.

Finally, it can be helpful to team up with others who are studying for the same test. Your actual studying should be done in as isolated an environment as possible, but the work of organizing the information and setting up the study plan can be divided up. In between study sessions, you can discuss with your teammates the concepts that you're all studying and quiz each other on the details. Just be sure that your teammates are as serious about the test as you are. If you find that your study time is being replaced with social time, you might need to find a new team.

Secret Key #2 – Make Your Studying Count

You're devoting a lot of time and effort to preparing for this test, so you want to be absolutely certain it will pay off. This means doing more than just reading the content and hoping you can remember it on test day. It's important to make every minute of study count. There are two main areas you can focus on to make your studying count.

Retention

It doesn't matter how much time you study if you can't remember the material. You need to make sure you are retaining the concepts. To check your retention of the information you're learning, try recalling it at later times with minimal prompting. Try carrying around flashcards and glance at one or two from time to time or ask a friend who's also studying for the test to quiz you.

To enhance your retention, look for ways to put the information into practice so that you can apply it rather than simply recalling it. If you're using the information in practical ways, it will be much easier to remember. Similarly, it helps to solidify a concept in your mind if you're not only reading it to yourself but also explaining it to someone else. Ask a friend to let you teach them about a concept you're a little shaky on (or speak aloud to an imaginary audience if necessary). As you try to summarize, define, give examples, and answer your friend's questions, you'll understand the concepts better and they will stay with you longer. Finally, step back for a big picture view and ask yourself how each piece of information fits with the whole subject. When you link the different concepts together and see them working together as a whole, it's easier to remember the individual components.

Finally, practice showing your work on any multi-step problems, even if you're just studying. Writing out each step you take to solve a problem will help solidify the process in your mind, and you'll be more likely to remember it during the test.

Modality

Modality simply refers to the means or method by which you study. Choosing a study modality that fits your own individual learning style is crucial. No two people learn best in exactly the same way, so it's important to know your strengths and use them to your advantage.

For example, if you learn best by visualization, focus on visualizing a concept in your mind and draw an image or a diagram. Try color-coding your notes, illustrating them, or creating symbols that will trigger your mind to recall a learned concept. If you learn best by hearing or discussing information, find a study partner who learns the same way or read aloud to yourself. Think about how to put the information in your own words. Imagine that you are giving a lecture on the topic and record yourself so you can listen to it later.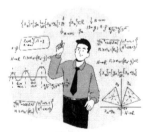

For any learning style, flashcards can be helpful. Organize the information so you can take advantage of spare moments to review. Underline key words or phrases. Use different colors for different categories. Mnemonic devices (such as creating a short list in which every item starts with the same letter) can also help with retention. Find what works best for you and use it to store the information in your mind most effectively and easily.

3

Secret Key #3 – Practice the Right Way

Your success on test day depends not only on how many hours you put into preparing, but also on whether you prepared the right way. It's good to check along the way to see if your studying is paying off. One of the most effective ways to do this is by taking practice tests to evaluate your progress. Practice tests are useful because they show exactly where you need to improve. Every time you take a practice test, pay special attention to these three groups of questions:

- The questions you got wrong
- The questions you had to guess on, even if you guessed right
- The questions you found difficult or slow to work through

This will show you exactly what your weak areas are, and where you need to devote more study time. Ask yourself why each of these questions gave you trouble. Was it because you didn't understand the material? Was it because you didn't remember the vocabulary? Do you need more repetitions on this type of question to build speed and confidence? Dig into those questions and figure out how you can strengthen your weak areas as you go back to review the material.

 Additionally, many practice tests have a section explaining the answer choices. It can be tempting to read the explanation and think that you now have a good understanding of the concept. However, an explanation likely only covers part of the question's broader context. Even if the explanation makes perfect sense, **go back and investigate** every concept related to the question until you're positive you have a thorough understanding.

As you go along, keep in mind that the practice test is just that: practice. Memorizing these questions and answers will not be very helpful on the actual test because it is unlikely to have any of the same exact questions. If you only know the right answers to the sample questions, you won't be prepared for the real thing. **Study the concepts** until you understand them fully, and then you'll be able to answer any question that shows up on the test.

It's important to wait on the practice tests until you're ready. If you take a test on your first day of study, you may be overwhelmed by the amount of material covered and how much you need to learn. Work up to it gradually.

On test day, you'll need to be prepared for answering questions, managing your time, and using the test-taking strategies you've learned. It's a lot to balance, like a mental marathon that will have a big impact on your future. Like training for a marathon, you'll need to start slowly and work your way up. When test day arrives, you'll be ready.

Start with the strategies you've read in the first two Secret Keys—plan your course and study in the way that works best for you. If you have time, consider using multiple study resources to get different approaches to the same concepts. It can be helpful to see difficult concepts from more than one angle. Then find a good source for practice tests. Many times, the test website will suggest potential study resources or provide sample tests.

Practice Test Strategy

If you're able to find at least three practice tests, we recommend this strategy:

UNTIMED AND OPEN-BOOK PRACTICE

Take the first test with no time constraints and with your notes and study guide handy. Take your time and focus on applying the strategies you've learned.

TIMED AND OPEN-BOOK PRACTICE

Take the second practice test open-book as well, but set a timer and practice pacing yourself to finish in time.

TIMED AND CLOSED-BOOK PRACTICE

Take any other practice tests as if it were test day. Set a timer and put away your study materials. Sit at a table or desk in a quiet room, imagine yourself at the testing center, and answer questions as quickly and accurately as possible.

Keep repeating timed and closed-book tests on a regular basis until you run out of practice tests or it's time for the actual test. Your mind will be ready for the schedule and stress of test day, and you'll be able to focus on recalling the material you've learned.

Secret Key #4 – Pace Yourself

Once you're fully prepared for the material on the test, your biggest challenge on test day will be managing your time. Just knowing that the clock is ticking can make you panic even if you have plenty of time left. Work on pacing yourself so you can build confidence against the time constraints of the exam. Pacing is a difficult skill to master, especially in a high-pressure environment, so **practice is vital**.

Set time expectations for your pace based on how much time is available. For example, if a section has 60 questions and the time limit is 30 minutes, you know you have to average 30 seconds or less per question in order to answer them all. Although 30 seconds is the hard limit, set 25 seconds per question as your goal, so you reserve extra time to spend on harder questions. When you budget extra time for the harder questions, you no longer have any reason to stress when those questions take longer to answer.

Don't let this time expectation distract you from working through the test at a calm, steady pace, but keep it in mind so you don't spend too much time on any one question. Recognize that taking extra time on one question you don't understand may keep you from answering two that you do understand later in the test. If your time limit for a question is up and you're still not sure of the answer, mark it and move on, and come back to it later if the time and the test format allow. If the testing format doesn't allow you to return to earlier questions, just make an educated guess; then put it out of your mind and move on.

On the easier questions, be careful not to rush. It may seem wise to hurry through them so you have more time for the challenging ones, but it's not worth missing one if you know the concept and just didn't take the time to read the question fully. Work efficiently but make sure you understand the question and have looked at all of the answer choices, since more than one may seem right at first.

Even if you're paying attention to the time, you may find yourself a little behind at some point. You should speed up to get back on track, but do so wisely. Don't panic; just take a few seconds less on each question until you're caught up. Don't guess without thinking, but do look through the answer choices and eliminate any you know are wrong. If you can get down to two choices, it is often worthwhile to guess from those. Once you've chosen an answer, move on and don't dwell on any that you skipped or had to hurry through. If a question was taking too long, chances are it was one of the harder ones, so you weren't as likely to get it right anyway.

On the other hand, if you find yourself getting ahead of schedule, it may be beneficial to slow down a little. The more quickly you work, the more likely you are to make a careless mistake that will affect your score. You've budgeted time for each question, so don't be afraid to spend that time. Practice an efficient but careful pace to get the most out of the time you have.

Secret Key #5 – Have a Plan for Guessing

When you're taking the test, you may find yourself stuck on a question. Some of the answer choices seem better than others, but you don't see the one answer choice that is obviously correct. What do you do?

The scenario described above is very common, yet most test takers have not effectively prepared for it. Developing and practicing a plan for guessing may be one of the single most effective uses of your time as you get ready for the exam.

In developing your plan for guessing, there are three questions to address:

- When should you start the guessing process?
- How should you narrow down the choices?
- Which answer should you choose?

When to Start the Guessing Process

Unless your plan for guessing is to select C every time (which, despite its merits, is not what we recommend), you need to leave yourself enough time to apply your answer elimination strategies. Since you have a limited amount of time for each question, that means that if you're going to give yourself the best shot at guessing correctly, you have to decide quickly whether or not you will guess.

Of course, the best-case scenario is that you don't have to guess at all, so first, see if you can answer the question based on your knowledge of the subject and basic reasoning skills. Focus on the key words in the question and try to jog your memory of related topics. Give yourself a chance to bring the knowledge to mind, but once you realize that you don't have (or you can't access) the knowledge you need to answer the question, it's time to start the guessing process.

It's almost always better to start the guessing process too early than too late. It only takes a few seconds to remember something and answer the question from knowledge. Carefully eliminating wrong answer choices takes longer. Plus, going through the process of eliminating answer choices can actually help jog your memory.

Summary: Start the guessing process as soon as you decide that you can't answer the question based on your knowledge.

How to Narrow Down the Choices

The next chapter in this book (**Test-Taking Strategies**) includes a wide range of strategies for how to approach questions and how to look for answer choices to eliminate. You will definitely want to read those carefully, practice them, and figure out which ones work best for you. Here though, we're going to address a mindset rather than a particular strategy.

Your odds of guessing an answer correctly depend on how many options you are choosing from.

Number of options left	5	4	3	2	1
Odds of guessing correctly	20%	25%	33%	50%	100%

You can see from this chart just how valuable it is to be able to eliminate incorrect answers and make an educated guess, but there are two things that many test takers do that cause them to miss out on the benefits of guessing:

- Accidentally eliminating the correct answer
- Selecting an answer based on an impression

We'll look at the first one here, and the second one in the next section.

To avoid accidentally eliminating the correct answer, we recommend a thought exercise called **the $5 challenge**. In this challenge, you only eliminate an answer choice from contention if you are willing to bet $5 on it being wrong. Why $5? Five dollars is a small but not insignificant amount of money. It's an amount you could afford to lose but wouldn't want to throw away. And while losing

$5 once might not hurt too much, doing it twenty times will set you back $100. In the same way, each small decision you make—eliminating a choice here, guessing on a question there—won't by itself impact your score very much, but when you put them all together, they can make a big difference. By holding each answer choice elimination decision to a higher standard, you can reduce the risk of accidentally eliminating the correct answer.

The $5 challenge can also be applied in a positive sense: If you are willing to bet $5 that an answer choice *is* correct, go ahead and mark it as correct.

Summary: Only eliminate an answer choice if you are willing to bet $5 that it is wrong.

Which Answer to Choose

You're taking the test. You've run into a hard question and decided you'll have to guess. You've eliminated all the answer choices you're willing to bet $5 on. Now you have to pick an answer. Why do we even need to talk about this? Why can't you just pick whichever one you feel like when the time comes?

The answer to these questions is that if you don't come into the test with a plan, you'll rely on your impression to select an answer choice, and if you do that, you risk falling into a trap. The test writers know that everyone who takes their test will be guessing on some of the questions, so they intentionally write wrong answer choices to seem plausible. You still have to pick an answer though, and if the wrong answer choices are designed to look right, how can you ever be sure that you're not falling for their trap? The best solution we've found to this dilemma is to take the decision out of your hands entirely. Here is the process we recommend:

Once you've eliminated any choices that you are confident (willing to bet $5) are wrong, select the first remaining choice as your answer.

Whether you choose to select the first remaining choice, the second, or the last, the important thing is that you use some preselected standard. Using this approach guarantees that you will not be enticed into selecting an answer choice that looks right, because you are not basing your decision on how the answer choices look.

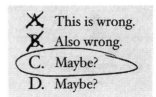

This is not meant to make you question your knowledge. Instead, it is to help you recognize the difference between your knowledge and your impressions. There's a huge difference between thinking an answer is right because of what you know, and thinking an answer is right because it looks or sounds like it should be right.

Summary: To ensure that your selection is appropriately random, make a predetermined selection from among all answer choices you have not eliminated.

Test-Taking Strategies

This section contains a list of test-taking strategies that you may find helpful as you work through the test. By taking what you know and applying logical thought, you can maximize your chances of answering any question correctly!

It is very important to realize that every question is different and every person is different: no single strategy will work on every question, and no single strategy will work for every person. That's why we've included all of them here, so you can try them out and determine which ones work best for different types of questions and which ones work best for you.

Question Strategies

⌀ READ CAREFULLY

Read the question and the answer choices carefully. Don't miss the question because you misread the terms. You have plenty of time to read each question thoroughly and make sure you understand what is being asked. Yet a happy medium must be attained, so don't waste too much time. You must read carefully and efficiently.

⌀ CONTEXTUAL CLUES

Look for contextual clues. If the question includes a word you are not familiar with, look at the immediate context for some indication of what the word might mean. Contextual clues can often give you all the information you need to decipher the meaning of an unfamiliar word. Even if you can't determine the meaning, you may be able to narrow down the possibilities enough to make a solid guess at the answer to the question.

⌀ PREFIXES

If you're having trouble with a word in the question or answer choices, try dissecting it. Take advantage of every clue that the word might include. Prefixes can be a huge help. Usually, they allow you to determine a basic meaning. *Pre-* means before, *post-* means after, *pro-* is positive, *de-* is negative. From prefixes, you can get an idea of the general meaning of the word and try to put it into context.

⌀ HEDGE WORDS

Watch out for critical hedge words, such as *likely, may, can, sometimes, often, almost, mostly, usually, generally, rarely,* and *sometimes*. Question writers insert these hedge phrases to cover every possibility. Often an answer choice will be wrong simply because it leaves no room for exception. Be on guard for answer choices that have definitive words such as *exactly* and *always*.

⌀ SWITCHBACK WORDS

Stay alert for *switchbacks*. These are the words and phrases frequently used to alert you to shifts in thought. The most common switchback words are *but, although,* and *however*. Others include *nevertheless, on the other hand, even though, while, in spite of, despite,* and *regardless of*. Switchback words are important to catch because they can change the direction of the question or an answer choice.

⊘ FACE VALUE

When in doubt, use common sense. Accept the situation in the problem at face value. Don't read too much into it. These problems will not require you to make wild assumptions. If you have to go beyond creativity and warp time or space in order to have an answer choice fit the question, then you should move on and consider the other answer choices. These are normal problems rooted in reality. The applicable relationship or explanation may not be readily apparent, but it is there for you to figure out. Use your common sense to interpret anything that isn't clear.

Answer Choice Strategies

⊘ ANSWER SELECTION

The most thorough way to pick an answer choice is to identify and eliminate wrong answers until only one is left, then confirm it is the correct answer. Sometimes an answer choice may immediately seem right, but be careful. The test writers will usually put more than one reasonable answer choice on each question, so take a second to read all of them and make sure that the other choices are not equally obvious. As long as you have time left, it is better to read every answer choice than to pick the first one that looks right without checking the others.

⊘ ANSWER CHOICE FAMILIES

An answer choice family consists of two (in rare cases, three) answer choices that are very similar in construction and cannot all be true at the same time. If you see two answer choices that are direct opposites or parallels, one of them is usually the correct answer. For instance, if one answer choice says that quantity x increases and another either says that quantity x decreases (opposite) or says that quantity y increases (parallel), then those answer choices would fall into the same family. An answer choice that doesn't match the construction of the answer choice family is more likely to be incorrect. Most questions will not have answer choice families, but when they do appear, you should be prepared to recognize them.

⊘ ELIMINATE ANSWERS

Eliminate answer choices as soon as you realize they are wrong, but make sure you consider all possibilities. If you are eliminating answer choices and realize that the last one you are left with is also wrong, don't panic. Start over and consider each choice again. There may be something you missed the first time that you will realize on the second pass.

⊘ AVOID FACT TRAPS

Don't be distracted by an answer choice that is factually true but doesn't answer the question. You are looking for the choice that answers the question. Stay focused on what the question is asking for so you don't accidentally pick an answer that is true but incorrect. Always go back to the question and make sure the answer choice you've selected actually answers the question and is not merely a true statement.

⊘ EXTREME STATEMENTS

In general, you should avoid answers that put forth extreme actions as standard practice or proclaim controversial ideas as established fact. An answer choice that states the "process should be used in certain situations, if…" is much more likely to be correct than one that states the "process should be discontinued completely." The first is a calm rational statement and doesn't even make a definitive, uncompromising stance, using a hedge word *if* to provide wiggle room, whereas the second choice is far more extreme.

☑ BENCHMARK

As you read through the answer choices and you come across one that seems to answer the question well, mentally select that answer choice. This is not your final answer, but it's the one that will help you evaluate the other answer choices. The one that you selected is your benchmark or standard for judging each of the other answer choices. Every other answer choice must be compared to your benchmark. That choice is correct until proven otherwise by another answer choice beating it. If you find a better answer, then that one becomes your new benchmark. Once you've decided that no other choice answers the question as well as your benchmark, you have your final answer.

☑ PREDICT THE ANSWER

Before you even start looking at the answer choices, it is often best to try to predict the answer. When you come up with the answer on your own, it is easier to avoid distractions and traps because you will know exactly what to look for. The right answer choice is unlikely to be word-for-word what you came up with, but it should be a close match. Even if you are confident that you have the right answer, you should still take the time to read each option before moving on.

General Strategies

☑ TOUGH QUESTIONS

If you are stumped on a problem or it appears too hard or too difficult, don't waste time. Move on! Remember though, if you can quickly check for obviously incorrect answer choices, your chances of guessing correctly are greatly improved. Before you completely give up, at least try to knock out a couple of possible answers. Eliminate what you can and then guess at the remaining answer choices before moving on.

☑ CHECK YOUR WORK

Since you will probably not know every term listed and the answer to every question, it is important that you get credit for the ones that you do know. Don't miss any questions through careless mistakes. If at all possible, try to take a second to look back over your answer selection and make sure you've selected the correct answer choice and haven't made a costly careless mistake (such as marking an answer choice that you didn't mean to mark). This quick double check should more than pay for itself in caught mistakes for the time it costs.

☑ PACE YOURSELF

It's easy to be overwhelmed when you're looking at a page full of questions; your mind is confused and full of random thoughts, and the clock is ticking down faster than you would like. Calm down and maintain the pace that you have set for yourself. Especially as you get down to the last few minutes of the test, don't let the small numbers on the clock make you panic. As long as you are on track by monitoring your pace, you are guaranteed to have time for each question.

☑ DON'T RUSH

It is very easy to make errors when you are in a hurry. Maintaining a fast pace in answering questions is pointless if it makes you miss questions that you would have gotten right otherwise. Test writers like to include distracting information and wrong answers that seem right. Taking a little extra time to avoid careless mistakes can make all the difference in your test score. Find a pace that allows you to be confident in the answers that you select.

⊘ Keep Moving

Panicking will not help you pass the test, so do your best to stay calm and keep moving. Taking deep breaths and going through the answer elimination steps you practiced can help to break through a stress barrier and keep your pace.

Final Notes

The combination of a solid foundation of content knowledge and the confidence that comes from practicing your plan for applying that knowledge is the key to maximizing your performance on test day. As your foundation of content knowledge is built up and strengthened, you'll find that the strategies included in this chapter become more and more effective in helping you quickly sift through the distractions and traps of the test to isolate the correct answer.

Now that you're preparing to move forward into the test content chapters of this book, be sure to keep your goal in mind. As you read, think about how you will be able to apply this information on the test. If you've already seen sample questions for the test and you have an idea of the question format and style, try to come up with questions of your own that you can answer based on what you're reading. This will give you valuable practice applying your knowledge in the same ways you can expect to on test day.

Good luck and good studying!

14

Quantitative

Numbers and Operations

CLASSIFICATIONS OF NUMBERS

Numbers are the basic building blocks of mathematics. Specific features of numbers are identified by the following terms:

Integer – any positive or negative whole number, including zero. Integers do not include fractions $\left(\frac{1}{3}\right)$, decimals (0.56), or mixed numbers $\left(7\frac{3}{4}\right)$.

Prime number – any whole number greater than 1 that has only two factors, itself and 1; that is, a number that can be divided evenly only by 1 and itself.

Composite number – any whole number greater than 1 that has more than two different factors; in other words, any whole number that is not a prime number. For example: The composite number 8 has the factors of 1, 2, 4, and 8.

Even number – any integer that can be divided by 2 without leaving a remainder. For example: 2, 4, 6, 8, and so on.

Odd number – any integer that cannot be divided evenly by 2. For example: 3, 5, 7, 9, and so on.

Decimal number – any number that uses a decimal point to show the part of the number that is less than one. Example: 1.234.

Decimal point – a symbol used to separate the ones place from the tenths place in decimals or dollars from cents in currency.

Decimal place – the position of a number to the right of the decimal point. In the decimal 0.123, the 1 is in the first place to the right of the decimal point, indicating tenths; the 2 is in the second place, indicating hundredths; and the 3 is in the third place, indicating thousandths.

The **decimal**, or base 10, system is a number system that uses ten different digits (0, 1, 2, 3, 4, 5, 6, 7, 8, 9). An example of a number system that uses something other than ten digits is the **binary**, or base 2, number system, used by computers, which uses only the numbers 0 and 1. It is thought that the decimal system originated because people had only their 10 fingers for counting.

Rational numbers include all integers, decimals, and fractions. Any terminating or repeating decimal number is a rational number.

Irrational numbers cannot be written as fractions or decimals because the number of decimal places is infinite and there is no recurring pattern of digits within the number. For example, pi (π)

begins with 3.141592 and continues without terminating or repeating, so pi is an irrational number.

Real numbers are the set of all rational and irrational numbers.

Review Video: <u>Classification of Numbers</u>
Visit mometrix.com/academy and enter code: 461071
Review Video: <u>Rational and Irrational Numbers</u>
Visit mometrix.com/academy and enter code: 280645
Review Video: <u>Prime and Composite Numbers</u>
Visit mometrix.com/academy and enter code: 565581

ABSOLUTE VALUE

A precursor to working with negative numbers is understanding what **absolute values** are. A number's absolute value is simply the distance away from zero a number is on the number line. The absolute value of a number is always positive and is written $|x|$. For example, the absolute value of 3, written as $|3|$, is 3 because the distance between 0 and 3 on a number line is three units. Likewise, the absolute value of –3, written as $|-3|$, is 3 because the distance between 0 and –3 on a number line is three units. So, $|3| = |-3|$.

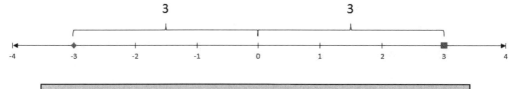

Review Video: <u>Absolute Value</u>
Visit mometrix.com/academy and enter code: 314669

OPERATIONS

Mathematical expressions consist of a combination of values and operations. An **operation** is simply a mathematical process that takes some value(s) as input(s) and produces an output. Elementary operations are often written in the following form: *value operation value*. For instance, in the expression $1 + 2$ the values are 1 and 2 and the operation is addition. Performing the operation gives the output of 3. In this way we can say that $1 + 2$ and 3 are equal, or $1 + 2 = 3$.

ADDITION

Addition increases the value of one quantity by the value of another quantity (both called **addends**). For example, $2 + 4 = 6$; $8 + 9 = 17$. The result is called the **sum**. With addition, the order does not matter, $4 + 2 = 2 + 4$.

When adding signed numbers, if the signs are the same simply add the absolute values of the addends and apply the original sign to the sum. For example, $(+4) + (+8) = +12$ and $(-4) + (-8) = -12$. When the original signs are different, take the absolute values of the addends and subtract the smaller value from the larger value, then apply the original sign of the larger value to the difference. For instance, $(+4) + (-8) = -4$ and $(-4) + (+8) = +4$.

SUBTRACTION

Subtraction is the opposite operation to addition; it decreases the value of one quantity (the **minuend**) by the value of another quantity (the **subtrahend**). For example, $6 - 4 = 2$; $17 - 8 = 9$. The result is called the **difference**. Note that with subtraction, the order does matter, $6 - 4 \neq 4 - 6$.

For subtracting signed numbers, change the sign of the subtrahend and then follow the same rules used for addition. For example, $(+4) - (+8) = (+4) + (-8) = -4$.

MULTIPLICATION

Multiplication can be thought of as repeated addition. One number (the **multiplier**) indicates how many times to add the other number (the **multiplicand**) to itself. For example, 3×2 (three times two) $= 2 + 2 + 2 = 6$. With multiplication, the order does not matter: $2 \times 3 = 3 \times 2$ or $3 + 3 = 2 + 2 + 2$, either way the result (the **product**) is the same.

If the signs are the same the product is positive when multiplying signed numbers. For example, $(+4) \times (+8) = +32$ and $(-4) \times (-8) = +32$. If the signs are opposite, the product is negative. For example, $(+4) \times (-8) = -32$ and $(-4) \times (+8) = -32$. When more than two factors are multiplied together, the sign of the product is determined by how many negative factors are present. If there are an odd number of negative factors then the product is negative, whereas an even number of negative factors indicates a positive product. For instance, $(+4) \times (-8) \times (-2) = +64$ and $(-4) \times (-8) \times (-2) = -64$.

DIVISION

Division is the opposite operation to multiplication; one number (the **divisor**) tells us how many parts to divide the other number (the **dividend**) into. The result of division is called the **quotient**. For example, $20 \div 4 = 5$; if 20 is split into 4 equal parts, each part is 5. With division, the order of the numbers does matter, $20 \div 4 \neq 4 \div 20$.

The rules for dividing signed numbers are similar to multiplying signed numbers. If the dividend and divisor have the same sign, the quotient is positive. If the dividend and divisor have opposite signs, the quotient is negative. For example, $(-4) \div (+8) = -0.5$.

> **Review Video: Mathematical Operations**
> Visit mometrix.com/academy and enter code: 208095

PARENTHESES

Parentheses are used to designate which operations should be done first when there are multiple operations. Example: $4 - (2 + 1) = 1$; the parentheses tell us that we must add 2 and 1, and then subtract the sum from 4, rather than subtracting 2 from 4 and then adding 1 (this would give us an answer of 3).

> **Review Video: Mathematical Parentheses**
> Visit mometrix.com/academy and enter code: 978600

EXPONENTS

An **exponent** is a superscript number placed next to another number at the top right. It indicates how many times the base number is to be multiplied by itself. Exponents provide a shorthand way to write what would be a longer mathematical expression, for example: $2^4 = 2 \times 2 \times 2 \times 2$. A number with an exponent of 2 is said to be "squared," while a number with an exponent of 3 is said to be "cubed." The value of a number raised to an exponent is called its power. So, 8^4 is read as "8 to the 4th power," or "8 raised to the power of 4."

The properties of exponents are as follows:

Property	Description
$a^1 = a$	Any number to the power of 1 is equal to itself
$1^n = 1$	The number 1 raised to any power is equal to 1
$a^0 = 1$	Any number raised to the power of 0 is equal to 1
$a^n \times a^m = a^{n+m}$	Add exponents to multiply powers of the same base number
$a^n \div a^m = a^{n-m}$	Subtract exponents to divide powers of the same base number
$(a^n)^m = a^{n \times m}$	When a power is raised to a power, the exponents are multiplied
$(a \times b)^n = a^n \times b^n$	Multiplication and division operations inside parentheses can be raised to
$(a \div b)^n = a^n \div b^n$	a power. This is the same as each term being raised to that power.
$a^{-n} = \dfrac{1}{a^n}$	A negative exponent is the same as the reciprocal of a positive exponent

Note that exponents do not have to be integers. Fractional or decimal exponents follow all the rules above as well. Example: $5^{\frac{1}{4}} \times 5^{\frac{3}{4}} = 5^{\frac{1}{4}+\frac{3}{4}} = 5^1 = 5$.

> **Review Video: What is an Exponent?**
> Visit mometrix.com/academy and enter code: 600998
>
> **Review Video: Laws of Exponents**
> Visit mometrix.com/academy and enter code: 532558

ROOTS

A **root**, such as a square root, is another way of writing a fractional exponent. Instead of using a superscript, roots use the radical symbol ($\sqrt{\ }$) to indicate the operation. A radical will have a number underneath the bar, and may sometimes have a number in the upper left: $\sqrt[n]{a}$, read as "the nth root of a." The relationship between radical notation and exponent notation can be described by this equation: $\sqrt[n]{a} = a^{\frac{1}{n}}$. The two special cases of $n = 2$ and $n = 3$ are called square roots and cube roots. If there is no number to the upper left, it is understood to be a square root ($n = 2$). Nearly all of the roots you encounter will be square roots. A square root is the same as a number raised to the one-half power. When we say that a is the square root of b ($a = \sqrt{b}$), we mean that a multiplied by itself equals b: ($a \times a = b$).

A **perfect square** is a number that has an integer for its square root. There are 10 perfect squares from 1 to 100: 1, 4, 9, 16, 25, 36, 49, 64, 81, 100 (the squares of integers 1 through 10).

> **Review Video: Roots**
> Visit mometrix.com/academy and enter code: 795655
>
> **Review Video: Square Root and Perfect Squares**
> Visit mometrix.com/academy and enter code: 648063

ORDER OF OPERATIONS

The **order of operations** is a set of rules that dictates the order in which we must perform each operation in an expression so that we will evaluate it accurately. If we have an expression that includes multiple different operations, the order of operations tells us which operations to do first.

The most common mnemonic for the order of operations is **PEMDAS**, or "Please Excuse My Dear Aunt Sally." PEMDAS stands for parentheses, exponents, multiplication, division, addition, and subtraction. It is important to understand that multiplication and division have equal precedence, as do addition and subtraction, so those pairs of operations are simply worked from left to right in order.

For example, evaluating the expression $5 + 20 \div 4 \times (2 + 3) - 6$ using the correct order of operations would be done like this:

- **P:** Perform the operations inside the parentheses: $(2 + 3) = 5$
- **E:** Simplify the exponents.
  - The equation now looks like this: $5 + 20 \div 4 \times 5 - 6$
- **MD:** Perform multiplication and division from left to right: $20 \div 4 = 5$; then $5 \times 5 = 25$
  - The equation now looks like this: $5 + 25 - 6$
- **AS:** Perform addition and subtraction from left to right: $5 + 25 = 30$; then $30 - 6 = 24$

Review Video: Order of Operations
Visit mometrix.com/academy and enter code: 259675

SUBTRACTION WITH REGROUPING

A great way to make use of some of the features built into the decimal system would be regrouping when attempting longform subtraction operations. When subtracting within a place value, sometimes the minuend is smaller than the subtrahend, **regrouping** enables you to 'borrow' a unit from a place value to the left in order to get a positive difference. For example, consider subtracting 189 from 525 with regrouping.

Review Video: Subtracting Large Numbers
Visit mometrix.com/academy and enter code: 603350

First, set up the subtraction problem in vertical form:

$$\begin{array}{r} 525 \\ - \ 189 \end{array}$$

Notice that the numbers in the ones and tens columns of 525 are smaller than the numbers in the ones and tens columns of 189. This means you will need to use regrouping to perform subtraction:

$$\begin{array}{ccc} 5 & 2 & 5 \\ - \quad 1 & 8 & 9 \end{array}$$

To subtract 9 from 5 in the ones column you will need to borrow from the 2 in the tens columns:

$$\begin{array}{ccc} 5 & 1 & 15 \\ - \quad 1 & 8 & 9 \\ \hline & & 6 \end{array}$$

Next, to subtract 8 from 1 in the tens column you will need to borrow from the 5 in the hundreds column:

$$
\begin{array}{rrr}
4 & 11 & 15 \\
- \quad 1 & 8 & 9 \\
\hline
& 3 & 6 \\
\end{array}
$$

Last, subtract the 1 from the 4 in the hundreds column:

$$
\begin{array}{rrr}
4 & 11 & 15 \\
- \quad 1 & 8 & 9 \\
\hline
3 & 3 & 6 \\
\end{array}
$$

PRACTICE

P1. Simplify the following expressions with exponents:

   (a) 37^0
   (b) 1^{30}
   (c) $2^3 \times 2^4 \times 2^x$
   (d) $(3^x)^3$
   (e) $(12 \div 3)^2$

PRACTICE SOLUTIONS

P1. Using the properties of exponents and the proper order of operations:

   (a) Any number raised to the power of 0 is equal to 1: $37^0 = 1$
   (b) The number 1 raised to any power is equal to 1: $1^{30} = 1$
   (c) Add exponents to multiply powers of the same base: $2^3 \times 2^4 \times 2^x = 2^{(3+4+x)} = 2^{(7+x)}$
   (d) When a power is raised to a power, the exponents are multiplied: $(3^x)^3 = 3^{3x}$
   (e) Perform the operation inside the parentheses first: $(12 \div 3)^2 = 4^2 = 16$

Rational Numbers

FRACTIONS

A **fraction** is a number that is expressed as one integer written above another integer, with a dividing line between them $\left(\frac{x}{y}\right)$. It represents the **quotient** of the two numbers "x divided by y." It can also be thought of as x out of y equal parts.

The top number of a fraction is called the **numerator**, and it represents the number of parts under consideration. The 1 in $\frac{1}{4}$ means that 1 part out of the whole is being considered in the calculation. The bottom number of a fraction is called the **denominator**, and it represents the total number of equal parts. The 4 in $\frac{1}{4}$ means that the whole consists of 4 equal parts. A fraction cannot have a denominator of zero; this is referred to as "*undefined.*"

Fractions can be manipulated, without changing the value of the fraction, by multiplying or dividing (but not adding or subtracting) both the numerator and denominator by the same number. If you divide both numbers by a common factor, you are **reducing** or simplifying the fraction. Two fractions that have the same value but are expressed differently are known as **equivalent**

fractions. For example, $\frac{2}{10}, \frac{3}{15}, \frac{4}{20}$, and $\frac{5}{25}$ are all equivalent fractions. They can also all be reduced or simplified to $\frac{1}{5}$.

When two fractions are manipulated so that they have the same denominator, this is known as finding a **common denominator**. The number chosen to be that common denominator should be the least common multiple of the two original denominators. Example: $\frac{3}{4}$ and $\frac{5}{6}$; the least common multiple of 4 and 6 is 12. Manipulating to achieve the common denominator: $\frac{3}{4} = \frac{9}{12}$; $\frac{5}{6} = \frac{10}{12}$.

> **Review Video: Overview of Fractions**
> Visit mometrix.com/academy and enter code: 262335

PROPER FRACTIONS AND MIXED NUMBERS

A fraction whose denominator is greater than its numerator is known as a **proper fraction**, while a fraction whose numerator is greater than its denominator is known as an **improper fraction**. Proper fractions have values *less than one* and improper fractions have values *greater than one*.

A **mixed number** is a number that contains both an integer and a fraction. Any improper fraction can be rewritten as a mixed number. Example: $\frac{8}{3} = \frac{6}{3} + \frac{2}{3} = 2 + \frac{2}{3} = 2\frac{2}{3}$. Similarly, any mixed number can be rewritten as an improper fraction. Example: $1\frac{3}{5} = 1 + \frac{3}{5} = \frac{5}{5} + \frac{3}{5} = \frac{8}{5}$.

> **Review Video: Improper Fractions and Mixed Numbers**
> Visit mometrix.com/academy and enter code: 211077

OPERATIONS WITH FRACTIONS
ADDING AND SUBTRACTING FRACTIONS

If two fractions have a common denominator, they can be added or subtracted simply by adding or subtracting the two numerators and retaining the same denominator. If the two fractions do not already have the same denominator, one or both of them must be manipulated to achieve a common denominator before they can be added or subtracted. Example: $\frac{1}{2} + \frac{1}{4} = \frac{2}{4} + \frac{1}{4} = \frac{3}{4}$.

> **Review Video: Adding and Subtracting Fractions**
> Visit mometrix.com/academy and enter code: 378080

MULTIPLYING FRACTIONS

Two fractions can be multiplied by multiplying the two numerators to find the new numerator and the two denominators to find the new denominator. Example: $\frac{1}{3} \times \frac{2}{3} = \frac{1\times2}{3\times3} = \frac{2}{9}$.

DIVIDING FRACTIONS

Two fractions can be divided by flipping the numerator and denominator of the second fraction and then proceeding as though it were a multiplication. Example: $\frac{2}{3} \div \frac{3}{4} = \frac{2}{3} \times \frac{4}{3} = \frac{8}{9}$.

> **Review Video: Multiplying and Dividing Fractions**
> Visit mometrix.com/academy and enter code: 473632

MULTIPLYING A MIXED NUMBER BY A WHOLE NUMBER OR A DECIMAL

When multiplying a mixed number by something, it is usually best to convert it to an improper fraction first. Additionally, if the multiplicand is a decimal, it is most often simplest to convert it to a fraction. For instance, to multiply $4\frac{3}{8}$ by 3.5, begin by rewriting each quantity as a whole number plus a proper fraction. Remember, a mixed number is a fraction added to a whole number and a decimal is a representation of the sum of fractions, specifically tenths, hundredths, thousandths, and so on:

$$4\frac{3}{8} \times 3.5 = \left(4 + \frac{3}{8}\right) \times \left(3 + \frac{1}{2}\right)$$

Next, the quantities being added need to be expressed with the same denominator. This is achieved by multiplying and dividing the whole number by the denominator of the fraction. Recall that a whole number is equivalent to that number divided by 1:

$$= \left(\frac{4}{1} \times \frac{8}{8} + \frac{3}{8}\right) \times \left(\frac{3}{1} \times \frac{2}{2} + \frac{1}{2}\right)$$

When multiplying fractions, remember to multiply the numerators and denominators separately:

$$= \left(\frac{4 \times 8}{1 \times 8} + \frac{3}{8}\right) \times \left(\frac{3 \times 2}{1 \times 2} + \frac{1}{2}\right)$$

$$= \left(\frac{32}{8} + \frac{3}{8}\right) \times \left(\frac{6}{2} + \frac{1}{2}\right)$$

Now that the fractions have the same denominators, they can be added:

$$= \frac{35}{8} \times \frac{7}{2}$$

Finally, perform the last multiplication and then simplify:

$$= \frac{35 \times 7}{8 \times 2} = \frac{245}{16} = \frac{240}{16} + \frac{5}{16} = 15\frac{5}{16}$$

DECIMALS

Decimals are one way to represent parts of a whole. Using the place value system, each digit to the right of a decimal point denotes the number of units of a corresponding *negative* power of ten. For example, consider the decimal 0.24. We can use a model to represent the decimal. Since a dime is worth one-tenth of a dollar and a penny is worth one-hundredth of a dollar, one possible model to represent this fraction is to have 2 dimes representing the 2 in the tenths place and 4 pennies representing the 4 in the hundredths place:

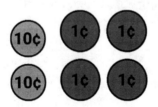

To write the decimal as a fraction, put the decimal in the numerator with 1 in the denominator. Multiply the numerator and denominator by tens until there are no more decimal places. Then simplify the fraction to lowest terms. For example, converting 0.24 to a fraction:

$$0.24 = \frac{0.24}{1} = \frac{0.24 \times 100}{1 \times 100} = \frac{24}{100} = \frac{6}{25}$$

> **Review Video: Decimals**
> Visit mometrix.com/academy and enter code: 837268

OPERATIONS WITH DECIMALS
ADDING AND SUBTRACTING DECIMALS

When adding and subtracting decimals, the decimal points must always be aligned. Adding decimals is just like adding regular whole numbers. Example: $4.5 + 2 = 6.5$.

If the problem-solver does not properly align the decimal points, an incorrect answer of 4.7 may result. An easy way to add decimals is to align all of the decimal points in a vertical column visually. This will allow you to see exactly where the decimal should be placed in the final answer. Begin adding from right to left. Add each column in turn, making sure to carry the number to the left if a column adds up to more than 9. The same rules apply to the subtraction of decimals.

> **Review Video: Adding and Subtracting Decimals**
> Visit mometrix.com/academy and enter code: 381101

MULTIPLYING DECIMALS

A simple multiplication problem has two components: a **multiplicand** and a **multiplier**. When multiplying decimals, work as though the numbers were whole rather than decimals. Once the final product is calculated, count the number of places to the right of the decimal in both the multiplicand and the multiplier. Then, count that number of places from the right of the product and place the decimal in that position.

For example, 12.3×2.56 has a total of three places to the right of the respective decimals. Multiply 123×256 to get 31488. Now, beginning on the right, count three places to the left and insert the decimal. The final product will be 31.488.

> **Review Video: Multiplying Decimals**
> Visit mometrix.com/academy and enter code: 731574

DIVIDING DECIMALS

Every division problem has a **divisor** and a **dividend**. The dividend is the number that is being divided. In the problem $14 \div 7$, 14 is the dividend and 7 is the divisor. In a division problem with decimals, the divisor must be converted into a whole number. Begin by moving the decimal in the divisor to the right until a whole number is created. Next, move the decimal in the dividend the same number of spaces to the right. For example, 4.9 into 24.5 would become 49 into 245. The decimal was moved one space to the right to create a whole number in the divisor, and then the same was done for the dividend. Once the whole numbers are created, the problem is carried out normally: $245 \div 49 = 5$.

> **Review Video: Dividing Decimals**
> Visit mometrix.com/academy and enter code: 560690

PERCENTAGES

Percentages can be thought of as fractions that are based on a whole of 100; that is, one whole is equal to 100%. The word **percent** means "per hundred." Percentage problems are often presented in three main ways:

- Find what percentage of some number another number is.
  - Example: What percentage of 40 is 8?
- Find what number is some percentage of a given number.
  - Example: What number is 20% of 40?
- Find what number another number is a given percentage of.
  - Example: What number is 8 20% of?

There are three components in each of these cases: a **whole** (W), a **part** (P), and a **percentage** (%). These are related by the equation: $P = W \times \%$. This can easily be rearranged into other forms that may suit different questions better: $\% = \frac{P}{W}$ and $W = \frac{P}{\%}$. Percentage problems are often also word problems. As such, a large part of solving them is figuring out which quantities are what. For example, consider the following word problem:

In a school cafeteria, 7 students choose pizza, 9 choose hamburgers, and 4 choose tacos. What percentage of student choose tacos?

To find the whole, you must first add all of the parts: $7 + 9 + 4 = 20$. The percentage can then be found by dividing the part by the whole ($\% = \frac{P}{W}$): $\frac{4}{20} = \frac{20}{100} = 20\%$.

> **Review Video: Computation with Percentages**
> Visit mometrix.com/academy and enter code: 693099

CONVERTING BETWEEN PERCENTAGES, FRACTIONS, AND DECIMALS

Converting decimals to percentages and percentages to decimals is as simple as moving the decimal point. To *convert from a decimal to a percentage*, move the decimal point **two places to the right**. To *convert from a percentage to a decimal*, move it **two places to the left**. It may be helpful to remember that the percentage number will always be larger than the equivalent decimal number. For example:

$$0.23 = 23\% \quad 5.34 = 534\% \quad 0.007 = 0.7\%$$
$$700\% = 7.00 \quad 86\% = 0.86 \quad 0.15\% = 0.0015$$

To convert a fraction to a decimal, simply divide the numerator by the denominator in the fraction. To convert a decimal to a fraction, put the decimal in the numerator with 1 in the denominator. Multiply the numerator and denominator by tens until there are no more decimal places. Then simplify the fraction to lowest terms. For example, converting 0.24 to a fraction:

$$0.24 = \frac{0.24}{1} = \frac{0.24 \times 100}{1 \times 100} = \frac{24}{100} = \frac{6}{25}$$

Fractions can be converted to a percentage by finding equivalent fractions with a denominator of 100. For example:

$$\frac{7}{10} = \frac{70}{100} = 70\% \qquad \frac{1}{4} = \frac{25}{100} = 25\%$$

To convert a percentage to a fraction, divide the percentage number by 100 and reduce the fraction to its simplest possible terms. For example:

$$60\% = \frac{60}{100} = \frac{3}{5} \qquad 96\% = \frac{96}{100} = \frac{24}{25}$$

> **Review Video: <u>Converting Fractions to Percentages and Decimals</u>**
> Visit mometrix.com/academy and enter code: 306233
>
> **Review Video: <u>Converting Percentages to Decimals and Fractions</u>**
> Visit mometrix.com/academy and enter code: 287297
>
> **Review Video: <u>Converting Decimals to Fractions and Percentages</u>**
> Visit mometrix.com/academy and enter code: 986765
>
> **Review Video: <u>Converting Decimals, Improper Fractions, and Mixed Numbers</u>**
> Visit mometrix.com/academy and enter code: 696924

RATIONAL NUMBERS

The term **rational** means that the number can be expressed as a ratio or fraction. That is, a number, r, is rational if and only if it can be represented by a fraction $\frac{a}{b}$ where a and b are integers and b does not equal 0. The set of rational numbers includes integers and decimals. If there is no finite way to represent a value with a fraction of integers, then the number is **irrational**. Common examples of irrational numbers include: $\sqrt{5}$, $\left(1 + \sqrt{2}\right)$, and π.

> **Review Video: <u>Rational and Irrational Numbers</u>**
> Visit mometrix.com/academy and enter code: 280645
>
> **Review Video: <u>Ordering Rational Numbers</u>**
> Visit mometrix.com/academy and enter code: 419578

PRACTICE

P1. What is 30% of 120?

P2. What is 150% of 20?

P3. What is 14.5% of 96?

P4. Simplify the following expressions:

(a) $\left(\frac{2}{5}\right)/\left(\frac{4}{7}\right)$

(b) $\frac{7}{8} - \frac{8}{16}$

(c) $\frac{1}{2} + \left(3\left(\frac{3}{4}\right) - 2\right) + 4$

(d) $0.22 + 0.5 - (5.5 + 3.3 \div 3)$

(e) $\frac{3}{2} + (4(0.5) - 0.75) + 2$

P5. Convert the following to a fraction and to a decimal: **(a)** 15%; **(b)** 24.36%

P6. Convert the following to a decimal and to a percentage. **(a)** 4/5; **(b)** $3\frac{2}{5}$

P7. A woman's age is thirteen more than half of 60. How old is the woman?

P8. A patient was given pain medicine at a dosage of 0.22 grams. The patient's dosage was then increased to 0.80 grams. By how much was the patient's dosage increased?

P9. At a hotel, $\frac{3}{4}$ of the 100 rooms are occupied today. Yesterday, $\frac{4}{5}$ of the 100 rooms were occupied. On which day were more of the rooms occupied and by how much more?

P10. At a school, 40% of the teachers teach English. If 20 teachers teach English, how many teachers work at the school?

P11. A patient was given blood pressure medicine at a dosage of 2 grams. The patient's dosage was then decreased to 0.45 grams. By how much was the patient's dosage decreased?

P12. Two weeks ago, $\frac{2}{3}$ of the 60 customers at a skate shop were male. Last week, $\frac{3}{6}$ of the 80 customers were male. During which week were there more male customers?

P13. Jane ate lunch at a local restaurant. She ordered a $4.99 appetizer, a $12.50 entrée, and a $1.25 soda. If she wants to tip her server 20%, how much money will she spend in all?

P14. According to a survey, about 82% of engineers were highly satisfied with their job. If 145 engineers were surveyed, how many reported that they were highly satisfied?

P15. A patient was given 40 mg of a certain medicine. Later, the patient's dosage was increased to 45 mg. What was the percent increase in his medication?

P16. Order the following rational numbers from least to greatest: 0.55, 17%, $\sqrt{25}$, $\frac{64}{4}$, $\frac{25}{50}$, 3.

P17. Order the following rational numbers from greatest to least: 0.3, 27%, $\sqrt{100}$, $\frac{72}{9}$, $\frac{1}{9}$, 4.5.

P18. Perform the following multiplication. Write each answer as a mixed number.

(a) $\left(1\frac{11}{16}\right) \times 4$

(b) $\left(12\frac{1}{3}\right) \times 1.1$

(c) $3.71 \times \left(6\frac{1}{5}\right)$

P19. Suppose you are making doughnuts and you want to triple the recipe you have. If the following list is the original amounts for the ingredients, what would be the amounts for the tripled recipe?

$1\frac{3}{4}$	cup	Flour
$1\frac{1}{4}$	tsp	Baking powder
$\frac{3}{4}$	tsp	Salt
$\frac{3}{8}$	cup	Sugar
$1\frac{1}{2}$	Tbsp	Butter
2	large	Eggs
$\frac{3}{4}$	tsp	Vanilla extract
$\frac{3}{8}$	cup	Sour cream

PRACTICE SOLUTIONS

P1. The word *of* indicates multiplication, so 30% of 120 is found by multiplying 120 by 30%. Change 30% to a decimal, then multiply: $120 \times 0.3 = 36$

P2. The word *of* indicates multiplication, so 150% of 20 is found by multiplying 20 by 150%. Change 150% to a decimal, then multiply: $20 \times 1.5 = 30$

P3. Change 14.5% to a decimal before multiplying: $0.145 \times 96 = 13.92$

P4. Follow the order of operations and utilize properties of fractions to solve each:

(a) Rewrite the problem as a multiplication problem: $\frac{2}{5} \times \frac{7}{4} = \frac{2\times7}{5\times4} = \frac{14}{20}$. Make sure the fraction is reduced to lowest terms. Both 14 and 20 can be divided by 2.

$$\frac{14}{20} = \frac{14 \div 2}{20 \div 2} = \frac{7}{10}$$

(b) The denominators of $\frac{7}{8}$ and $\frac{8}{16}$ are 8 and 16, respectively. The lowest common denominator of 8 and 16 is 16 because 16 is the least common multiple of 8 and 16. Convert the first fraction to its equivalent with the newly found common denominator of 16: $\frac{7 \times 2}{8 \times 2} = \frac{14}{16}$. Now that the fractions have the same denominator, you can subtract them.

$$\frac{14}{16} - \frac{8}{16} = \frac{6}{16} = \frac{3}{8}$$

(c) When simplifying expressions, first perform operations within groups. Within the set of parentheses are multiplication and subtraction operations. Perform the multiplication first to

27

get $\frac{1}{2} + \left(\frac{9}{4} - 2\right) + 4$. Then, subtract two to obtain $\frac{1}{2} + \frac{1}{4} + 4$. Finally, perform addition from left to right:

$$\frac{1}{2} + \frac{1}{4} + 4 = \frac{2}{4} + \frac{1}{4} + \frac{16}{4} = \frac{19}{4} = 4\frac{3}{4}$$

(d) First, evaluate the terms in the parentheses $(5.5 + 3.3 \div 3)$ using order of operations. $3.3 \div 3 = 1.1$, and $5.5 + 1.1 = 6.6$. Next, rewrite the problem: $0.22 + 0.5 - 6.6$. Finally, add and subtract from left to right: $0.22 + 0.5 = 0.72$; $0.72 - 6.6 = -5.88$. The answer is -5.88.

(e) First, simplify within the parentheses, then change the fraction to a decimal and perform addition from left to right:

$$\frac{3}{2} + (2 - 0.75) + 2 =$$

$$\frac{3}{2} + 1.25 + 2 =$$

$$1.5 + 1.25 + 2 = 4.75$$

P5. (a) 15% can be written as $\frac{15}{100}$. Both 15 and 100 can be divided by 5: $\frac{15 \div 5}{100 \div 5} = \frac{3}{20}$

When converting from a percentage to a decimal, drop the percent sign and move the decimal point two places to the left: $15\% = 0.15$

(b) 24.36% written as a fraction is $\frac{24.36}{100}$, or $\frac{2436}{10,000}$, which reduces to $\frac{609}{2500}$. 24.36% written as a decimal is 0.2436. Recall that dividing by 100 moves the decimal two places to the left.

P6. (a) Recall that in the decimal system the first decimal place is one tenth: $\frac{4 \times 2}{5 \times 2} = \frac{8}{10} = 0.8$

Percent means "per hundred." $\frac{4 \times 20}{5 \times 20} = \frac{80}{100} = 80\%$

(b) The mixed number $3\frac{2}{5}$ has a whole number and a fractional part. The fractional part $\frac{2}{5}$ can be written as a decimal by dividing 5 into 2, which gives 0.4. Adding the whole to the part gives 3.4.

To find the equivalent percentage, multiply the decimal by 100. $3.4(100) = 340\%$. Notice that this percentage is greater than 100%. This makes sense because the original mixed number $3\frac{2}{5}$ is greater than 1.

P7. "More than" indicates addition, and "of" indicates multiplication. The expression can be written as $\frac{1}{2}(60) + 13$. So, the woman's age is equal to $\frac{1}{2}(60) + 13 = 30 + 13 = 43$. The woman is 43 years old.

P8. The first step is to determine what operation (addition, subtraction, multiplication, or division) the problem requires. Notice the keywords and phrases "by how much" and "increased." "Increased" means that you go from a smaller amount to a larger amount. This change can be found by subtracting the smaller amount from the larger amount: 0.80 grams– 0.22 grams = 0.58 grams.

Remember to line up the decimal when subtracting:

$$
\begin{array}{r}
0.80 \\
-\ \ 0.22 \\
\hline
0.58
\end{array}
$$

P9. First, find the number of rooms occupied each day. To do so, multiply the fraction of rooms occupied by the number of rooms available:

$$\text{Number occupied} = \text{Fraction occupied} \times \text{Total number}$$

$$\text{Number of rooms occupied today} = \frac{3}{4} \times 100 = 75$$

$$\text{Number of rooms occupied} = \frac{4}{5} \times 100 = 80$$

The difference in the number of rooms occupied is: $80 - 75 = 5$ rooms

P10. To answer this problem, first think about the number of teachers that work at the school. Will it be more or less than the number of teachers who work in a specific department such as English? More teachers work at the school, so the number you find to answer this question will be greater than 20.

40% of the teachers are English teachers. "Of" indicates multiplication, and words like "is" and "are" indicate equivalence. Translating the problem into a mathematical sentence gives $40\% \times t = 20$, where t represents the total number of teachers. Solving for t gives $t = \frac{20}{40\%} = \frac{20}{0.40} = 50$. Fifty teachers work at the school.

P11. The decrease is represented by the difference between the two amounts:

$$2 \text{ grams} - 0.45 \text{ grams} = 1.55 \text{ grams}.$$

Remember to line up the decimal point before subtracting.

$$
\begin{array}{r}
2.00 \\
-\ \ 0.45 \\
\hline
1.55
\end{array}
$$

P12. First, you need to find the number of male customers that were in the skate shop each week. You are given this amount in terms of fractions. To find the actual number of male customers, multiply the fraction of male customers by the number of customers in the store.

$$\text{Actual number of male customers} = \text{fraction of male customers} \times \text{total customers}$$

$$\text{Number of male customers two weeks ago} = \frac{2}{3} \times 60 = \frac{120}{3} = 40$$

$$\text{Number of male customers last week} = \frac{3}{6} \times 80 = \frac{1}{2} \times 80 = \frac{80}{2} = 40$$

The number of male customers was the same both weeks.

P13. To find total amount, first find the sum of the items she ordered from the menu and then add 20% of this sum to the total.

$$\$4.99 + \$12.50 + \$1.25 = \$18.74$$

$$\$18.74 \times 20\% = (0.20)(\$18.74) = \$3.748 \approx \$3.75$$

$$\text{Total} = \$18.74 + \$3.75 = \$22.49$$

P14. 82% of 145 is $0.82 \times 145 = 118.9$. Because you can't have 0.9 of a person, we must round up to say that 119 engineers reported that they were highly satisfied with their jobs.

P15. To find the percent increase, first compare the original and increased amounts. The original amount was 40 mg, and the increased amount is 45 mg, so the dosage of medication was increased by 5 mg ($45 - 40 = 5$). Note, however, that the question asks not by how much the dosage increased but by what percentage it increased.

$$\text{Percent increase} = \frac{\text{new amount} - \text{original amount}}{\text{original amount}} \times 100\%$$

$$= \frac{45 \text{ mg} - 40 \text{ mg}}{40 \text{ mg}} \times 100\% = \frac{5}{40} \times 100\% = 0.125 \times 100\% = 12.5\%$$

P16. Recall that the term rational simply means that the number can be expressed as a ratio or fraction. Notice that each of the numbers in the problem can be written as a decimal or integer:

$$17\% = 0.17$$

$$\sqrt{25} = 5$$

$$\frac{64}{4} = 16$$

$$\frac{25}{50} = \frac{1}{2} = 0.5$$

So, the answer is $17\%, \frac{25}{50}, 0.55, 3, \sqrt{25}, \frac{64}{4}$.

P17. Converting all the numbers to integers and decimals makes it easier to compare the values:

$$27\% = 0.27$$

$$\sqrt{100} = 10$$

$$\frac{72}{9} = 8$$

$$\frac{1}{9} \approx 0.11$$

So, the answer is $\sqrt{100}, \frac{72}{9}, 4.5, 0.3, 27\%, \frac{1}{9}$.

Review Video: <u>Ordering Rational Numbers</u>
Visit mometrix.com/academy and enter code: 419578

P18. For each, convert improper fractions, adjust to a common denominator, perform the operations, and then simplify:

(a) Sometimes, you can skip converting the denominator and just distribute the multiplication.

$$\left(1\frac{11}{16}\right) \times 4 = \left(1 + \frac{11}{16}\right) \times 4$$

$$= 1 \times 4 + \frac{11}{16} \times 4$$

$$= 4 + \frac{11}{16} \times \frac{4}{1}$$

$$= 4 + \frac{44}{16} = 4 + \frac{11}{4} = 4 + 2\frac{3}{4} = 6\frac{3}{4}$$

(b)

$$\left(12\frac{1}{3}\right) \times 1.1 = \left(12 + \frac{1}{3}\right) \times \left(1 + \frac{1}{10}\right)$$

$$= \left(\frac{12}{1} \times \frac{3}{3} + \frac{1}{3}\right) \times \left(\frac{10}{10} + \frac{1}{10}\right)$$

$$= \left(\frac{36}{3} + \frac{1}{3}\right) \times \frac{11}{10}$$

$$= \frac{37}{3} \times \frac{11}{10}$$

$$= \frac{407}{30} = \frac{390}{30} + \frac{17}{30} = 13\frac{17}{30}$$

(c)

$$3.71 \times \left(6\frac{1}{5}\right) = \left(3 + \frac{71}{100}\right) \times \left(6 + \frac{1}{5}\right)$$

$$= \left(\frac{300}{100} + \frac{71}{100}\right) \times \left(\frac{6}{1} \times \frac{5}{5} + \frac{1}{5}\right)$$

$$= \frac{371}{100} \times \left(\frac{30}{5} + \frac{1}{5}\right)$$

$$= \frac{371}{100} \times \frac{31}{5}$$

$$= \frac{11501}{500} = \frac{11500}{500} + \frac{1}{500} = 23\frac{1}{500}$$

P19. Fortunately, some of the amounts are duplicated, so we do not need to figure out every amount.

$$1\frac{3}{4} \times 3 = (1 \times 3) + \left(\frac{3}{4} \times 3\right)$$
$$= 3 + \frac{9}{4}$$
$$= 3 + 2\frac{1}{4}$$
$$= 5\frac{1}{4}$$

$$1\frac{1}{4} \times 3 = (1 \times 3) + \left(\frac{1}{4} \times 3\right)$$
$$= 3 + \frac{3}{4}$$
$$= 3\frac{3}{4}$$

$$\frac{3}{4} \times 3 = \frac{3}{4} \times 3$$
$$= \frac{9}{4}$$
$$= 2\frac{1}{4}$$

$$\frac{3}{8} \times 3 = \frac{3}{8} \times 3$$
$$= \frac{9}{8}$$
$$= 1\frac{1}{8}$$

$$1\frac{1}{2} \times 3 = 1 \times 3 + \frac{1}{2} \times 3$$
$$= 3 + \frac{3}{2}$$
$$= 3 + 1\frac{1}{2}$$
$$= 4\frac{1}{2}$$

$$2 \times 3 = 6$$

So, the result for the triple recipe is:

$5\frac{1}{4}$	cup	Flour
$3\frac{3}{4}$	tsp	Baking powder
$2\frac{1}{4}$	tsp	Salt
$1\frac{1}{8}$	cup	Sugar
$4\frac{1}{2}$	Tbsp	Butter
6	large	Eggs
$2\frac{1}{4}$	tsp	Vanilla extract
$1\frac{1}{8}$	cup	Sour cream

Proportions and Ratios

PROPORTIONS

A proportion is a relationship between two quantities that dictates how one changes when the other changes. A **direct proportion** describes a relationship in which a quantity increases by a set amount for every increase in the other quantity, or decreases by that same amount for every decrease in the other quantity. Example: Assuming a constant driving speed, the time required for a car trip increases as the distance of the trip increases. The distance to be traveled and the time required to travel are directly proportional.

An **inverse proportion** is a relationship in which an increase in one quantity is accompanied by a decrease in the other, or vice versa. Example: the time required for a car trip decreases as the speed

increases, and increases as the speed decreases, so the time required is inversely proportional to the speed of the car.

RATIOS

A **ratio** is a comparison of two quantities in a particular order. Example: If there are 14 computers in a lab, and the class has 20 students, there is a student to computer ratio of 20 to 14, commonly written as 20:14. Ratios are normally reduced to their smallest whole number representation, so 20:14 would be reduced to 10:7 by dividing both sides by 2.

CONSTANT OF PROPORTIONALITY

When two quantities have a proportional relationship, there exists a **constant of proportionality** between the quantities. The product of this constant and one of the quantities is equal to the other quantity. For example, if one lemon costs $0.25, two lemons cost $0.50, and three lemons cost $0.75, there is a proportional relationship between the total cost of lemons and the number of lemons purchased. The constant of proportionality is the **unit price**, namely $0.25/lemon. Notice that the total price of lemons, t, can be found by multiplying the unit price of lemons, p, and the number of lemons, n: $t = pn$.

WORK/UNIT RATE

Unit rate expresses a quantity of one thing in terms of one unit of another. For example, if you travel 30 miles every two hours, a unit rate expresses this comparison in terms of one hour: in one hour you travel 15 miles, so your unit rate is 15 miles per hour. Other examples are how much one ounce of food costs (price per ounce) or figuring out how much one egg costs out of the dozen (price per 1 egg, instead of price per 12 eggs). The denominator of a unit rate is always 1. Unit rates are used to compare different situations to solve problems. For example, to make sure you get the best deal when deciding which kind of soda to buy, you can find the unit rate of each. If soda #1 costs $1.50 for a 1-liter bottle, and soda #2 costs $2.75 for a 2-liter bottle, it would be a better deal to buy soda #2, because its unit rate is only $1.375 per 1-liter, which is cheaper than soda #1. Unit rates can also help determine the length of time a given event will take. For example, if you can paint 2 rooms in 4.5 hours, you can determine how long it will take you to paint 5 rooms by solving for the unit rate per room and then multiplying that by 5.

SLOPE

On a graph with two points, (x_1, y_1) and (x_2, y_2), the **slope** is found with the formula $m = \frac{y_2 - y_1}{x_2 - x_1}$; where $x_1 \neq x_2$ and m stands for slope. If the value of the slope is **positive**, the line has an *upward direction* from left to right. If the value of the slope is **negative**, the line has a *downward direction* from left to right. Consider the following example:

A new book goes on sale in bookstores and online stores. In the first month, 5,000 copies of the book are sold. Over time, the book continues to grow in popularity. The data for the number of copies sold is in the table below.

# of Months on Sale	1	2	3	4	5
# of Copies Sold (In Thousands)	5	10	15	20	25

So, the number of copies that are sold and the time that the book is on sale is a proportional relationship. In this example, an equation can be used to show the data: $y = 5x$, where x is the number of months that the book is on sale, and y is the number of copies sold. So, the slope of the corresponding line is $\frac{\text{rise}}{\text{run}} = \frac{5}{1} = 5$.

> **Review Video: Finding the Slope of a Line**
> Visit mometrix.com/academy and enter code: 766664

FINDING AN UNKNOWN IN EQUIVALENT EXPRESSIONS

It is often necessary to apply information given about a rate or proportion to a new scenario. For example, if you know that Jedha can run a marathon (26 miles) in 3 hours, how long would it take her to run 10 miles at the same pace? Start by setting up equivalent expressions:

$$\frac{26 \text{ mi}}{3 \text{ hr}} = \frac{10 \text{ mi}}{x \text{ hr}}$$

Now, cross multiply and, solve for x:

$$26x = 30$$
$$x = \frac{30}{26} = \frac{15}{13}$$
$$x \cong 1.15 \text{ hrs } or \text{ 1 hr 9 min}$$

So, at this pace, Jedha could run 10 miles in about 1.15 hours or about 1 hour and 9 minutes.

> **Review Video: Cross Multiply Fractions**
> Visit mometrix.com/academy and enter code: 893904

PRACTICE

P1. Solve the following for x.

(a) $\frac{45}{12} = \frac{15}{x}$

(b) $\frac{0.50}{2} = \frac{1.50}{x}$

(c) $\frac{40}{8} = \frac{x}{24}$

P2. At a school, for every 20 female students there are 15 male students. This same student ratio happens to exist at another school. If there are 100 female students at the second school, how many male students are there?

P3. In a hospital emergency room, there are 4 nurses for every 12 patients. What is the ratio of nurses to patients? If the nurse-to-patient ratio remains constant, how many nurses must be present to care for 24 patients?

P4. In a bank, the banker-to-customer ratio is 1:2. If seven bankers are on duty, how many customers are currently in the bank?

P5. Janice made $40 during the first 5 hours she spent babysitting. She will continue to earn money at this rate until she finishes babysitting in 3 more hours. Find how much money Janice earns per hour and the total she earned babysitting.

P6. The McDonalds are taking a family road trip, driving 300 miles to their cabin. It took them 2 hours to drive the first 120 miles. They will drive at the same speed all the way to their cabin. Find the speed at which the McDonalds are driving and how much longer it will take them to get to their cabin.

P7. It takes Andy 10 minutes to read 6 pages of his book. He has already read 150 pages in his book that is 210 pages long. Find how long it takes Andy to read 1 page and also find how long it will take him to finish his book if he continues to read at the same speed.

PRACTICE SOLUTIONS

P1. First, cross multiply; then, solve for x:

(a) $45x = 12 \times 15$
$45x = 180$
$x = \frac{180}{45} = 4$

(b) $0.5x = 1.5 \times 2$
$0.5x = 3$
$x = \frac{3}{0.5} = 6$

(c) $8x = 40 \times 24$
$8x = 960$
$x = \frac{960}{8} = 120$

P2. One way to find the number of male students is to set up and solve a proportion.

$$\frac{\text{number of female students}}{\text{number of male students}} = \frac{20}{15} = \frac{100}{\text{number of male students}}$$

Represent the unknown number of male students as the variable x: $\frac{20}{15} = \frac{100}{x}$

Cross multiply and then solve for x:

$$20x = 15 \times 100$$
$$x = \frac{1500}{20}$$
$$x = 75$$

P3. The ratio of nurses to patients can be written as 4 to 12, 4:12, or $\frac{4}{12}$. Because four and twelve have a common factor of four, the ratio should be reduced to 1:3, which means that there is one nurse present for every three patients. If this ratio remains constant, there must be eight nurses present to care for 24 patients.

P4. Use proportional reasoning or set up a proportion to solve. Because there are twice as many customers as bankers, there must be fourteen customers when seven bankers are on duty. Setting up and solving a proportion gives the same result:

$$\frac{\text{number of bankers}}{\text{number of customers}} = \frac{1}{2} = \frac{7}{\text{number of customers}}$$

Represent the unknown number of customers as the variable x: $\frac{1}{2} = \frac{7}{x}$.

To solve for x, cross multiply: $1 \times x = 7 \times 2$, so $x = 14$.

P5. Janice earns $8 per hour. This can be found by taking her initial amount earned, $40, and dividing it by the number of hours worked, 5. Since $\frac{40}{5} = 8$, Janice makes $8 in one hour. This can also be found by finding the unit rate, money earned per hour: $\frac{40}{5} = \frac{x}{1}$. Since cross multiplying yields $5x = 40$, and division by 5 shows that $x = 8$, Janice earns $8 per hour.

Janice will earn $64 babysitting in her 8 total hours (adding the first 5 hours to the remaining 3 gives the 8 hour total). Since Janice earns $8 per hour and she worked 8 hours, $\frac{\$8}{\text{hr}} \times 8 \text{ hrs} = \$64$. This can also be found by setting up a proportion comparing money earned to babysitting hours. Since she earns $40 for 5 hours and since the rate is constant, she will earn a proportional amount in 8 hours: $\frac{40}{5} = \frac{x}{8}$. Cross multiplying will yield $5x = 320$, and division by 5 shows that $x = 64$.

P6. The McDonalds are driving 60 miles per hour. This can be found by setting up a proportion to find the unit rate, the number of miles they drive per one hour: $\frac{120}{2} = \frac{x}{1}$. Cross multiplying yields $2x = 120$ and division by 2 shows that $x = 60$.

Since the McDonalds will drive this same speed for the remaining miles, it will take them another 3 hours to get to their cabin. This can be found by first finding how many miles the McDonalds have left to drive, which is $300 - 120 = 180$. The McDonalds are driving at 60 miles per hour, so a proportion can be set up to determine how many hours it will take them to drive 180 miles: $\frac{180}{x} = \frac{60}{1}$. Cross multiplying yields $60x = 180$, and division by 60 shows that $x = 3$. This can also be found by using the formula $D = r \times t$ (or distance = rate × time), where $180 = 60 \times t$, and division by 60 shows that $t = 3$.

P7. It takes Andy 10 minutes to read 6 pages, $\frac{10}{6} = 1\frac{2}{3}$ minutes, which is 1 minute and 40 seconds.

Next, determine how many pages Andy has left to read, $210 - 150 = 60$. Since it is now known that it takes him $1\frac{2}{3}$ minutes to read each page, then that rate must be multiplied by however many pages he has left to read (60) to find the time he'll need: $60 \times 1\frac{2}{3} = 100$, so it will take him 100 minutes, or 1 hour and 40 minutes, to read the rest of his book.

Measurement

ROUNDING AND ESTIMATION

Rounding is reducing the digits in a number while still trying to keep the value similar. The result will be less accurate but in a simpler form and easier to use. Whole numbers can be rounded to the nearest ten, hundred, or thousand.

When you are asked to estimate the solution to a problem, you will need to provide only an approximate figure or **estimation** for your answer. In this situation, you will need to round each number in the calculation to the level indicated (nearest hundred, nearest thousand, etc.) or to a level that makes sense for the numbers involved. When estimating a sum **all numbers must be rounded to the same level**. You cannot round one number to the nearest thousand while rounding another to the nearest hundred.

> **Review Video: Rounding and Estimation**
> Visit mometrix.com/academy and enter code: 126243

PRACTICE

P1. Round each number to the indicated degree:

(a) Round to the nearest ten: 11; 47; 118

(b) Round to the nearest hundred: 78; 980; 248

(c) Round each number to the nearest thousand: 302; 1274; 3756

P2. Estimate the solution to $345,932 + 96,369$ by rounding each number to the nearest ten thousand.

P3. A runner's heart beats 422 times over the course of six minutes. About how many times did the runner's heart beat during each minute?

PRACTICE SOLUTIONS

P1. (a) When rounding to the nearest ten, anything ending in 5 or greater rounds up. So, 11 rounds to 10, 47 rounds to 50, and 118 rounds to 120.

(b) When rounding to the nearest hundred, anything ending in 50 or greater rounds up. So, 78 rounds to 100, 980 rounds to 1,000, and 248 rounds to 200.

(c) When rounding to the nearest thousand, anything ending in 500 or greater rounds up. So, 302 rounds to 0, 1274 rounds to 1,000, and 3,756 rounds to 4,000.

P2. Start by rounding each number to the nearest ten thousand: 345,932 becomes 350,000, and 96,369 becomes 100,000. Then, add the rounded numbers: $350,000 + 100,000 = 450,000$. So, the answer is approximately 450,000. The exact answer would be $345,932 + 96,369 = 442,301$. So, the estimate of 450,000 is a similar value to the exact answer.

P3. "About how many" indicates that you need to estimate the solution. In this case, look at the numbers you are given. 422 can be rounded down to 420, which is easily divisible by 6. A good estimate is $420 \div 6 = 70$ beats per minute. More accurately, the patient's heart rate was just over 70 beats per minute since his heart actually beat a little more than 420 times in six minutes.

Sequences

A **sequence** is a set of numbers that continues on in a defined pattern. The function that defines a sequence has a domain composed of the set of positive integers. Each member of the sequence is an element, or individual term. Each element is identified by the notation a_n, where a is the term of the sequence, and n is the integer identifying which term in the sequence a is. There are two different ways to represent a sequence that contains the element a_n. The first is the simple notation $\{a_n\}$. The expanded notation of a sequence is $a_1, a_2, a_3, \dots a_n, \dots$. Notice that the expanded form does not end with the nth term. There is no indication that the nth term is the last term in the sequence, only that the nth term is an element of the sequence.

ARITHMETIC SEQUENCES

An **arithmetic sequence**, or arithmetic progression, is a special kind of sequence in which each term has a specific quantity, called the common difference, that is added to the previous term. The common difference may be positive or negative. The general form of an arithmetic sequence containing n terms is $a_1, a_1 + d, a_1 + 2d, \dots, a_1 + (n-1)d$, where d is the common difference. The formula for the general term of an arithmetic sequence is $a_n = a_1 + (n-1)d$, where a_n is the term you are looking for and d is the common difference. To find the sum of the first n terms of an arithmetic sequence, use the formula $s_n = \frac{n}{2}(a_1 + a_n)$.

> **Review Video: Arithmetic Sequence**
> Visit mometrix.com/academy and enter code: 676885

MONOTONIC SEQUENCES

A **monotonic sequence** is a sequence that is either nonincreasing or nondecreasing. A **nonincreasing** sequence is one whose terms either get progressively smaller in value or remain the same - a sequence that is bounded above. This means that all elements of the sequence must be less than a given real number. A **nondecreasing** sequence is one whose terms either get progressively larger in value or remain the same - a sequence that is bounded below. This means that all elements of the sequence must be greater than a given real number.

RECURSIVE SEQUENCES

When one element of a sequence is defined in terms of a previous element or elements of the sequence, the sequence is a **recursive sequence**. For example, given the recursive definition $a_1 = 1; a_2 = 1; a_n = a_{n-1} + a_{n-2}$ for all $n > 2$, you get the sequence $1, 1, 2, 3, 5, 8, \dots$. This particular sequence is known as the Fibonacci sequence, and is defined as the numbers zero and one, and a continuing sequence of numbers, with each number in the sequence equal to the sum of the two previous numbers. It is important to note that the Fibonacci sequence can also be defined as the first two terms being equal to one, with the remaining terms equal to the sum of the previous two terms. Both definitions are considered correct in mathematics. Make sure you know which definition you are working with when dealing with Fibonacci numbers.

Sometimes one term of a sequence with a recursive definition can be found without knowing the previous terms of the sequence. This case is known as a **closed-form** expression for a recursive definition. In this case, an alternate formula will apply to the sequence to generate the same sequence of numbers. However, not all sequences based on recursive definitions will have a closed-form expression. Some sequences will require the use of the recursive definition.

GOLDEN RATIO AND FIBONACCI SEQUENCE

The golden ratio is approximately 1.6180339887498948482... and is often represented by the Greek letter phi, Φ. The exact value of Φ is $(1 + \sqrt{5})/2$ and it is one of the solutions to $x - \frac{1}{x} = 1$. The golden ratio is represented within the Fibonacci sequence, since the ratio of a term to the previous term approaches Φ as the sequence approaches infinity:

n	a_n	a_{n-1}	$\dfrac{a_n}{a_{n-1}}$
3	2	1	2
4	3	2	1.5
5	5	3	$1.\overline{6}$
6	8	5	1.6
7	13	8	1.625
8	21	13	$1.\overline{615384}$
9	34	21	$1.\overline{619047}$
⋮	⋮	⋮	⋮
20	6765	4181	1.618033963

GEOMETRIC SEQUENCES

A **geometric sequence**, or geometric progression, is a special kind of sequence in which each term has a specific quantity, called the common ratio, multiplied by the previous term. The common ratio may be positive or negative. The general form of a geometric sequence containing n terms is $a_1, a_1r, a_1r^2, \ldots, a_1r^{n-1}$, where r is the common ratio. The formula for the general term of a geometric sequence is $a_n = a_1r^{n-1}$, where a_n is the term you are looking for and r is the common ratio. To find the sum of the first n terms of a geometric sequence, use the formula $s_n = \frac{a_1(1-r^n)}{1-r}$.

Any function with the set of all natural numbers as the domain is also called a sequence. An element of a sequence is denoted by the symbol a_n, which represents the nth element of sequence a. Sequences may be arithmetic or geometric, and may be defined by a recursive definition, closed-form expression or both. Arithmetic and geometric sequences both have recursive definitions based on the first term of the sequence, as well as both having formulas to find the sum of the first n terms in the sequence, assuming you know what the first term is. The sum of all the terms in a sequence is called a **series**. Consider the following example of a geometric sequence: Andy opens a savings account with $10. During each subsequent week, he plans to double the amount deposited during the previous week.

Sequence: 10, 20, 40, 80, 160, ...

Function: $a_n = 10 \times 2^{n-1}$

The sequence is a geometric sequence, with a common ratio of 2. All geometric sequences represent exponential functions. The nth term in any geometric sequence is represented by the general form, $a_n = a_1 \times r^{n-1}$, where a_n represents the value of the nth term, a_1 represents the value of the initial term, r represents the common ratio, and n represents the number of terms. Thus, substituting the initial value of 10 and common ratio of 2 gives the function, $a_n = 10 \times 2^{n-1}$.

LIMIT OF A SEQUENCE

Some sequences will have a **limit**, or a value the sequence approaches or sometimes even reaches but never passes. A sequence that has a limit is known as a convergent sequence because all the values of the sequence seemingly converge at that point. Sequences that do not converge at a particular limit are divergent sequences. The easiest way to determine whether a sequence converges or diverges is to find the limit of the sequence. If the limit is a real number, the sequence is a convergent sequence. If the limit is infinity, the sequence is a divergent sequence.

Remember the following rules for finding limits:

- $\lim\limits_{n \to \infty} k = k$, for all real numbers k
- $\lim\limits_{n \to \infty} \dfrac{1}{n} = 0$
- $\lim\limits_{n \to \infty} n = \infty$
- $\lim\limits_{n \to \infty} \dfrac{k}{n^p} = 0$, for all real numbers k and positive rational numbers p
- The limit of the sums of two sequences is equal to the sum of the limits of the two sequences: $\lim\limits_{n \to \infty} (a_n + b_n) = \lim\limits_{n \to \infty} a_n + \lim\limits_{n \to \infty} b_n$.
- The limit of the difference between two sequences is equal to the difference between the limits of the two sequences: $\lim\limits_{n \to \infty} (a_n - b_n) = \lim\limits_{n \to \infty} a_n - \lim\limits_{n \to \infty} b_n$
- The limit of the product of two sequences is equal to the product of the limits of the two sequences: $\lim\limits_{n \to \infty} (a_n \times b_n) = \lim\limits_{n \to \infty} a_n \times \lim\limits_{n \to \infty} b_n$
- The limit of the quotient of two sequences is equal to the quotient of the limits of the two sequences, with some exceptions: $\lim\limits_{n \to \infty} \left(\dfrac{a_n}{b_n} \right) = \dfrac{\lim\limits_{n \to \infty} a_n}{\lim\limits_{n \to \infty} b_n}$. In the quotient formula, it is important to consider that $b_n \neq 0$ and $\lim\limits_{n \to \infty} b_n \neq 0$.
- The limit of a sequence multiplied by a scalar is equal to the scalar multiplied by the limit of the sequence: $\lim\limits_{n \to \infty} k a_n = k \lim\limits_{n \to \infty} a_n$, where k is any real number.

INFINITE SERIES

An **infinite series**, also referred to as just a series, is a series of partial sums of a defined sequence. Each infinite sequence represents an infinite series according to the equation $\sum_{n=1}^{\infty} a_n = a_1 + a_2 + a_3 + \cdots + a_n + \cdots$. This notation can be shortened to $\sum_{n=1}^{\infty} a_n$ or $\sum a_n$. Every series is a sequence of partial sums, where the first partial sum is equal to the first element of the series, the second partial sum is equal to the sum of the first two elements of the series, and the nth partial sum is equal to the sum of the first n elements of the series.

Every infinite sequence of partial sums (infinite series) either converges or diverges. Like the test for convergence in a sequence, finding the limit of the sequence of partial sums will indicate whether it is a converging series or a diverging series. If there exists a real number S such that $\lim\limits_{n \to \infty} S_n = S$, where S_n is the sequence of partial sums, then the series converges. If the limit equals infinity, then the series diverges. If $\lim\limits_{n \to \infty} S_n = S$ and S is a real number, then S is also the convergence value of the series.

To find the sum as n approaches infinity for the sum of two convergent series, find the sum as n approaches infinity for each individual series and add the results.

$$\sum_{n=1}^{\infty} (a_n + b_n) = \sum_{n=1}^{\infty} a_n + \sum_{n=1}^{\infty} b_n$$

To find the sum as n approaches infinity for the difference between two convergent series, find the sum as n approaches infinity for each individual series and subtract the results.

$$\sum_{n=1}^{\infty} (a_n - b_n) = \sum_{n=1}^{\infty} a_n - \sum_{n=1}^{\infty} b_n$$

To find the sum as n approaches infinity for the product of a constant, also called a scalar, and a convergent series, find the sum as n approaches infinity for the series and multiply the result by the scalar.

$$\sum_{n=1}^{\infty} k a_n = k \sum_{n=1}^{\infty} a_n$$

The **n^{th} term test for divergence** involves taking the limit of the nth term of a sequence and determining whether or not the limit is equal to zero. If the limit of the nth term is not equal to zero, then the series is a diverging series. This test only works to prove divergence, however. If the nth term is equal to zero, the test is inconclusive.

PRACTICE

P1. Suppose Rachel has \$4,500 in her account in month 1. With each passing month, her account is one-half of what it was during the previous month. What would be a formula for the value of her account in any future month?

P2. Determine if the following geometric sequences converge or diverge:

(a) $a_n = 500(3^{n-1})$; where $n = 1,2,3,\dots$

(b) $a_n = 5(1^{n-1})$; where $n = 1,2,3,\dots$

(c) $a_n = 50((-1)^{n-1})$; where $n = 1,2,3,\dots$

(d) $a_n = 5000\left(\left(\frac{1}{5}\right)^{n-1}\right)$; where $n = 1,2,3,\dots$

P3. Determine a recursive expression for the following sequences:

(a) $3, 7, 19, 55, 163, \dots$

(b) $8, 6, 5, 4.5, 4.25, \dots$

PRACTICE SOLUTIONS

P1. The sequence: 4,500, 2,250, 1,125, 562.50, 281.25, ... is geometric, since there is a common ratio of $\frac{1}{2}$. Thus, this sequence represents an exponential function. All geometric sequences represent exponential functions. Recall the general form of a geometric sequence is $a_n = a_1 \times r^{n-1}$, and substituting the initial value of 4,500 and common ratio of $\frac{1}{2}$ gives $a_n = 4,500 \times \left(\frac{1}{2}\right)^{n-1}$.

P2. (a) $\lim_{n\to\infty} a_n \to 500(3^{\infty-1}) \to 500(\infty) \to \infty$. This sequence diverges.

(b) $\lim_{n\to\infty} a_n \to 5(1^{\infty-1}) \to 5(1) \to 5$. This sequence converges.

(c) $\lim\limits_{n \to \infty} a_n \to 50((-1)^{\infty-1}) \to 50((-1)^{\infty}) \to undefined$. Since -1 raised to an integer power is either -1 or +1 this sequence just oscilates and does not converge. However, it is bounded above and below, so it does not diverge either.

(d) $\lim\limits_{n \to \infty} a_n \to 5000\left(\left(\frac{1}{5}\right)^{\infty-1}\right) \to 500(0) \to 0$. This sequence converges.

P3. (a) Use a table to determine the pattern:

n	1	2	3	4	5
a_n	3	7	19	55	163
$d_n = a_n - a_{n-1}$	-	4	12	36	108
$r_n = \dfrac{d_n}{d_{n-1}}$	-	-	3	3	3

Since the difference between successive terms is increasing at a uniform rate, we can use that to the guess at a sequence: $a_n = 3a_{n-1} + d$. Substitute the first terms to find d:

$$7 = 3(3) + d$$
$$-2 = d$$

Thus, the recursive form would be $a_n = 3a_{n-1} - 2$

(b) Use a table to determine the pattern:

n	1	2	3	4	5
a_n	8	6	5	4.5	4.25
$d_n = a_n - a_{n-1}$	-	2	1	0.5	0.25
$r_n = \dfrac{d_n}{d_{n-1}}$	-	-	$\dfrac{1}{2}$	$\dfrac{1}{2}$	$\dfrac{1}{2}$

Since the difference between successive terms is increasing at a uniform rate, we can use that to the guess at a sequence: $a_n = \frac{a_{n-1}}{2} + d$. Substitute the first terms to find d:

$$6 = \frac{8}{2} + d$$
$$2 = d$$

Thus, the recursive form would be $a_n = \frac{a_{n-1}}{2} + 2$

Expressions, Equations and Inequalities

LINEAR EQUATIONS

Equations that can be written as $ax + b = 0$, where $a \neq 0$ are referred to as **one variable linear equations**. A solution to such an equation is called a **root**. In the case where we have the equation $5x + 10 = 0$, if we solve for x we get a solution of $x = -2$. In other words, the root of the equation is -2. This is found by first subtracting 10 from both sides, which gives $5x = -10$. Next, simply divide both sides by the coefficient of the variable, in this case 5, to get $x = -2$. This can be checked by plugging -2 back into the original equation $(5)(-2) + 10 = -10 + 10 = 0$.

The **solution set** is the set of all solutions of an equation. In our example, the solution set would simply be -2. If there were more solutions (there usually are in multivariable equations) then they would also be included in the solution set. When an equation has no true solutions, this is referred to as an **empty set**. Equations with identical solution sets are **equivalent equations**. An **identity** is a term whose value or determinant is equal to 1.

Linear equations can be written many ways. Below is a list of some forms linear equations can take:

- **Standard Form**: $Ax + By = C$; the slope is $\frac{-A}{B}$ and the y-intercept is $\frac{C}{B}$
- **Slope Intercept Form**: $y = mx + b$, where m is the slope and b is the y-intercept
- **Point-Slope Form**: $y - y_1 = m(x - x_1)$, where m is the slope and (x_1, y_1) is a point on the line
- **Two-Point Form**: $\frac{y-y_1}{x-x_1} = \frac{y_2-y_1}{x_2-x_1}$, where (x_1, y_1) and (x_2, y_2) are two points on the given line
- **Intercept Form**: $\frac{x}{x_1} + \frac{y}{y_1} = 1$, where $(x_1, 0)$ is the point at which a line intersects the x-axis, and $(0, y_1)$ is the point at which the same line intersects the y-axis

SOLVING ONE-VARIABLE LINEAR EQUATIONS

Multiply all terms by the lowest common denominator to eliminate any fractions. Look for addition or subtraction to undo so you can isolate the variable on one side of the equal sign. Divide both sides by the coefficient of the variable. When you have a value for the variable, substitute this value into the original equation to make sure you have a true equation. Consider the following example:

Kim's savings are represented by the table below. Represent her savings, using an equation.

X (Months)	Y (Total Savings)
2	$1,300
5	$2,050
9	$3,050
11	$3,550
16	$4,800

The table shows a function with a constant rate of change, or slope, of 250. Given the points on the table, the slopes can be calculated as $(2,050 - 1,300)/(5 - 2)$, $(3,050 - 2,050)/(9 - 5)$, $(3,550 - 3,050)/(11 - 9)$, and $(4,800 - 3,550)/(16 - 11)$, each of which equals 250. Thus, the table shows a constant rate of change, indicating a linear function. The slope-intercept form of a linear equation is written as $y = mx + b$, where m represents the slope and b represents the y-intercept. Substituting the slope into this form gives $y = 250x + b$. Substituting corresponding x- and y-values from any point into this equation will give the y-intercept, or b. Using the point, (2, 1,300), gives $1,300 = 250(2) + b$, which simplifies as b = 800. Thus, her savings may be represented by the equation, $y = 250x + 800$.

RULES FOR MANIPULATING EQUATIONS

LIKE TERMS

Like terms are terms in an equation that have the same variable, regardless of whether or not they also have the same coefficient. This includes terms that *lack* a variable; all constants (i.e. numbers without variables) are considered like terms. If the equation involves terms with a variable raised to different powers, the like terms are those that have the variable raised to the same power.

For example, consider the equation $x^2 + 3x + 2 = 2x^2 + x - 7 + 2x$. In this equation, 2 and –7 are like terms; they are both constants. $3x$, x, and $2x$ are like terms: they all include the variable x raised to the first power. x^2 and $2x^2$ are like terms; they both include the variable x, raised to the second power. $2x$ and $2x^2$ are not like terms; although they both involve the variable x, the variable is not raised to the same power in both terms. The fact that they have the same coefficient, 2, is not relevant.

CARRYING OUT THE SAME OPERATION ON BOTH SIDES OF AN EQUATION

When solving an equation, the general procedure is to carry out a series of operations on both sides of an equation, choosing operations that will tend to simplify the equation when doing so. The reason why the same operation must be carried out on both sides of the equation is because that leaves the meaning of the equation unchanged, and yields a result that is equivalent to the original equation. This would not be the case if we carried out an operation on one side of an equation and not the other. Consider what an equation means: it is a statement that two values or expressions are equal. If we carry out the same operation on both sides of the equation—add 3 to both sides, for example—then the two sides of the equation are changed in the same way, and so remain equal. If we do that to only one side of the equation—add 3 to one side but not the other—then that wouldn't be true; if we change one side of the equation but not the other then the two sides are no longer equal.

ADVANTAGE OF COMBINING LIKE TERMS

Combining like terms refers to adding or subtracting like terms—terms with the same variable—and therefore reducing sets of like terms to a single term. The main advantage of doing this is that it simplifies the equation. Often combining like terms can be done as the first step in solving an equation, though it can also be done later, such as after distributing terms in a product.

For example, consider the equation $2(x + 3) + 3(2 + x + 3) = -4$. The 2 and the 3 in the second set of parentheses are like terms, and we can combine them, yielding $2(x + 3) + 3(x + 5) = -4$. Now we can carry out the multiplications implied by the parentheses, distributing outer 2 and 3 accordingly: $2x + 6 + 3x + 15 = -4$. The $2x$ and the $3x$ are like terms, and we can add them together: $5x + 6 + 15 = -4$. Now, the constants 6, 15, and –4 are also like terms, and we can combine them as well: subtracting 6 and 15 from both sides of the equation, we get $5x = -4 - 6 - 15$, or $5x = -25$, which simplifies further to $x = -5$.

> **Review Video: Simplifying Equations by Combining Like Terms**
> Visit mometrix.com/academy and enter code: 668506

CANCELING TERMS ON OPPOSITE SIDES OF AN EQUATION

Two terms on opposite sides of an equation can be canceled if and only if they *exactly* match each other. They must have the same variable raised to the same power and the same coefficient. For example, in the equation $3x + 2x^2 + 6 = 2x^2 - 6$, $2x^2$ appears on both sides of the equation, and can be canceled, leaving $3x + 6 = -6$. The 6 on each side of the equation cannot be canceled, because it is added on one side of the equation and subtracted on the other. While they cannot be canceled, however, the 6 and –6 are like terms and can be combined, yielding $3x = -12$, which simplifies further to $x = -4$.

It's also important to note that the terms to be canceled must be independent terms and cannot be part of a larger term. For example, consider the equation $2(x + 6) = 3(x + 4) + 1$. We cannot cancel the xs, because even though they match each other they are part of the larger terms $2(x + 6)$ and $3(x + 4)$. We must first distribute the 2 and 3, yielding $2x + 12 = 3x + 12 + 1$. Now we see that the terms with the x's do not match, but the 12's do, and can be canceled, leaving $2x = 3x + 1$, which simplifies to $x = -1$.

> **Review Video: <u>Rules for Manipulating Equations</u>**
> Visit mometrix.com/academy and enter code: 838871

PROCESS FOR MANIPULATING EQUATIONS

ISOLATING VARIABLES

To **isolate a variable** means to manipulate the equation so that the variable appears by itself on one side of the equation, and does not appear at all on the other side. Generally, an equation or inequality is considered to be solved once the variable is isolated and the other side of the equation or inequality is simplified as much as possible. In the case of a two-variable equation or inequality, only one variable need be isolated; it will not usually be possible to simultaneously isolate both variables.

For a linear equation—an equation in which the variable only appears raised to the first power— isolating a variable can be done by first moving all the terms with the variable to one side of the equation and all other terms to the other side. (*Moving* a term really means adding the inverse of the term to both sides; when a term is *moved* to the other side of the equation its sign is flipped.) Then combine like terms on each side. Finally, divide both sides by the coefficient of the variable, if applicable. The steps need not necessarily be done in this order, but this order will always work.

> **Review Video: <u>Solving Equations with Variables on Both Sides</u>**
> Visit mometrix.com/academy and enter code: 402497

EQUATIONS WITH MORE THAN ONE SOLUTION

Some types of non-linear equation, such as equations involving squares of variables, may have more than one solution. For example, the equation $x^2 = 4$ has two solutions: 2 and –2. Equations with absolute values can also have multiple solutions: $|x| = 1$ has the solutions $x = 1$ and $x = -1$.

It is also possible for a linear equation to have more than one solution, but only if the equation is true regardless of the value of the variable. In this case, the equation is considered to have infinitely many solutions, because any possible value of the variable is a solution. We know a linear equation has infinitely many solutions if when we combine like terms the variables cancel, leaving a true statement. For example, consider the equation $2(3x + 5) = x + 5(x + 2)$. Distributing, we get $6x + 10 = x + 5x + 10$; combining like terms gives $6x + 10 = 6x + 10$, and the $6x$ terms cancel to leave $10 = 10$. This is clearly true, so the original equation is true for any value of x. We could also have canceled the 10s leaving $0 = 0$, but again this is clearly true—in general if both sides of the equation match exactly, it has infinitely many solutions.

EQUATIONS WITH NO SOLUTION

Some types of non-linear equation, such as equations involving squares of variables, may have no solution. For example, the equation $x^2 = -2$ has no solutions in the real numbers, because the square of any real number must be positive. Similarly, $|x| = -1$ has no solution, because the absolute value of a number is always positive.

It is also possible for an equation to have no solution even if does not involve any powers greater than one or absolute values or other special functions. For example, the equation $2(x + 3) + x = 3x$ has no solution. We can see that if we try to solve it: first we distribute, leaving $2x + 6 + x = 3x$. But now if we try to combine all the terms with the variable, we find that they cancel: we have $3x$ on the left and $3x$ on the right, canceling to leave us with $6 = 0$. This is clearly false. In general, whenever the variable terms in an equation cancel leaving different constants on both sides, it means that the equation has no solution. (If we are left with the *same* constant on both sides, the equation has infinitely many solutions instead.)

FEATURES OF EQUATIONS THAT REQUIRE SPECIAL TREATMENT
LINEAR EQUATIONS

A linear equation is an equation in which variables only appear by themselves: not multiplied together, not with exponents other than one, and not inside absolute value signs or any other functions. For example, the equation $x + 1 - 3x = 5 - x$ is a linear equation: while x appears multiple times, it never appears with an exponent other than one, or inside any function. The two-variable equation $2x - 3y = 5 + 2x$ is also a linear equation. In contrast, the equation $x^2 - 5 = 3x$ is *not* a linear equation, because it involves the term x^2. $\sqrt{x} = 5$ is not a linear equation, because it involves a square root. $(x - 1)^2 = 4$ is not a linear equation because even though there's no exponent on the x directly, it appears as part of an expression that is squared. The two-variable equation $x + xy - y = 5$ is not a linear equation because it includes the term xy, where two variables are multiplied together.

Linear equations can always be solved (or shown to have no solution) by combining like terms and performing simple operations on both sides of the equation. Some non-linear equations can also be solved by similar methods, but others may require more advanced methods of solution, if they can be solved analytically at all.

SOLVING EQUATIONS INVOLVING ROOTS

In an equation involving roots, the first step is to isolate the term with the root, if possible, and then raise both sides of the equation to the appropriate power to eliminate it. Consider an example equation, $2\sqrt{x + 1} - 1 = 3$. In this case, begin by adding 1 to both sides, yielding $2\sqrt{x + 1} = 4$, and then dividing both sides by 2, yielding $\sqrt{x + 1} = 2$. Now square both sides, yielding $x + 1 = 4$. Finally, subtracting 1 from both sides yields $x = 3$.

Squaring both sides of an equation may, however, yield a spurious solution—a solution to the squared equation that is *not* a solution of the original equation. It's therefore necessary to plug the solution back into the original equation to make sure it works. In this case, it does: $2\sqrt{3 + 1} - 1 = 2\sqrt{4} - 1 = 2(2) - 1 = 4 - 1 = 3$.

The same procedure applies for roots other than square roots. For example, given the equation $3 + \sqrt[3]{2x} = 5$, we can first subtract 3 from both sides, yielding $\sqrt[3]{2x} = 2$ and isolating the root. Raising both sides to the third power yields $2x = 2^3$, i.e. $2x = 8$. We can now divide both sides by 2 to get $x = 4$.

Review Video: Solving Equations Involving Roots
Visit mometrix.com/academy and enter code: 297670

SOLVING EQUATIONS WITH EXPONENTS

To solve an equation involving an exponent, the first step is to isolate the variable with the exponent. We can then take the appropriate root of both sides to eliminate the exponent. For instance, for the equation $2x^3 + 17 = 5x^3 - 7$, we can subtract $5x^3$ from both sides to get $-3x^3 + 17 = -7$, and then subtract 17 from both sides to get $-3x^3 = -24$. Finally, we can divide both sides by -3 to get $x^3 = 8$. Finally, we can take the cube root of both sides to get $x = \sqrt[3]{8} = 2$.

One important but often overlooked point is that equations with an exponent greater than 1 may have more than one answer. The solution to $x^2 = 9$ isn't simply $x = 3$; it's $x = \pm 3$: that is, $x = 3$ or $x = -3$. For a slightly more complicated example, consider the equation $(x - 1)^2 - 1 = 3$. Adding one to both sides yields $(x - 1)^2 = 4$; taking the square root of both sides yields $x - 1 = 2$. We can then add 1 to both sides to get $x = 3$. However, there's a second solution: we also have the possibility that $x - 1 = -2$, in which case $x = -1$. Both $x = 3$ and $x = -1$ are valid solutions, as can be verified by substituting them both into the original equation.

> **Review Video: Solving Equations with Exponents**
> Visit mometrix.com/academy and enter code: 514557

SOLVING EQUATIONS WITH ABSOLUTE VALUES

When solving an equation with an absolute value, the first step is to isolate the absolute value term. We then consider the two possibilities: when the expression inside the absolute value is positive or when it is negative. In the former case, the expression in the absolute value equals the expression on the other side of the equation; in the latter, it equals the additive inverse of that expression—the expression times negative one. We consider each case separately, and finally check for spurious solutions.

For instance, consider solving $|2x - 1| + x = 5$ for x. We can first isolate the absolute value by moving the x to the other side: $|2x - 1| = -x + 5$. Now, we have two possibilities. First, that $2x - 1$ is positive, and hence $2x - 1 = -x + 5$. Rearranging and combining like terms yields $3x = 6$, and hence $x = 2$. The other possibility is that $2x - 1$ is negative, and hence $2x - 1 = -(-x + 5) = x - 5$. In this case, rearranging and combining like terms yields $x = -4$. Substituting $x = 2$ and $x = -4$ back into the original equation, we see that they are both valid solutions.

Note that the absolute value of a sum or difference applies to the sum or difference as a whole, not to the individual terms: in general, $|2x - 1|$ is not equal to $|2x + 1|$ or to $|2x| - 1$.

SPURIOUS SOLUTIONS

A **spurious solution** may arise when we square both sides of an equation as a step in solving it, or under certain other operations on the equation. It is a solution to the squared or otherwise modified equation that is *not* a solution of the original equation. To identify a spurious solution, it's useful when you solve an equation involving roots or absolute values to plug the solution back into the original equation to make sure it's valid.

CHOOSING WHICH VARIABLE TO ISOLATE IN TWO-VARIABLE EQUATIONS

Similar to methods for a one-variable equation, solving a two-variable equation involves isolating a variable: manipulating the equation so that a variable appears by itself on one side of the equation, and not at all on the other side. However, in a two-variable equation, you will usually only be able to isolate one of the variables; the other variable may appear on the other side along with constant terms, or with exponents or other functions.

Often one variable will be much more easily isolated than the other, and therefore that's the variable you should choose. If one variable appears with various exponents, and the other is only raised to the first power, the latter variable is the one to isolate: given the equation $a^2 + 2b = a^3 + b + 3$, the b only appears to the first power, whereas a appears squared and cubed, so b is the variable that can be solved for: combining like terms and isolating the b on the left side of the equation, we get $b = a^3 - a^2 + 3$. If both variables are equally easy to isolate, then it's best to isolate the independent variable, if one is defined; if the two variables are x and y, the convention is that y is the independent variable.

> **Review Video: Solving Equations with Variables on Both Sides**
> Visit mometrix.com/academy and enter code: 402497

WORKING WITH INEQUALITIES

Commonly in algebra and other upper-level fields of math you find yourself working with mathematical expressions that do not equal each other. The statement comparing such expressions with symbols such as < (less than) or > (greater than) is called an *inequality*. An example of an inequality is $7x > 5$. To solve for x, simply divide both sides by 7 and the solution is shown to be $x > \frac{5}{7}$. Graphs of the solution set of inequalities are represented on a number line. Open circles are used to show that an expression approaches a number but is never quite equal to that number.

> **Review Video: Solving Multi-Step Inequalities**
> Visit mometrix.com/academy and enter code: 347842

Conditional inequalities are those with certain values for the variable that will make the condition true and other values for the variable where the condition will be false. **Absolute inequalities** can have any real number as the value for the variable to make the condition true, while there is no real number value for the variable that will make the condition false. Solving inequalities is done by following the same rules as for solving equations with the exception that when multiplying or dividing by a negative number the direction of the inequality sign must be flipped or reversed. **Double inequalities** are situations where two inequality statements apply to the same variable expression. An example of this is $-c < ax + b < c$.

> **Review Video: Conditional and Absolute Inequalities**
> Visit mometrix.com/academy and enter code: 980164

DETERMINING SOLUTIONS TO INEQUALITIES

To determine whether a coordinate is a solution of an inequality, you can substitute the values of the coordinate into the inequality, simplify, and check whether the resulting statement holds true. For instance, to determine whether $(-2, 4)$ is a solution of the inequality $y \geq -2x + 3$, substitute the values into the inequality, $4 \geq -2(-2) + 3$. Simplify the right side of the inequality and the result is $4 \geq 7$, which is a false statement. Therefore, the coordinate is not a solution of the inequality. You can also use this method to determine which part of the graph of an inequality is shaded. The graph of $y \geq -2x + 3$ includes the solid line $y = -2x + 3$ and, since it excludes the point $(-2, 4)$ to the left of the line, it is shaded to the right of the line.

FLIPPING INEQUALITY SIGNS

When given an inequality, we can always turn the entire inequality around, swapping the two sides of the inequality and changing the inequality sign. For instance, $x + 2 > 2x - 3$ is equivalent to $2x - 3 < x + 2$. Aside from that, normally the inequality does not change if we carry out the same

48

operation on both sides of the inequality. There is, however, one principal exception: if we *multiply* or *divide* both sides of the inequality by a *negative number*, the inequality is flipped. For example, if we take the inequality $-2x < 6$ and divide both sides by -2, the inequality flips and we are left with $x > -3$. This *only* applies to multiplication and division, and only with negative numbers. Multiplying or dividing both sides by a positive number, or adding or subtracting any number regardless of sign, does not flip the inequality. Another special case that flips the inequality sign is when reciprocals are used. For instance, $3 > 2$ but the relation of the reciprocals is $\frac{1}{2} < \frac{1}{3}$.

COMPOUND INEQUALITIES

A **compound inequality** is an equality that consists of two inequalities combined with *and* or *or*. The two components of a proper compound inequality must be of opposite type: that is, one must be greater than (or greater than or equal to), the other less than (or less than or equal to). For instance, "$x + 1 < 2$ or $x + 1 > 3$" is a compound inequality, as is "$2x \geq 4$ and $2x \leq 6$." An *and* inequality can be written more compactly by having one inequality on each side of the common part: "$2x \geq 1$ and $2x \leq 6$," can also be written as $1 \leq 2x \leq 6$.

In order for the compound inequality to be meaningful, the two parts of an *and* inequality must overlap; otherwise no numbers satisfy the inequality. On the other hand, if the two parts of an *or* inequality overlap, then *all* numbers satisfy the inequality and as such is usually not meaningful.

Solving a compound inequality requires solving each part separately. For example, given the compound inequality "$x + 1 < 2$ or $x + 1 > 3$," the first inequality, $x + 1 < 2$, reduces to $x < 1$, and the second part, $x + 1 > 3$, reduces to $x > 2$, so the whole compound inequality can be written as "$x < 1$ or $x > 2$." Similarly, $1 \leq 2x \leq 6$ can be solved by dividing each term by 2, yielding $\frac{1}{2} \leq x \leq 3$.

> **Review Video: Compound Inequalities**
> Visit mometrix.com/academy and enter code: 786318

SOLVING INEQUALITIES INVOLVING ABSOLUTE VALUES

To solve an inequality involving an absolute value, first isolate the term with the absolute value. Then proceed to treat the two cases separately as with an absolute value equation, but flipping the inequality in the case where the expression in the absolute value is negative (since that essentially involves multiplying both sides by -1.) The two cases are then combined into a compound inequality; if the absolute value is on the greater side of the inequality, then it is an *or* compound inequality, if on the lesser side, then it's an *and*.

Consider the inequality $2 + |x - 1| \geq 3$. We can isolate the absolute value term by subtracting 2 from both sides: $|x - 1| \geq 1$. Now, we're left with the two cases $x - 1 \geq 1$ or $x - 1 \leq -1$: note that in the latter, negative case, the inequality is flipped. $x - 1 \geq 1$ reduces to $x \geq 2$, and $x - 1 \leq -1$ reduces to $x \leq 0$. Since in the inequality $|x - 1| \geq 1$ the absolute value is on the greater side, the two cases combine into an *or* compound inequality, so the final, solved inequality is "$x \leq 0$ or $x \geq 2$."

> **Review Video: Solving Absolute Value Inequalities**
> Visit mometrix.com/academy and enter code: 997008

SOLVING INEQUALITIES INVOLVING SQUARE ROOTS

Solving an inequality with a square root involves two parts. First, we solve the inequality as if it were an equation, isolating the square root and then squaring both sides of the equation. Second, we restrict the solution to the set of values of x for which the value inside the square root sign is non-negative.

For example, in the inequality, $\sqrt{x-2}+1 < 5$, we can isolate the square root by subtracting 1 from both sides, yielding $\sqrt{x-2} < 4$. Squaring both sides of the inequality yields $x-2 < 16$, so $x < 18$. Since we can't take the square root of a negative number, we also require the part inside the square root to be non-negative. In this case, that means $x-2 \geq 0$. Adding 2 to both sides of the inequality yields $x \geq 2$. Our final answer is a compound inequality combining the two simple inequalities: $x \geq 2$ and $x < 18$, or $2 \leq x < 18$.

Note that we only get a compound inequality if the two simple inequalities are in opposite directions; otherwise we take the one that is more restrictive.

The same technique can be used for other even roots, such as fourth roots. It is *not*, however, used for cube roots or other odd roots—negative numbers *do* have cube roots, so the condition that the quantity inside the root sign cannot be negative does not apply.

> **Review Video: Solving Inequalities Involving Square Roots**
> Visit mometrix.com/academy and enter code: 800288

SPECIAL CIRCUMSTANCES

Sometimes an inequality involving an absolute value or an even exponent is true for all values of x, and we don't need to do any further work to solve it. This is true if the inequality, once the absolute value or exponent term is isolated, says that term is greater than a negative number (or greater than or equal to zero). Since an absolute value or a number raised to an even exponent is *always* non-negative, this inequality is always true.

GRAPHICAL SOLUTIONS TO EQUATIONS AND INEQUALITIES

When equations are shown graphically, they are usually shown on a **Cartesian coordinate plane**. The Cartesian coordinate plane consists of two number lines placed perpendicular to each other, and intersecting at the zero point, also known as the origin. The horizontal number line is known as the x-axis, with positive values to the right of the origin, and negative values to the left of the origin. The vertical number line is known as the y-axis, with positive values above the origin, and negative values below the origin. Any point on the plane can be identified by an ordered pair in the form (x, y), called coordinates. The x-value of the coordinate is called the abscissa, and the y-value of the coordinate is called the ordinate. The two number lines divide the plane into **four quadrants**: I, II, III, and IV.

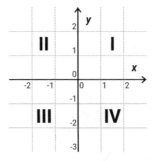

Note that in quadrant I $x > 0$ and $y > 0$, in quadrant II $x < 0$ and $y > 0$, in quadrant III $x < 0$ and $y < 0$, and in quadrant IV $x > 0$ and $y < 0$.

Recall that if the value of the slope of a line is positive, the line slopes upward from left to right. If the value of the slope is negative, the line slopes downward from left to right. If the y-coordinates are the same for two points on a line, the slope is 0 and the line is a **horizontal line**. If the x-coordinates are the same for two points on a line, there is no slope and the line is a **vertical line**. Two or more lines that have equivalent slopes are **parallel lines**. **Perpendicular lines** have slopes that are negative reciprocals of each other, such as $\frac{a}{b}$ and $\frac{-b}{a}$.

> **Review Video: Cartesian Coordinate Plane and Graphing**
> Visit mometrix.com/academy and enter code: 115173

GRAPHING SIMPLE INEQUALITIES

To graph a simple inequality, we first mark on the number line the value that signifies the end point of the inequality. If the inequality is strict (involves a less than or greater than), we use a hollow circle; if it is not strict (less than or equal to or greater than or equal to), we use a solid circle. We then fill in the part of the number line that satisfies the inequality: to the left of the marked point for less than (or less than or equal to), to the right for greater than (or greater than or equal to).

For example, we would graph the inequality $x < 5$ by putting a hollow circle at 5 and filling in the part of the line to the left:

GRAPHING COMPOUND INEQUALITIES

To graph a compound inequality, we fill in both parts of the inequality for an *or* inequality, or the overlap between them for an *and* inequality. More specifically, we start by plotting the endpoints of each inequality on the number line. For an *or* inequality, we then fill in the appropriate side of the line for each inequality. Typically, the two component inequalities do not overlap, that means the shaded part is *outside* the two points. For an *and* inequality, we instead fill in the part of the line that meets both inequalities.

For the inequality "$x \leq -3$ or $x > 4$," we first put a solid circle at –3 and a hollow circle at 4. We then fill the parts of the line *outside* these circles:

GRAPHING INEQUALITIES INCLUDING ABSOLUTE VALUES

An inequality with an absolute value can be converted to a compound inequality. To graph the inequality, first convert it to a compound inequality, and then graph that normally. If the absolute value is on the greater side of the inequality, we end up with an *or* inequality; we plot the endpoints of the inequality on the number line and fill in the part of the line *outside* those points. If the absolute value is on the smaller side of the inequality, we end up with an *and* inequality; we plot the endpoints of the inequality on the number line and fill in the part of the line *between* those points.

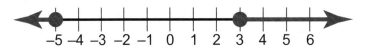

For example, the inequality $|x + 1| \geq 4$ can be rewritten as $x \geq 3$ or $x \leq -5$. We place solid circles at the points 3 and -5 and fill in the part of the line *outside* them:

GRAPHING EQUATIONS IN TWO VARIABLES

One way of graphing an equation in two variables is to plot enough points to get an idea for its shape, and then draw the appropriate curve through those points. A point can be plotted by substituting in a value for one variable and solving for the other. If the equation is linear, we only need two points, and can then draw a straight line between them.

For example, consider the equation $y = 2x - 1$. This is a linear equation—both variables only appear raised to the first power—so we only need two points. When $x = 0$, $y = 2(0) - 1 = -1$. When $x = 2$, $y = 2(2) - 1 = 3$. We can therefore choose the points $(0, -1)$ and $(2, 3)$, and draw a line between them:

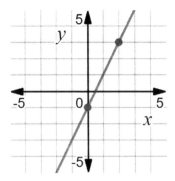

Review Video: Graphing Linear Equations
Visit mometrix.com/academy and enter code: 479576

Review Video: Graphing Linear Functions
Visit mometrix.com/academy and enter code: 699478

GRAPHING INEQUALITIES IN TWO VARIABLES

To graph an inequality in two variables, we first graph the border of the inequality. This means graphing the equation that we get if we replace the inequality sign with an equals sign. If the inequality is strict (> or <), we graph the border with a dashed or dotted line; if it is not strict ($\geq$ or $\leq$), we use a solid line. We can then test any point not on the border to see if it satisfies the inequality. If it does, we shade in that side of the border; if not, we shade in the other side. As an example, consider $y > 2x + 2$. To graph this inequality, we first graph the border, $y = 2x + 2$. Since it is a strict inequality, we use a dashed line. Then, we choose a test point. This can be any point not on the border; in this case, we will choose the origin, $(0, 0)$. (This makes the calculation easy and is generally a good choice unless the border passes through the origin.) Putting this into the original inequality, we get $0 > 2(0) + 2$, i.e. $0 > 2$. This is *not* true, so we shade in the side of the border that does *not* include the point $(0, 0)$:

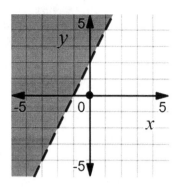

GRAPHING COMPOUND INEQUALITIES IN TWO VARIABLES

One way to graph a compound inequality in two variables is to first graph each of the component inequalities. For an *and* inequality, we then shade in only the parts where the two graphs overlap; for an *or* inequality, we shade in any region that pertains to either of the individual inequalities.

Consider the graph of "$y \geq x - 1$ *and* $y \leq -x$":

We first shade in the individual inequalities:

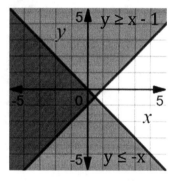

Now, since the compound inequality has an *and*, we only leave shaded the overlap—the part that pertains to *both* inequalities:

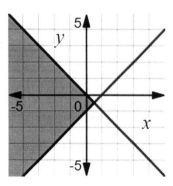

If instead the inequality had been "$y \geq x - 1 \ or \ y \leq -x$," our final graph would involve the *total* shaded area:

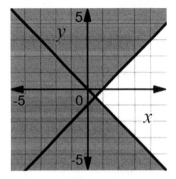

SOLVING SYSTEMS OF EQUATIONS

Systems of equations are a set of simultaneous equations that all use the same variables. A solution to a system of equations must be true for each equation in the system. **Consistent systems** are those with at least one solution. **Inconsistent systems** are systems of equations that have no solution.

SUBSTITUTION

To solve a system of linear equations by **substitution**, start with the easier equation and solve for one of the variables. Express this variable in terms of the other variable. Substitute this expression in the other equation and solve for the other variable. The solution should be expressed in the form (x, y). Substitute the values into both of the original equations to check your answer. Consider the following system of equations:

$$x + 6y = 15$$
$$3x - 12y = 18$$

Solving the first equation for x: $x = 15 - 6y$

Substitute this value in place of x in the second equation, and solve for y:

$$3(15 - 6y) - 12y = 18$$
$$45 - 18y - 12y = 18$$
$$30y = 27$$
$$y = \frac{27}{30} = \frac{9}{10} = 0.9$$

Plug this value for y back into the first equation to solve for x:

$$x = 15 - 6(0.9) = 15 - 5.4 = 9.6$$

Check both equations if you have time:

$$9.6 + 6(0.9) = 15 \qquad 3(9.6) - 12(0.9) = 18$$
$$9.6 + 5.4 = 15 \qquad 28.8 - 10.8 = 18$$
$$15 = 15 \qquad 18 = 18$$

Therefore, the solution is (9.6, 0.9).

Review Video: The Substitution Method
Visit mometrix.com/academy and enter code: 565151

Review Video: Substitution and Elimination
Visit mometrix.com/academy and enter code: 958611

ELIMINATION

To solve a system of equations using **elimination**, begin by rewriting both equations in standard form $Ax + By = C$. Check to see if the coefficients of one pair of like variables add to zero. If not, multiply one or both of the equations by a non-zero number to make one set of like variables add to zero. Add the two equations to solve for one of the variables. Substitute this value into one of the original equations to solve for the other variable. Check your work by substituting into the other equation. Now, consider solving the following system using the elimination method:

$$5x + 6y = 4$$
$$x + 2y = 4$$

If we multiply the second equation by -3, we can eliminate the y terms:

$$5x + 6y = 4$$
$$-3x - 6y = -12$$

Add the equations together and solve for x:

$$2x = -8$$
$$x = \frac{-8}{2} = -4$$

Plug the value for x back in to either of the original equations and solve for y:

$$-4 + 2y = 4$$
$$y = \frac{4+4}{2} = 4$$

Check both equations if you have time:

$$5(-4) + 6(4) = 4 \qquad -4 + 2(4) = 4$$
$$-20 + 24 = 4 \qquad -4 + 8 = 4$$
$$4 = 4 \qquad 4 = 4$$

Therefore, the solution is (-4, 4).

GRAPHICALLY

To solve a system of linear equations **graphically**, plot both equations on the same graph. The solution of the equations is the point where both lines cross. If the lines do not cross (are parallel), then there is **no solution**.

For example, consider the following system of equations:

$$y = 2x + 7$$
$$y = -x + 1$$

Since these equations are given in slope-intercept form, they are easy to graph; the y intercepts of the lines are $(0, 7)$ and $(0, 1)$. The respective slopes are 2 and –1, thus the graphs look like this:

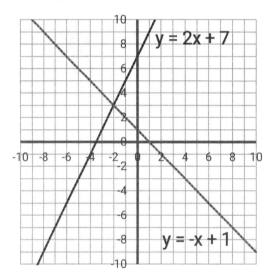

The two lines intersect at the point $(-2, 3)$, thus this is the solution to the system of equations.

Solving a system graphically is generally only practical if both coordinates of the solution are integers; otherwise the intersection will lie between gridlines on the graph and the coordinates will be difficult or impossible to determine exactly. It also helps if, as in this example, the equations are in slope-intercept form or some other form that makes them easy to graph. Otherwise, another method of solution (by substitution or elimination) is likely to be more useful.

SOLVING SYSTEMS OF EQUATIONS USING THE TRACE FEATURE

Using the **trace feature** on a calculator requires that you rewrite each equation, isolating the y-variable on one side of the equal sign. Enter both equations in the graphing calculator and plot the graphs simultaneously. Use the trace cursor to find where the two lines cross. Use the zoom feature if necessary, to obtain more accurate results. Always check your answer by substituting into the original equations. The trace method is likely to be less accurate than other methods due to the resolution of graphing calculators, but is a useful tool to provide an approximate answer.

CALCULATIONS USING POINTS

Sometimes you need to perform calculations using only points on a graph as input data. Using points, you can determine what the **midpoint** and **distance** are. If you know the equation for a line you can calculate the distance between the line and the point.

To find the **midpoint** of two points (x_1, y_1) and (x_2, y_2), average the x-coordinates to get the x-coordinate of the midpoint, and average the y-coordinates to get the y-coordinate of the midpoint. The formula is: $\left(\frac{x_1 + x_2}{2}, \frac{y_1 + y_2}{2}\right)$.

The **distance** between two points is the same as the length of the hypotenuse of a right triangle with the two given points as endpoints, and the two sides of the right triangle parallel to the x-axis and y-axis, respectively. The length of the segment parallel to the x-axis is the difference between the x-coordinates of the two points. The length of the segment parallel to the y-axis is the difference between the y-coordinates of the two points. Use the Pythagorean theorem $a^2 + b^2 = c^2$ or $c = \sqrt{a^2 + b^2}$ to find the distance. The formula is $d = \sqrt{(x_2 - x_1)^2 + (y_2 - y_1)^2}$.

When a line is in the format $Ax + By + C = 0$, where A, B, and C are coefficients, you can use a point (x_1, y_1) not on the line and apply the formula $d = \frac{|Ax_1 + By_1 + C|}{\sqrt{A^2 + B^2}}$ to find the distance between the line and the point (x_1, y_1).

> **Review Video: Calculations Using Points on a Graph**
> Visit mometrix.com/academy and enter code: 883228

PRACTICE

P1. Seeing the equation $2x + 4 = 4x + 7$, a student divides the first terms on each side by 2, yielding $x + 4 = 2x + 7$, and then combines like terms to get $x = -3$. However, this is incorrect, as can be seen by substituting –3 into the original equation. Explain what is wrong with the student's reasoning.

P2. Describe the steps necessary to solve the equation $2x + 1 - x = 4 + 3x + 7$.

P3. Describe the steps necessary to solve the equation $2(x + 5) = 7(4 - x)$.

P4. Find all real solutions to the equation $1 - \sqrt{x} = 2$.

P5. Find all real solutions to the equation $|x + 1| = 2x + 5$.

P6. Solve for x: $-x + 2\sqrt{x + 5} + 1 = 3$.

P7. Ray earns $10 an hour at his job. Write an equation for his earnings as a function of time spent working. Determine how long Ray has to work in order to earn $360.

P8. Simplify the following: $3x + 2 + 2y = 5y - 7 + |2x - 1|$

P9. Analyze the following inequalities:

    (a) $2 - |x + 1| < 3$
    (b) $2(x - 1)^2 + 7 \leq 1$

P10. Graph the following on a number line:

    (a) $x \geq 3$
    (b) $-2 \leq x \leq 6$
    (c) $|x| < 2$

P11. Graph $y = x^2 - 3x + 2$.

P12. Solve the following systems of equations:

    (a) $3x + 4y = 9$
        $-12x + 7y = 10$

    (b) $-3x + 2y = -1$
        $4x - 5y = 6$

P13. Find the distance and midpoint between points (2, 4) and (8,6).

PRACTICE SOLUTIONS

P1. As stated, it's easy to verify that the student's solution is incorrect: $2(-3) + 4 = -2$ and $4(-3) + 7 = -5$; clearly $-2 \neq -5$. The mistake was in the first step, which illustrates a common type of error in solving equations. The student tried to simplify the two variable terms by dividing them by 2. However, it's not valid to multiply or divide only one term on each side of an equation by a number; when multiplying or dividing, the operation must be applied to *every* term in the equation. So, dividing by 2 would yield not $x + 4 = 2x + 7$, but $x + 2 = 2x + \frac{7}{2}$. While this is now valid, that fraction is inconvenient to work with, so this may not be the best first step in solving the equation. Rather, it may have been better to first combine like terms: subtracting $4x$ from both sides yields $-2x + 4 = 7$; subtracting 4 from both sides yields $-2x = 3$; and *now* we can divide both sides by –2 to get $x = -\frac{3}{2}$.

P2. Our ultimate goal is to isolate the variable, x. To that end we first move all the terms containing x to the left side of the equation, and all the constant terms to the right side. Note that when we move a term to the other side of the equation its sign changes. We are therefore now left with $2x - x - 3x = 4 + 7 - 1$.

Next, we combine the like terms on each side of the equation, adding and subtracting the terms as appropriate. This leaves us with $-2x = 10$.

At this point, we're almost done; all that remains is to divide both sides by -2 to leave the x by itself. We now have our solution, $x = -5$. We can verify that this is a correct solution by substituting it back into the original equation.

P3. Generally, in equations that have a sum or difference of terms multiplied by another value or expression, the first step is to multiply those terms, distributing as necessary: $2(x + 5) = 2(x) + 2(5) = 2x + 10$, and $7(4 - x) = 7(4) - 7(x) = 28 - 7x$. So, the equation becomes $2x + 10 = 28 - 7x$. We can now add $7x$ to both sides to eliminate the variable from the right-hand side: $9x + 10 = 28$. Similarly, we can subtract 10 from both sides to move all the constants to the right: $9x = 18$. Finally, we can divide both sides by 9, yielding the final answer, $x = 2$.

P4. It's not hard to isolate the root: subtract one from both sides, yielding $-\sqrt{x} = 1$. Finally, multiply both sides by –1, yielding $\sqrt{x} = -1$. Squaring both sides of the equation yields $x = 1$.

However, if we plug this back into the original equation, we get $1 - \sqrt{1} = 2$, which is false. Therefore $x = 1$ is a spurious solution, and the equation has no real solutions.

P5. This equation has two possibilities: $x + 1 = 2x + 5$, which simplifies to $x = -4$; or $x + 1 = -(2x + 5) = -2x - 5$, which simplifies to $x = -2$. However, if we try substituting both values back into the original equation, we see that only $x = -2$ yields a true statement. $x = -4$ is a spurious solution; $x = -2$ is the only valid solution to the equation.

P6. Start by isolating the term with the root. We can do that by moving the $-x$ and the 1 to the other side, yielding $2\sqrt{x + 5} = 3 + x - 1$, or $2\sqrt{x + 5} = x + 2$. Dividing both sides of the equation by 2 would give us a fractional term that could be messy to deal with, so we won't do that for now. Instead, we square both sides of the equation; note that on the left-hand side the 2 is outside the square root sign, so we have to square it. As a result, we get $4(x + 5) = (x + 2)^2$. Expanding both sides gives us $4x + 20 = x^2 + 4x + 4$. In this case, we see that we have $4x$ on both sides, so we can cancel the $4x$ (which is what allows us to solve this equation despite the different powers of x). We now have $20 = x^2 + 4$, or $x^2 = 16$. Since the variable is raised to an even power, we need to take the positive and negative roots, so $x = \pm 4$: that is, $x = 4$ or $x = -4$. Substituting both values into the original equation, we see that $x = 4$ satisfies the equation but $x = -4$ does not; hence $x = -4$ is a spurious solution, and the only solution to the equation is $x = 4$.

P7. The number of dollars that Ray earns is dependent on the number of hours he works, so earnings will be represented by the dependent variable y and hours worked will be represented by the independent variable x. He earns 10 dollars per hour worked, so his earning can be calculated as $y = 10x$. To calculate the number of hours Ray must work in order to earn \$360, plug in 360 for y and solve for x:

$$360 = 10x$$
$$x = \frac{360}{10} = 36$$

P8. To simplify this equation, we must isolate one of its variables on one side of the equation. In this case, the x appears under an absolute value sign, which makes it difficult to isolate. The y, on the other hand, only appears without an exponent—the equation is linear in y. We will therefore choose to isolate the y. The first step, then, is to move all the terms with y to the left side of the equation, which we can do by subtracting $5y$ from both sides:

$$3x + 2 - 3y = -7 + |2x - 1|$$

We can then move all the terms that do *not* include y to the right side of the equation, by subtracting $3x$ and 2 from both sides of the equation:

$$-3y = -3x - 9 + |2x - 1|$$

Finally, we can isolate the y by dividing both sides by –3.

$$y = x + 3 - \frac{1}{3}|2x - 1|$$

This is as far as we can simplify the equation; we cannot combine the terms inside and outside the absolute value sign. We can therefore consider the equation to be solved.

P9. (a) Subtracting 2 from both sides yields $-|x + 1| < 1$; multiplying by -1—and flipping the inequality, since we're multiplying by a negative number—yields $|x + 1| > -1$. But since the absolute value cannot be negative, it's *always* greater than –1, so this inequality is true for all values of x.

(b) Subtracting 7 from both sides yields $2(x - 1)^2 \leq -6$; dividing by 2 yields $(x - 1)^2 \leq -3$. But $(x - 1)^2$ must be nonnegative, and hence cannot be less than or equal to –3; this inequality has no solution.

P10. (a) We would graph the inequality $x \geq 3$ by putting a solid circle at 3 and filling in the part of the line to the right:

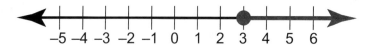

(b) The inequality $-2 \leq x \leq 6$ is equivalent to "$x \geq -2$ and $x \leq 6$." To plot this compound inequality, we first put solid circles at –2 and 6, and then fill in the part of the line *between* these circles:

(c) The inequality $|x| < 2$ can be rewritten as "$x > -2$ and $x < 2$." We place hollow circles at the points –2 and 2 and fill in the part of the line between them:

P11. The equation $y = x^2 - 3x + 2$ is not linear, so we may need more points to get an idea of its shape. By substituting in different values of x, we find the points $(0, 2)$, $(1, 0)$, $(2, 0)$, and $(3, 2)$. That may be enough to give us an idea of the shape, though we can find more points if we're still not sure:

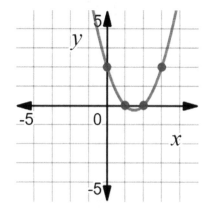

P12. (a) If we multiply the first equation by 4, we can eliminate the x terms:

$$12x + 16y = 36$$
$$-12x + 7y = 10$$

Add the equations together and solve for y:

$$23y = 46$$
$$y = 2$$

Plug the value for y back in to either of the original equations and solve for x:

$$3x + 4(2) = 10$$
$$x = \frac{10 - 8}{3} = \frac{2}{3}$$

The solution is $\left(\frac{2}{3}, 2\right)$

(b) Solving the first equation for y:

$$-3x + 2y = -1$$
$$2y = 3x - 1$$
$$y = \frac{3x - 1}{2}$$

Substitute this expression in place of y in the second equation, and solve for x:

$$4x - 5\left(\frac{3x - 1}{2}\right) = 6$$
$$4x - \frac{15x}{2} + \frac{5}{2} = 6$$
$$8x - 15x + 5 = 12$$
$$-7x = 7$$
$$x = -1$$

Plug the value for x back in to either of the original equations and solve for y:

$$-3(-1) + 2y = -1$$
$$3 + 2y = -1$$
$$2y = -4$$
$$y = -2$$

The solution is $(-1, -2)$

P13. Use the formulas for distance and midpoint:

$$\text{Distance} = \sqrt{(x_2 - x_1)^2 + (y_2 - y_1)^2}$$
$$= \sqrt{(8 - 2)^2 + (6 - 4)^2}$$
$$= \sqrt{(6)^2 + (2)^2}$$
$$= \sqrt{36 + 4}$$
$$= \sqrt{40} \text{ or } 2\sqrt{10}$$

$$\text{Midpoint} = \left(\frac{x_1 + x_2}{2}, \frac{y_1 + y_2}{2}\right)$$
$$= \left(\frac{2 + 8}{2}, \frac{4 + 6}{2}\right)$$
$$= \left(\frac{10}{2}, \frac{10}{2}\right)$$
$$= (5,5)$$

Polynomial Algebra

POLYNOMIALS

Equations are made up of monomials and polynomials. A **monomial** is a single constant, variable, or product of constants and variables, such as 7, x, $2x$, or x^3y. There will never be addition or subtraction symbols in a monomial. Like monomials have like variables, but they may have different coefficients. **Polynomials** are algebraic expressions which use addition and subtraction to combine two or more monomials. Two terms make a **binomial**, three terms make a **trinomial**, etc. The **degree of a monomial** is the sum of the exponents of the variables. The **degree of a polynomial** is the highest degree of any individual term.

> **Review Video: Polynomials**
> Visit mometrix.com/academy and enter code: 305005

SIMPLIFYING POLYNOMIALS

Simplifying polynomials requires combining like terms. The like terms in a polynomial expression are those that have the same variable raised to the same power. It is often helpful to connect the like terms with arrows or lines in order to separate them from the other monomials. Once you have determined the like terms, you can rearrange the polynomial by placing them together. Remember to include the sign that is in front of each term. Once the like terms are placed together, you can apply each operation and simplify. When adding and subtracting polynomials, only add and subtract the **coefficient**, or the number part; the variable and exponent stay the same.

> **Review Video: Adding and Subtracting Polynomials**
> Visit mometrix.com/academy and enter code: 124088

THE FOIL METHOD

In general, multiplying polynomials is done by multiplying each term in one polynomial by each term in the other and adding the results. In the specific case for multiplying binomials, there is useful acronym, FOIL, that can help you make sure to cover each combination of terms. The **FOIL method** for $(Ax + By)(Cx + Dy)$ would be:

F	Multiply the *first* terms of each binomial	$(\overset{first}{\overbrace{Ax}} + By)(\overset{first}{\overbrace{Cx}} + Dy)$	ACx^2
O	Multiply the *outer* terms	$(\overset{outer}{\overbrace{Ax}} + By)(Cx + \overset{outer}{\overbrace{Dy}})$	$ADxy$
I	Multiply the *inner* terms	$(Ax + \underset{inner}{\underbrace{By}})(\underset{inner}{\underbrace{Cx}} + Dy)$	$BCxy$
L	Multiply the *last* terms of each binomial	$(Ax + \underset{last}{\underbrace{By}})(Cx + \underset{last}{\underbrace{Dy}})$	BDy^2

Then add up the result of each and combine like terms: $ACx^2 + (AD + BC)xy + BDy^2$.

For example, using the FOIL method on binomials $(x + 2)$ and $(x - 3)$:

$$\text{First:} \quad (\boxed{x} + 2)(\boxed{x} + (-3)) \;\rightarrow\; (x)(x) = x^2$$
$$\text{Outer:} \quad (\boxed{x} + 2)(x + \boxed{(-3)}) \;\rightarrow\; (x)(-3) = -3x$$
$$\text{Inner:} \quad (x + \boxed{2})(\boxed{x} + (-3)) \;\rightarrow\; (2)(x) = 2x$$
$$\text{Last:} \quad (x + \boxed{2})(x + \boxed{(-3)}) \;\rightarrow\; (2)(-3) = -6$$

This results in: $(x^2) + (-3x) + (2x) + (-6)$

Combine like terms: $x^2 + (-3 + 2)x + (-6) = x^2 - x - 6$

> **Review Video: <u>Multiplying Terms Using the FOIL Method</u>**
> Visit mometrix.com/academy and enter code: 854792

DIVIDING POLYNOMIALS

To divide polynomials, set up a long division problem, dividing a polynomial by either a monomial or another polynomial of equal or lesser degree.

When **dividing by a monomial**, divide each term of the polynomial by the monomial.

When **dividing by a polynomial**, begin by arranging the terms of each polynomial in order of one variable. You may arrange in ascending or descending order, but be consistent with both polynomials. To get the first term of the quotient, divide the first term of the dividend by the first term of the divisor. Multiply the first term of the quotient by the entire divisor and subtract that product from the dividend. Repeat for the second and successive terms until you either get a remainder of zero or a remainder whose degree is less than the degree of the divisor. If the quotient has a remainder, write the answer as a mixed expression in the form:

$$\text{quotient} + \frac{\text{remainder}}{\text{divisor}}$$

Mometrix

For example, we can evaluate the following expression in the same way as long division:

$$\frac{x^3 - 3x^2 - 2x + 5}{x - 5}$$

$$
\require{enclose}
\begin{array}{r}
x^2 + 2x + 8 \\
x - 5 \enclose{longdiv}{x^3 - 3x^2 - 2x + 5} \\
\underline{-(x^3 - 5x^2)} \\
2x^2 - 2x \\
\underline{-(2x^2 - 10x)} \\
8x + 5 \\
\underline{-(8x - 40)} \\
45
\end{array}
$$

$$\frac{x^3 - 3x^2 - 2x + 5}{x - 5} = x^2 + 2x + 8 + \frac{45}{x - 5}$$

When **factoring** a polynomial, first check for a common monomial factor, that is look to see if each coefficient has a common factor or if each term has an x in it. If the factor is a trinomial but not a perfect trinomial square, look for a factorable form, such as one of these:

$$x^2 + (a + b)x + ab = (x + a)(x + b)$$

$$(ac)x^2 + (ad + bc)x + bd = (ax + b)(cx + d)$$

For factors with four terms, look for groups to factor. Once you have found the factors, write the original polynomial as the product of all the factors. Make sure all of the polynomial factors are prime. Monomial factors may be *prime* or *composite*. Check your work by multiplying the factors to make sure you get the original polynomial.

Below are patterns of some special products to remember to help make factoring easier:

- Perfect trinomial squares: $x^2 + 2xy + y^2 = (x + y)^2$ or $x^2 - 2xy + y^2 = (x - y)^2$
- Difference between two squares: $x^2 - y^2 = (x + y)(x - y)$
- Sum of two cubes: $x^3 + y^3 = (x + y)(x^2 - xy + y^2)$
  - Note: the second factor is *not* the same as a perfect trinomial square, so do not try to factor it further.
- Difference between two cubes: $x^3 - y^3 = (x - y)(x^2 + xy + y^2)$
  - Again, the second factor is *not* the same as a perfect trinomial square.
- Perfect cubes: $x^3 + 3x^2y + 3xy^2 + y^3 = (x + y)^3$ and $x^3 - 3x^2y + 3xy^2 - y^3 = (x - y)^3$

RATIONAL EXPRESSIONS

Rational expressions are fractions with polynomials in both the numerator and the denominator; the value of the polynomial in the denominator cannot be equal to zero. Be sure to keep track of values that make the denominator of the original expression zero as the final result inherits the same restrictions. For example, a denominator of $x - 3$ indicates that the expression is not defined when $x = 3$ and as such, regardless of any operations done to the expression, it remains undefined there.

64

Copyright © Mometrix Media. You have been licensed one copy of this document for personal use only. Any other reproduction or redistribution is strictly prohibited. All rights reserved. This content is provided for test preparation purposes only and does not imply an endorsement by Mometrix of any particular political, scientific, or religious point of view.

To **add or subtract** rational expressions, first find the common denominator, then rewrite each fraction as an equivalent fraction with the common denominator. Finally, add or subtract the numerators to get the numerator of the answer, and keep the common denominator as the denominator of the answer.

When **multiplying** rational expressions factor each polynomial and cancel like factors (a factor which appears in both the numerator and the denominator). Then, multiply all remaining factors in the numerator to get the numerator of the product, and multiply the remaining factors in the denominator to get the denominator of the product. Remember: cancel entire factors, not individual terms.

To **divide** rational expressions, take the reciprocal of the divisor (the rational expression you are dividing by) and multiply by the dividend.

> **Review Video: Rational Expressions**
> Visit mometrix.com/academy and enter code: 415183

SIMPLIFYING RATIONAL EXPRESSIONS

To simplify a rational expression, factor the numerator and denominator completely. Factors that are the same and appear in the numerator and denominator have a ratio of 1. For example, look at the following expression:

$$\frac{x-1}{1-x^2}$$

The denominator, $(1-x^2)$, is a difference of squares. It can be factored as $(1-x)(1+x)$. The factor $1-x$ and the numerator $x-1$ are opposites and have a ratio of –1. Rewrite the numerator as $-1(1-x)$. So, the rational expression can be simplified as follows:

$$\frac{x-1}{1-x^2}=\frac{-1(1-x)}{(1-x)(1+x)}=\frac{-1}{1+x}$$

Note that since the original expression is only defined for $x \neq \{-1,1\}$, the simplified expression has the same restrictions.

> **Review Video: Reducing Rational Expressions**
> Visit mometrix.com/academy and enter code: 788868

SOLVING QUADRATIC EQUATIONS

Quadratic equations are a special set of trinomials of the form $y = ax^2 + bx + c$ that occur commonly in math and real world applications. The **roots** of a quadratic equation are the solutions that satisfy the equation when $y = 0$; in other words, where the graph touches the x-axis. There are several ways to determine these solutions including using the quadratic formula, factoring, completing the square, and graphing the function.

> **Review Video: Changing Constants in Graphs of Functions: Quadratic Equations**
> Visit mometrix.com/academy and enter code: 476276

QUADRATIC FORMULA

The **quadratic formula** is used to solve quadratic equations when other methods are more difficult. To use the quadratic formula to solve a quadratic equation, begin by rewriting the equation in standard form $ax^2 + bx + c = 0$, where a, b, and c are coefficients. Once you have identified the values of the coefficients, substitute those values into the quadratic formula:

$$x = \frac{-b \pm \sqrt{b^2 - 4ac}}{2a}$$

Evaluate the equation and simplify the expression. Again, check each root by substituting into the original equation. In the quadratic formula, the portion of the formula under the radical ($b^2 - 4ac$) is called the **discriminant**. If the discriminant is zero, there is only one root: $-\frac{b}{2a}$. If the discriminant is positive, there are two different real roots. If the discriminant is negative, there are no real roots, you will instead find complex roots. Often these solutions don't make sense in context and are ignored.

> **Review Video: Using the Quadratic Formula**
> Visit mometrix.com/academy and enter code: 163102

FACTORING

To solve a quadratic equation by factoring, begin by rewriting the equation in standard form, $x^2 + bx + c = 0$. Remember that the goal of factoring is to find numbers f and g such that $(x + f)(x + g) = x^2 + (f + g)x + fg$, in other words $(f + g) = b$ and $fg = c$ or . This can be a really useful method when b and c are integers. Determine the factors of c and look for pairs that could sum to b.

For example, consider finding the roots of $x^2 + 6x - 16 = 0$. The factors of -16 include, -4 and 4, -8 and 2, -2 and 8, -1 and 16, and 1 and -16. The factors that sum to 6 are -2 and 8. Write these factors as the product of two binomials, $0 = (x - 2)(x + 8)$. Finally, since these binomials multiply together to equal zero, set them each equal to zero and solve each for x. This results in $x - 2 = 0$, which simplifies to $x = 2$ and $x + 8 = 0$, which simplifies to $x = -8$. Therefore, the roots of the equation are 2 and -8.

> **Review Video: Factoring Quadratic Equations**
> Visit mometrix.com/academy and enter code: 336566

COMPLETING THE SQUARE

One way to find the roots of a quadratic equation is to find a way to manipulate it such that it follows the form of a perfect square ($x^2 + 2px + p^2$) by adding and subtracting a constant. This process is called **completing the square**. In other words, if are given a quadratic that is not a perfect square, $x^2 + bx + c = 0$, you can find a constant d that could be added in to make it a perfect square:

$$x^2 + bx + c + (d - d) = 0; \{\text{Let } b = 2p \text{ and } c + d = p^2\}$$

$$\text{then: } x^2 + 2px + p^2 - d = 0 \text{ and } d = \frac{b^2}{4} - c$$

Once you have completed the square you can find the roots of the resulting equation:

$$x^2 + 2px + p^2 - d = 0$$

$$(x + p)^2 = d$$

$$x + p = \pm\sqrt{d}$$

$$x = -p \pm \sqrt{d}$$

It is worth noting that substituting the original expressions into this solution gives the same result as the quadratic formula where $a = 1$:

$$x = -p \pm \sqrt{d} = -\frac{b}{2} \pm \sqrt{\frac{b^2}{4} - c} = -\frac{b}{2} \pm \frac{\sqrt{b^2 - 4c}}{2} = \frac{-b \pm \sqrt{b^2 - 4c}}{2}$$

Completing the square can be seen as arranging block representations of each of the terms to be as close to a square as possible and then filling in the gaps. For example, consider the quadratic expression $x^2 + 6x + 2$:

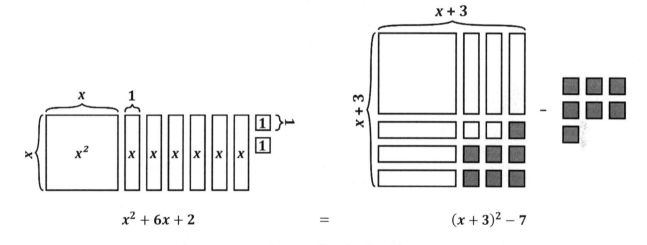

Review Video: **Completing the Square**
Visit mometrix.com/academy and enter code: 982479

USING GIVEN ROOTS TO FIND QUADRATIC EQUATION

One way to find the roots of a quadratic equation is to factor the equation and use the **zero product property**, setting each factor of the equation equal to zero to find the corresponding root. We can use this technique in reverse to find an equation given its roots. Each root corresponds to a linear equation which in turn corresponds to a factor of the quadratic equation.

For example, we can find a quadratic equation whose roots are $x = 2$ and $x = -1$. The root $x = 2$ corresponds to the equation $x - 2 = 0$, and the root $x = -1$ corresponds to the equation $x + 1 = 0$.

These two equations correspond to the factors $(x - 2)$ and $(x + 1)$, from which we can derive the equation $(x - 2)(x + 1) = 0$, or $x^2 - x - 2 = 0$.

Any integer multiple of this entire equation will also yield the same roots, as the integer will simply cancel out when the equation is factored. For example, $2x^2 - 2x - 4 = 0$ factors as $2(x - 2)(x + 1) = 0$.

SOLVING A SYSTEM OF EQUATIONS CONSISTING OF A LINEAR EQUATION AND A QUADRATIC EQUATION

ALGEBRAICALLY

Generally, the simplest way to solve a system of equations consisting of a linear equation and a quadratic equation algebraically is through the method of substitution. One possible strategy is to solve the linear equation for y and then substitute that expression into the quadratic equation. After expansion and combining like terms, this will result in a new quadratic equation for x which, like all quadratic equations, may have zero, one, or two solutions. Plugging each solution for x back into one of the original equations will then produce the corresponding value of y.

For example, consider the following system of equations:

$$x + y = 1$$
$$y = (x + 3)^2 - 2$$

We can solve the linear equation for y to yield $y = -x + 1$. Substituting this expression into the quadratic equation produces $-x + 1 = (x + 3)^2 - 2$. We can simplify this equation:

$$-x + 1 = (x + 3)^2 - 2$$
$$-x + 1 = x^2 + 6x + 9 - 2$$
$$-x + 1 = x^2 + 6x + 7$$
$$0 = x^2 + 7x + 6$$

This quadratic equation can be factored as $(x + 1)(x + 6) = 0$. It therefore has two solutions: $x_1 = -1$ and $x_2 = -6$. Plugging each of these back into the original linear equation yields $y_1 = -x_1 + 1 = -(-1) + 1 = 2$ and $y_2 = -x_2 + 1 = -(-6) + 1 = 7$. Thus, this system of equations has two solutions, $(-1, 2)$ and $(-6, 7)$.

It may help to check your work by putting each x and y value back into the original equations and verifying that they do provide a solution.

GRAPHICALLY

To solve a system of equations consisting of a linear equation and a quadratic equation graphically, plot both equations on the same graph. The linear equation will of course produce a straight line, while the quadratic equation will produce a parabola. These two graphs will intersect at zero, one, or two points; each point of intersection is a solution of the system.

For example, consider the following system of equations:

$$y = -2x + 2$$
$$y = -2x^2 + 4x + 2$$

The linear equation describes a line with a y-intercept of $(0, 2)$ and a slope of -2.

To graph the quadratic equation, we can first find the vertex of the parabola: the x-coordinate of the vertex is $h = -\dfrac{b}{2a} = -\dfrac{4}{2(-2)} = 1$, and the y coordinate is $k = -2(1)^2 + 4(1) + 2 = 4$. Thus, the vertex lies at $(1, 4)$. To get a feel for the rest of the parabola, we can plug in a few more values of x to find more points; by putting in $x = 2$ and $x = 3$ in the quadratic equation, we find that the points $(2, 2)$ and $(3, -4)$ lie on the parabola; by symmetry thus do $(0, 2)$ and $(-1, -4)$. We can now plot both equations:

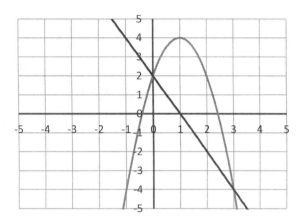

These two curves intersect at the points $(0, 2)$ and $(3, -4)$, thus these are the solutions of the equation.

> **Review Video: Solving a System of Equations Consisting of a Linear Equation and Quadratic Equations**
> Visit mometrix.com/academy and enter code: 194870

PRACTICE

P1. Expand the following polynomials:

(a) $(x + 3)(x - 7)(2x)$

(b) $(x + 2)^2(x - 2)^2$

(c) $(x^2 + 5x + 5)(3x - 1)$

P2. Find the roots of $y = 2x^2 + 8x + 4$.

P3. Find a quadratic equation with roots $x = 4$ and $x = -6$.

P4. Evaluate the following rational expressions:

(a) $\dfrac{x^3 - 2x^2 - 5x + 6}{3x + 6}$

(b) $\dfrac{x^2 + 4x + 4}{4 - x^2}$

PRACTICE SOLUTIONS

P1. (a) Apply the FOIL method and the distributive property of multiplication:

$$(x+3)(x-7)(2x) = (x^2 - 7x + 3x - 21)(2x)$$
$$= (x^2 - 4x - 21)(2x)$$
$$= 2x^3 - 8x^2 - 42x$$

(b) Note the difference of squares form:

$$(x+2)^2(x-2)^2 = (x+2)(x+2)(x-2)(x-2)$$
$$= [(x+2)(x-2)][(x+2)(x-2)]$$
$$= (x^2 - 4)(x^2 - 4)$$
$$= x^4 - 8x^2 + 16$$

(c) Multiply each pair of monomials and combine like terms:

$$(x^2 + 5x + 5)(3x - 1) = 3x^3 + 15x^2 + 15x - x^2 - 5x - 5$$
$$= 3x^3 + 14x^2 + 10x - 5$$

P2. First, substitute 0 in for y in the quadratic equation: $0 = 2x^2 + 8x + 4$

Next, try to factor the quadratic equation. Since $a \neq 1$, list the factors of ac, or 8:

$$(1, 8), (-1, -8), (2, 4), (-2, -4)$$

Look for the factors of ac that add up to b, or 8. Since none do, the equation cannot be factored with whole numbers. Substitute the values of a, b, and c into the quadratic formula, $x = \frac{-b \pm \sqrt{b^2 - 4ac}}{2a}$:

$$x = \frac{-8 \pm \sqrt{8^2 - 4(2)(4)}}{2(2)}$$

Use the order of operations to simplify:

$$x = \frac{-8 \pm \sqrt{64 - 32}}{4}$$
$$x = \frac{-8 \pm \sqrt{32}}{4}$$

Reduce and simplify:

$$x = \frac{-8 \pm \sqrt{(16)(2)}}{4}$$
$$x = \frac{-8 \pm 4\sqrt{2}}{4}$$
$$x = -2 \pm \sqrt{2}$$
$$x = \left(-2 + \sqrt{2}\right) \text{ and } \left(-2 - \sqrt{2}\right)$$

P3. The root $x = 4$ corresponds to the equation $x - 4 = 0$, and the root $x = -6$ corresponds to the equation $x + 6 = 0$. These two equations correspond to the factors $(x - 4)$ and $(x + 6)$, from which we can derive the equation $(x - 4)(x + 6) = 0$, or $x^2 + 2x - 24 = 0$.

P4. (a) Rather than trying to factor the fourth-degree polynomial, we can use long division:

$$\frac{x^3 - 2x^2 - 5x + 6}{3x + 6} = \frac{x^3 - 2x^2 - 5x + 6}{3(x + 2)}$$

$$
\begin{array}{r}
x^2 - 4x + 3 \\
x + 2 \overline{)\; x^3 - 2x^2 - 5x + 6} \\
\underline{x^3 + 2x^2} \\
-4x^2 - 5x \\
\underline{-4x^2 - 8x} \\
3x + 6 \\
\underline{3x + 6} \\
0
\end{array}
$$

$$\frac{x^3 - 2x^2 - 5x + 6}{3(x + 2)} = \frac{x^2 - 4x + 3}{3}$$

Note that since the original expression is only defined for $x \neq \{-2\}$, the simplified expression has the same restrictions.

(b) The denominator, $(4 - x^2)$, is a difference of squares. It can be factored as $(2 - x)(2 + x)$. The numerator, $(x^2 + 4x + 4)$, is a perfect square. It can be factored as $(x + 2)(x + 2)$. So, the rational expression can be simplified as follows:

$$\frac{x^2 + 4x + 4}{4 - x^2} = \frac{(x + 2)(x + 2)}{(2 - x)(2 + x)} = \frac{(x + 2)}{(2 - x)}$$

Note that since the original expression is only defined for $x \neq \{-2, 2\}$, the simplified expression has the same restrictions.

Geometry

LINES AND PLANES

A **point** is a fixed location in space; has no size or dimensions; commonly represented by a dot. A **line** is a set of points that extends infinitely in two opposite directions. It has length, but no width or depth. A line can be defined by any two distinct points that it contains. A **line segment** is a portion of a line that has definite endpoints. A **ray** is a portion of a line that extends from a single point on that line in one direction along the line. It has a definite beginning, but no ending.

Point   Line   Segment   Ray

Intersecting lines are lines that have exactly one point in common. **Concurrent lines** are multiple lines that intersect at a single point. **Perpendicular lines** are lines that intersect at right angles.

They are represented by the symbol ⊥. The shortest distance from a line to a point not on the line is a perpendicular segment from the point to the line. **Parallel lines** are lines in the same plane that have no points in common and never meet. It is possible for lines to be in different planes, have no points in common, and never meet, but they are not parallel because they are in different planes.

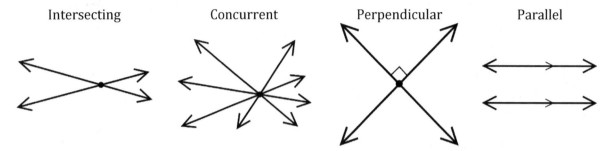

A **transversal** is a line that intersects at least two other lines, which may or may not be parallel to one another. A transversal that intersects parallel lines is a common occurrence in geometry. A **bisector** is a line or line segment that divides another line segment into two equal lengths. A **perpendicular bisector** of a line segment is composed of points that are equidistant from the endpoints of the segment it is dividing.

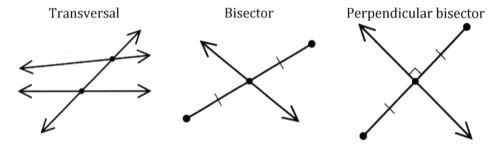

The **projection of a point on a line** is the point at which a perpendicular line drawn from the given point to the given line intersects the line. This is also the shortest distance from the given point to the line. The **projection of a segment on a line** is a segment whose endpoints are the points formed when perpendicular lines are drawn from the endpoints of the given segment to the given line. This is similar to the length a diagonal line appears to be when viewed from above.

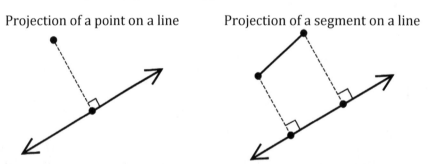

A **plane** is a two-dimensional flat surface defined by three non-collinear points. A plane extends an infinite distance in all directions in those two dimensions. It contains an infinite number of points, parallel lines and segments, intersecting lines and segments, as well as parallel or intersecting rays. A plane will never contain a three-dimensional figure or skew lines, lines that don't intersect and are not parallel. Two given planes are either parallel or they intersect at a line. A plane may

72

intersect a circular conic surface to form **conic sections**, such as a parabola, hyperbola, circle or ellipse.

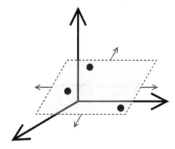

ANGLES

An **angle** is formed when two lines or line segments meet at a common point. It may be a common starting point for a pair of segments or rays, or it may be the intersection of lines. Angles are represented by the symbol ∠.

The **vertex** is the point at which two segments or rays meet to form an angle. If the angle is formed by intersecting rays, lines, and/or line segments, the vertex is the point at which four angles are formed. The pairs of angles opposite one another are called vertical angles, and their measures are equal.

- An **acute** angle is an angle with a degree measure less than 90°.
- A **right** angle is an angle with a degree measure of exactly 90°.
- An **obtuse** angle is an angle with a degree measure greater than 90° but less than 180°.
- A **straight angle** is an angle with a degree measure of exactly 180°. This is also a semicircle.
- A **reflex angle** is an angle with a degree measure greater than 180° but less than 360°.

A **full angle** is an angle with a degree measure of exactly 360°. This is also a circle.

Two angles whose sum is exactly 90° are said to be **complementary**. The two angles may or may not be adjacent. In a right triangle, the two acute angles are complementary.

Two angles whose sum is exactly 180° are said to be **supplementary**. The two angles may or may not be adjacent. Two intersecting lines always form two pairs of supplementary angles. Adjacent supplementary angles will always form a straight line.

Two angles that have the same vertex and share a side are said to be **adjacent**. Vertical angles are not adjacent because they share a vertex but no common side.

Adjacent
Share vertex and side

Not adjacent
Share part of side, but not vertex

When two parallel lines are cut by a transversal, the angles that are between the two parallel lines are **interior angles**. In the diagram below, angles 3, 4, 5, and 6 are interior angles.

When two parallel lines are cut by a transversal, the angles that are outside the parallel lines are **exterior angles**. In the diagram below, angles 1, 2, 7, and 8 are exterior angles.

When two parallel lines are cut by a transversal, the angles that are in the same position relative to the transversal and a parallel line are **corresponding angles**. The diagram below has four pairs of corresponding angles: angles 1 and 5; angles 2 and 6; angles 3 and 7; and angles 4 and 8. Corresponding angles formed by parallel lines are congruent.

When two parallel lines are cut by a transversal, the two interior angles that are on opposite sides of the transversal are called **alternate interior angles**. In the diagram below, there are two pairs of alternate interior angles: angles 3 and 6, and angles 4 and 5. Alternate interior angles formed by parallel lines are congruent.

When two parallel lines are cut by a transversal, the two exterior angles that are on opposite sides of the transversal are called **alternate exterior angles**.

In the diagram below, there are two pairs of alternate exterior angles: angles 1 and 8, and angles 2 and 7. Alternate exterior angles formed by parallel lines are congruent.

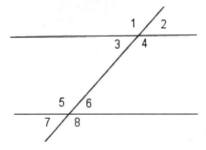

When two lines intersect, four angles are formed. The non-adjacent angles at this vertex are called vertical angles. Vertical angles are congruent. In the diagram, $\angle ABD \cong \angle CBE$ and $\angle ABC \cong \angle DBE$.

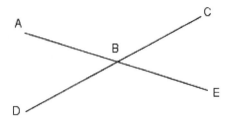

TRANSFORMATIONS

A **rotation** is a transformation that turns a figure around a point called the **center of rotation**, which can lie anywhere in the plane. If a line is drawn from a point on a figure to the center of rotation, and another line is drawn from the center to the rotated image of that point, the angle between the two lines is the **angle of rotation**. The vertex of the angle of rotation is the center of rotation.

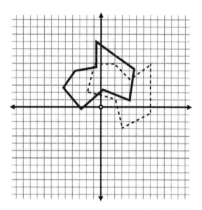

Review Video: Rotation
Visit mometrix.com/academy and enter code: 602600

A **translation** is a transformation which slides a figure from one position in the plane to another position in the plane. The original figure and the translated figure have the same size, shape, and orientation. A **dilation** is a transformation which proportionally stretches or shrinks a figure by a

scale factor. The dilated image is the same shape and orientation as the original image but a different size. A polygon and its dilated image are similar.

Translation

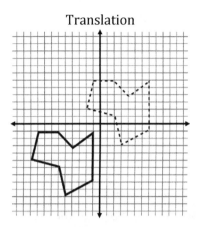

Dilation

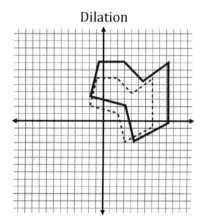

A **reflection of a figure over a line** (a "flip") creates a congruent image that is the same distance from the line as the original figure but on the opposite side. The **line of reflection** is the perpendicular bisector of any line segment drawn from a point on the original figure to its reflected image (unless the point and its reflected image happen to be the same point, which happens when a figure is reflected over one of its own sides). A **reflection of a figure over a point** (an inversion) in two dimensions is the same as the rotation of the figure 180° about that point. The image of the figure is congruent to the original figure. The **point of reflection** is the midpoint of a line segment which connects a point in the figure to its image (unless the point and its reflected image happen to be the same point, which happens when a figure is reflected in one of its own points).

Reflection of a figure over a line

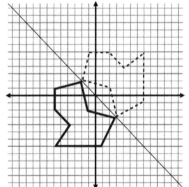

Reflection of a figure over a point

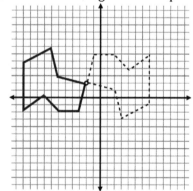

POLYGONS

A **polygon** is a closed, two-dimensional figure with three or more straight line segments called **sides**. The point at which two sides of a polygon intersect is called the **vertex**. In a polygon, the number of sides is always equal to the number of vertices. A polygon with all sides congruent and all angles equal is called a **regular polygon**. Common polygons are:

Triangle = 3 sides
Quadrilateral = 4 sides
Pentagon = 5 sides
Hexagon = 6 sides
Heptagon = 7 sides
Octagon = 8 sides
Nonagon = 9 sides
Decagon = 10 sides
Dodecagon = 12 sides

More generally, an *n*-gon is a polygon that has *n* angles and *n* sides.

The sum of the interior angles of an *n*-sided polygon is $(n - 2) \times 180°$. For example, in a triangle $n = 3$. So, the sum of the interior angles is $(3 - 2) \times 180° = 180°$. In a quadrilateral, $n = 4$, and the sum of the angles is $(4 - 2) \times 180° = 360°$.

> **Review Video: Intro to Polygons**
> Visit mometrix.com/academy and enter code: 271869
>
> **Review Video: Sum of Interior Angles**
> Visit mometrix.com/academy and enter code: 984991

A line segment from the center of a polygon that is perpendicular to a side of the polygon is called the **apothem**. A line segment from the center of a polygon to a vertex of the polygon is called a **radius**. In a regular polygon, the apothem can be used to find the area of the polygon using the formula $A = \frac{1}{2}ap$, where a is the apothem, and p is the perimeter.

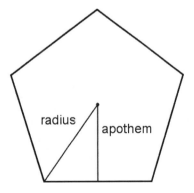

A **diagonal** is a line segment that joins two non-adjacent vertices of a polygon. The number of diagonals a polygon has can be found by using the formula:

$$\text{number of diagonals} = \frac{n(n - 3)}{2}$$

Note that *n* is the number of sides in the polygon. This formula works for all polygons, not just regular polygons.

QUADRILATERALS

A **quadrilateral** is a closed two-dimensional geometric figure that has four straight sides. The sum of the interior angles of any quadrilateral is 360°.

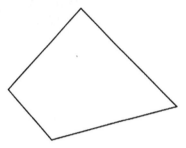

A **kite** is a quadrilateral with two pairs of adjacent sides that are congruent. A result of this is perpendicular diagonals. A kite can be concave or convex and has one line of symmetry.

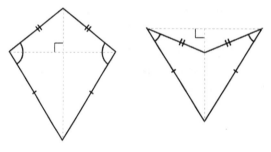

Trapezoid: A trapezoid is defined as a quadrilateral that has at least one pair of parallel sides. There are no rules for the second pair of sides. So, there are no rules for the diagonals and no lines of symmetry for a trapezoid.

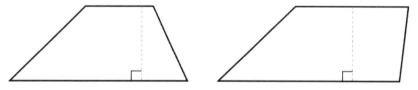

The **area of a trapezoid** is found by the formula $A = \frac{1}{2}h(b_1 + b_2)$, where *h* is the height (segment joining and perpendicular to the parallel bases), and b_1 and b_2 are the two parallel sides (bases). Do not use one of the other two sides as the height unless that side is also perpendicular to the parallel bases.

The **perimeter of a trapezoid** is found by the formula $P = a + b_1 + c + b_2$, where a, b_1, c, and b_2 are the four sides of the trapezoid.

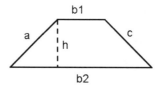

Review Video: **Area and Perimeter of a Trapezoid**
Visit mometrix.com/academy and enter code: 587523

Parallelogram: A quadrilateral that has two pairs of opposite parallel sides. As such it is a special type of trapezoid. The sides that are parallel are also congruent. The opposite interior angles are always congruent, and the consecutive interior angles are supplementary. The diagonals of a parallelogram divide each other. Each diagonal divides the parallelogram into two congruent triangles. A parallelogram has no line of symmetry, but does have 180-degree rotational symmetry about the midpoint.

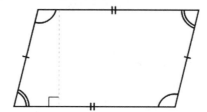

The **area of a parallelogram** is found by the formula $A = bh$, where b is the length of the base, and h is the height. Note that the base and height correspond to the length and width in a rectangle, so this formula would apply to rectangles as well. Do not confuse the height of a parallelogram with the length of the second side. The two are only the same measure in the case of a rectangle.

The **perimeter of a parallelogram** is found by the formula $P = 2a + 2b$ or $P = 2(a + b)$, where a and b are the lengths of the two sides.

Review Video: **Area and Perimeter of a Parallelogram**
Visit mometrix.com/academy and enter code: 718313
Review Video: **Diagonals of Parallelograms, Rectangles, and Rhombi**
Visit mometrix.com/academy and enter code: 320040

Isosceles trapezoid: A trapezoid with equal base angles. This gives rise to other properties including: the two nonparallel sides have the same length, the two non-base angles are also equal, and there is one line of symmetry through the midpoints of the parallel sides.

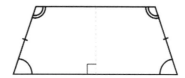

Rectangle: A quadrilateral with four right angles. All rectangles are parallelograms and trapezoids, but not all parallelograms or trapezoids are rectangles. The diagonals of a rectangle are congruent. Rectangles have 2 lines of symmetry (through each pair of opposing midpoints) and 180-degree rotational symmetry about the midpoint.

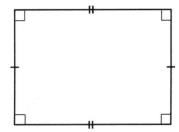

The **area of a rectangle** is found by the formula $A = lw$, where A is the area of the rectangle, l is the length (usually considered to be the longer side) and w is the width (usually considered to be the shorter side). The numbers for l and w are interchangeable.

The **perimeter of a rectangle** is found by the formula $P = 2l + 2w$ or $P = 2(l + w)$, where l is the length, and w is the width. It may be easier to add the length and width first and then double the result, as in the second formula.

Rhombus: A quadrilateral with four congruent sides. All rhombuses are parallelograms and kites; thus, they inherit all the properties of both types of quadrilaterals. The diagonals of a rhombus are perpendicular to each other. Rhombi have 2 lines of symmetry (along each of the diagonals) and 180-degree rotational symmetry. The **area of a rhombus** is half the product of the diagonals: $A = \frac{d_1 d_2}{2}$ and the perimeter of a rhombus is: $P = 2\sqrt{(d_1)^2 + (d_2)^2}$

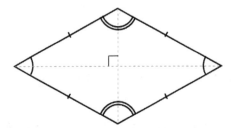

Square: A quadrilateral with four right angles and four congruent sides. Squares satisfy the criteria of all other types of quadrilaterals. The diagonals of a square are congruent and perpendicular to each other. Squares have 4 lines of symmetry (through each pair of opposing midpoints and along each of the diagonals) as well as 90-degree rotational symmetry about the midpoint.

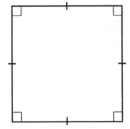

The **area of a square** is found by using the formula $A = s^2$, where s is the length of one side. The **perimeter of a square** is found by using the formula $P = 4s$, where s is the length of one side. Because all four sides are equal in a square, it is faster to multiply the length of one side by 4 than to add the same number four times. You could use the formulas for rectangles and get the same answer.

CIRCLES

The **center** of a circle is the single point from which every point on the circle is **equidistant**. The **radius** is a line segment that joins the center of the circle and any one point on the circle. All radii of a circle are equal. Circles that have the same center, but not the same length of radii are **concentric**. The **diameter** is a line segment that passes through the center of the circle and has both endpoints on the circle. The length of the diameter is exactly twice the length of the radius. Point O in the diagram below is the center of the circle, segments $\overline{OX}$, $\overline{OY}$, and $\overline{OZ}$ are radii, and segment $\overline{XZ}$ is a diamter.

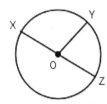

> **Review Video: Points of a Circle**
> Visit mometrix.com/academy and enter code: 420746
>
> **Review Video: The Diameter, Radius, and Circumference of Circles**
> Visit mometrix.com/academy and enter code: 448988

The **area of a circle** is found by the formula $A = \pi r^2$, where r is the length of the radius. If the diameter of the circle is given, remember to divide it in half to get the length of the radius before proceeding.

The **circumference** of a circle is found by the formula $C = 2\pi r$, where r is the radius. Again, remember to convert the diameter if you are given that measure rather than the radius.

> **Review Video: Area and Circumference of a Circle**
> Visit mometrix.com/academy and enter code: 243015

SOLIDS

The **surface area of a solid object** is the area of all sides or exterior surfaces. For objects such as prisms and pyramids, a further distinction is made between base surface area (B) and lateral surface area (LA). For a prism, the total surface area (SA) is $SA = LA + 2B$. For a pyramid or cone, the total surface area is $SA = LA + B$.

> **Review Video: How to Calculate the Volume of 3D Objects**
> Visit mometrix.com/academy and enter code: 163343

The **surface area of a sphere** can be found by the formula $A = 4\pi r^2$, where r is the radius. The volume is given by the formula $V = \frac{4}{3}\pi r^3$, where r is the radius. Both quantities are generally given in terms of π.

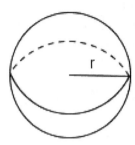

For a **rectangular prism**, the volume can be found by the formula $V = lwh$, where V is the volume, l is the length, w is the width, and h is the height. The surface area can be calculated as $SA = 2lw + 2hl + 2wh$ or $SA = 2(lw + hl + wh)$.

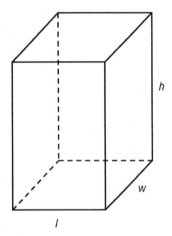

Review Video: <u>Volume and Surface Area of a Prism</u>
Visit mometrix.com/academy and enter code: 420158

The **volume of a cube** can be found by the formula $V = s^3$, where s is the length of a side. The surface area of a cube is calculated as $SA = 6s^2$, where SA is the total surface area and s is the length of a side. These formulas are the same as the ones used for the volume and surface area of a rectangular prism, but simplified since all three quantities (length, width, and height) are the same.

Review Video: <u>Volume and Surface Area of a Cube</u>
Visit mometrix.com/academy and enter code: 664455

The **volume of a cylinder** can be calculated by the formula $V = \pi r^2 h$, where r is the radius, and h is the height. The surface area of a cylinder can be found by the formula $SA = 2\pi r^2 + 2\pi rh$. The first term is the base area multiplied by two, and the second term is the perimeter of the base multiplied by the height.

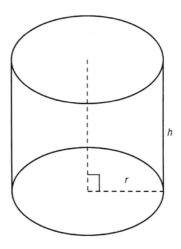

PRACTICE

P1. Find the measure of angles **(a)**, **(b)**, and **(c)** based on the figure with two parallel lines, two perpendicular lines and one transversal:

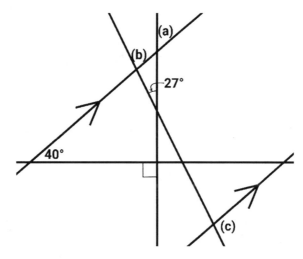

P2. Use the coordinate plane to reflect the figure below across the *y*-axis.

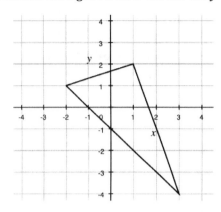

P3. Use the coordinate plane to enlarge the figure below by a factor of 2.

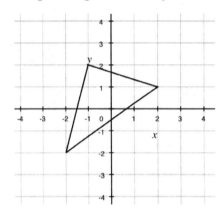

P4. Find the area and perimeter of the following quadrilaterals:

(a) A square with side length 2.5 cm.

(b) A parallelogram with height 3 m, base 4 m, and other side 6 m.

(c) A rhombus with diagonals 15 in and 20 in.

P5. Find the surface area and volume of a cylinder with radius 5 m and height 0.5 m.

PRACTICE SOLUTIONS

P1. (a) The vertical angle paired with (a) is part of a right triangle with the 40° angle. Thus the measure can be found:

$$90° = 40° + a$$
$$a = 50°$$

(b) The triangle formed by the supplementary angle to (b) is part of a triangle with the vertical angle paired with (a) and the given angle of 27°. Since $a = 50°$:

$$180° = (180° - b) + 50° + 27°$$
$$103° = 180° - b$$
$$-77° = -b$$
$$77° = b$$

(c) As they are part of a transversal crossing parallel lines, angles (b) and (c) are supplementary. Thus $c = 103°$

P2. To reflect the image across the y-axis, replace each x-coordinate of the points that are the vertex of the triangle, x, with its negative, $-x$.

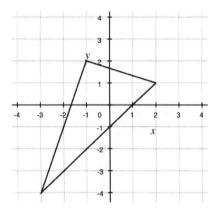

P3. An enlargement can be found by multiplying each coordinate of the coordinate pairs located at the triangle's vertices by 2. The original coordinates were $(-1, 2), (2, 1), (-2, -2)$, so the new coordinates are $(-2, 4), (4, 2), (-4, -4)$:

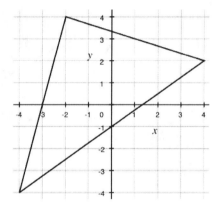

P4.　**(a)** $A = s^2 = (2.5 \text{ cm})^2 = 6.25 \text{ cm}^2; P = 4s = 4 \times 2.5 \text{ cm} = 10 \text{ cm}$

(b) $A = bh = (3 \text{ m})(4 \text{ m}) = 12 \text{ m}^2; P = 2a + 2b = 2 \times 6 \text{ m} + 2 \times 4 \text{ m} = 20 \text{ m}$

(c) $A = \frac{d_1 d_2}{2} = \frac{(15 \text{ in})(20 \text{ in})}{2} = 150 \text{ in}^2;$
$P = 2\sqrt{(d_1)^2 + (d_2)^2} = 2\sqrt{(15 \text{ in})^2 + (20 \text{ in})^2} = 2\sqrt{625 \text{ in}^2} = 50 \text{ in}$

P5. $SA = 2\pi r^2 + 2\pi rh = 2\pi(5 \text{ m})^2 + 2\pi(5 \text{ m})(0.5 \text{ m}) = 55\pi \text{ m}^2 \cong 172.79 \text{ m}^2;$
$V = \pi r^2 h = \pi(5 \text{ m})^2(0.5 \text{ m}) = 12.5\pi \text{ m}^3 \cong 39.27 \text{ m}^3$

Triangles

A **scalene triangle** is a triangle with no congruent sides. A scalene triangle will also have three angles of different measures. The angle with the largest measure is opposite the longest side, and the angle with the smallest measure is opposite the shortest side. An **acute triangle** is a triangle whose three angles are all less than 90°. If two of the angles are equal, the acute triangle is also an **isosceles triangle**. An isosceles triangle will also have two congruent angles opposite the two congruent sides. If the three angles are all equal, the acute triangle is also an **equilateral triangle**. An equilateral triangle will also have three congruent angles, each 60°. All equilateral triangles are also acute triangles. An **obtuse triangle** is a triangle with exactly one angle greater than 90°. The other two angles may or may not be equal. If the two remaining angles are equal, the obtuse triangle is also an isosceles triangle. A **right triangle** is a triangle with exactly one angle equal to 90°. All right triangles follow the Pythagorean theorem. A right triangle can never be acute or obtuse.

The table below illustrates how each descriptor places a different restriction on the triangle:

Angles / Sides	Acute: All angles < 90°	Obtuse: One angle > 90°	Right: One angle = 90°
Scalene: No equal side lengths	$90° > \angle a > \angle b > \angle c$ $x > y > z$	$\angle a > 90° > \angle b > \angle c$ $x > y > z$	$90° = \angle a > \angle b > \angle c$ $x > y > z$
Isosceles: Two equal side lengths	$90° > \angle a, \angle b, \text{or} \angle c$ $\angle b = \angle c, \quad y = z$	$\angle a > 90° > \angle b = \angle c$ $x > y = z$	$\angle a = 90°, \angle b = \angle c$ $= 45°$ $x > y = z$
Equilateral: Three equal side lengths	$60° = \angle a = \angle b = \angle c$ $x = y = z$		

> **Review Video: Introduction to Types of Triangles**
> Visit mometrix.com/academy and enter code: 511711

AREA AND PERIMETER OF A TRIANGLE

The **perimeter of any triangle** is found by summing the three side lengths; $P = a + b + c$. For an equilateral triangle, this is the same as $P = 3a$, where a is any side length, since all three sides are the same length.

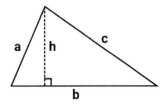

The **area of any triangle** can be found by taking half the product of one side length, referred to as the base and often given the variable b, and the perpendicular distance from that side to the opposite vertex, called the altitude or height and given the variable h. In equation form that is $A = \frac{1}{2}bh$. Another formula that works for any triangle is $A = \sqrt{s(s-a)(s-b)(s-c)}$, where s is the semiperimeter: $\frac{a+b+c}{2}$, and a, b, and c are the lengths of the three sides. Special cases include isosceles triangles: $A = \frac{1}{2}b\sqrt{a^2 - \frac{b^2}{4}}$, where b is the unique side and a is the length of one of the two congruent sides, and equilateral triangles: $A = \frac{\sqrt{3}}{4}a^2$, where a is the length of a side.

> **Review Video: Area and Perimeter of a Triangle**
> Visit mometrix.com/academy and enter code: 853779

PYTHAGOREAN THEOREM

The side of a triangle opposite the right angle is called the **hypotenuse**. The other two sides are called the legs. The Pythagorean theorem states a relationship among the legs and hypotenuse of a right triangle: $a^2 + b^2 = c^2$, where a and b are the lengths of the legs of a right triangle, and c is the length of the hypotenuse. Note that this formula will only work with right triangles.

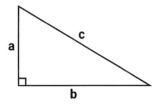

> **Review Video: Pythagorean Theorem**
> Visit mometrix.com/academy and enter code: 906576

PRACTICE

P1. Calculate the area of a triangle with side lengths of 7 ft, 8 ft, and 9 ft.

P2. Calculate the following values based on triangle MNO:

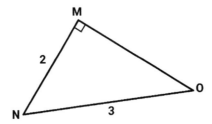

    (a) length of $\overline{MO}$

    (b) area of the triangle, if the units of the measurements are in miles

PRACTICE SOLUTIONS

P1. Given only side lengths, we can use the semi perimeter to the find the area based on the formula, $A = \sqrt{s(s-a)(s-b)(s-c)}$, where s is the semi perimeter, $\frac{a+b+c}{2} = \frac{7+8+9}{2} = 12$ ft:

$$A = \sqrt{12(12-7)(12-8)(12-9)}$$
$$= \sqrt{(12)(5)(4)(3)}$$
$$= 12\sqrt{5} \text{ ft}^2$$

P2. (a) Since triangle MNO is a right triangle, we can use the simple form of Pythagoras theorem to find the missing side length:

$$\left(\overline{MO}\right)^2 + 2^2 = 3^2$$
$$\left(\overline{MO}\right)^2 = 9 - 4$$
$$\overline{MO} = \sqrt{5}$$

    (b) Since triangle MNO is a right triangle, we can use either of the legs as the height and the other as the base in the simple formula for area of a triangle:

$$A = \frac{bh}{2}$$
$$= \frac{(2 \text{ mi})\left(\sqrt{5} \text{ mi}\right)}{2}$$
$$= \sqrt{5} \text{ mi}^2$$

Statistics

MEASURES OF CENTRAL TENDENCY

A **measure of central tendency** is a statistical value that gives a reasonable estimate for the center of a group of data. There are several different ways of describing the measure of central tendency. Each one has a unique way it is calculated, and each one gives a slightly different perspective on the data set. Whenever you give a measure of central tendency, always make sure the units are the same. If the data has different units, such as hours, minutes, and seconds, convert all the data to the same unit, and use the same unit in the measure of central tendency. If no units are given in the data, do not give units for the measure of central tendency.

MEAN

The **statistical mean** of a group of data is the same as the arithmetic average of that group. To find the mean of a set of data, first convert each value to the same units, if necessary. Then find the sum of all the values, and count the total number of data values, making sure you take into consideration each individual value. If a value appears more than once, count it more than once. Divide the sum of the values by the total number of values and apply the units, if any. Note that the mean does not have to be one of the data values in the set, and may not divide evenly.

$$\text{mean} = \frac{\text{sum of the data values}}{\text{quantity of data values}}$$

For instance, the mean of the data set {88, 72, 61, 90, 97, 68, 88, 79, 86, 93, 97, 71, 80, 84, 89} would be the sum of the fifteen numbers divided by 15:

$$\frac{88 + 72 + 61 + 90 + 97 + 68 + 88 + 79 + 86 + 93 + 97 + 71 + 80 + 84 + 89}{15} = \frac{1242}{15}$$
$$= 82.8$$

While the mean is relatively easy to calculate and averages are understood by most people, the mean can be very misleading if it is used as the sole measure of central tendency. If the data set has outliers (data values that are unusually high or unusually low compared to the rest of the data values), the mean can be very distorted, especially if the data set has a small number of values. If unusually high values are countered with unusually low values, the mean is not affected as much. For example, if five of twenty students in a class get a 100 on a test, but the other 15 students have an average of 60 on the same test, the class average would appear as 70. Whenever the mean is skewed by outliers, it is always a good idea to include the median as an alternate measure of central tendency.

A **weighted mean**, or weighted average, is a mean that uses "weighted" values. The formula is weighted mean $= \frac{w_1 x_1 + w_2 x_2 + w_3 x_3 \dots + w_n x_n}{w_1 + w_2 + w_3 + \dots + w_n}$. Weighted values, such as $w_1, w_2, w_3, \dots w_n$ are assigned to each member of the set $x_1, x_2, x_3, \dots x_n$. When calculating the weighted mean, make sure a weight value for each member of the set is used.

MEDIAN

The **statistical median** is the value in the middle of the set of data. To find the median, list all data values in order from smallest to largest or from largest to smallest. Any value that is repeated in the set must be listed the number of times it appears. If there are an odd number of data values, the median is the value in the middle of the list. If there is an even number of data values, the median is the arithmetic mean of the two middle values.

For example, the median of the data set {88, 72, 61, 90, 97, 68, 88, 79, 86, 93, 97, 71, 80, 84, 88} is 86 since the ordered set is {61, 68, 71, 72, 79, 80, 84, **86**, 88, 88, 88, 90, 93, 97, 97}.

The big disadvantage of using the median as a measure of central tendency is that is relies solely on a value's relative size as compared to the other values in the set. When the individual values in a set of data are evenly dispersed, the median can be an accurate tool. However, if there is a group of rather large values or a group of rather small values that are not offset by a different group of values, the information that can be inferred from the median may not be accurate because the distribution of values is skewed.

MODE

The **statistical mode** is the data value that occurs the greatest number of times in the data set. It is possible to have exactly one mode, more than one mode, or no mode. To find the mode of a set of data, arrange the data like you do to find the median (all values in order, listing all multiples of data values). Count the number of times each value appears in the data set. If all values appear an equal number of times, there is no mode. If one value appears more than any other value, that value is the mode. If two or more values appear the same number of times, but there are other values that appear fewer times and no values that appear more times, all of those values are the modes.

For example, the mode of the data set {**88**, 72, 61, 90, 97, 68, **88**, 79, 86, 93, 97, 71, 80, 84, **88**} is 88.

The main disadvantage of the mode is that the values of the other data in the set have no bearing on the mode. The mode may be the largest value, the smallest value, or a value anywhere in between in the set. The mode only tells which value or values, if any, occurred the greatest number of times. It does not give any suggestions about the remaining values in the set.

> **Review Video: Mean, Median, and Mode**
> Visit mometrix.com/academy and enter code: 286207

DATA ANALYSIS
SIMPLE REGRESSION

In statistics, **simple regression** is using an equation to represent a relation between an independent and a dependent variable. The independent variable is also referred to as the explanatory variable or the predictor, and is generally represented by the variable x in the equation. The dependent variable, usually represented by the variable y, is also referred to as the response variable. The equation may be any type of function – linear, quadratic, exponential, etc. The best way to handle this task is to use the regression feature of your graphing calculator. This will easily give you the curve of best fit and provide you with the coefficients and other information you need to derive an equation.

LINE OF BEST FIT

In a scatter plot, the **line of best fit** is the line that best shows the trends of the data. The line of best fit is given by the equation $\hat{y} = ax + b$, where a and b are the regression coefficients. The regression coefficient a is also the slope of the line of best fit, and b is also the y-coordinate of the point at which the line of best fit crosses the y-axis. Not every point on the scatter plot will be on the line of best fit. The differences between the y-values of the points in the scatter plot and the corresponding y-values according to the equation of the line of best fit are the residuals. The line of best fit is also called the least-squares regression line because it is also the line that has the lowest sum of the squares of the residuals.

CORRELATION COEFFICIENT

The **correlation coefficient** is the numerical value that indicates how strong the relationship is between the two variables of a linear regression equation. A correlation coefficient of –1 is a perfect negative correlation. A correlation coefficient of +1 is a perfect positive correlation. Correlation coefficients close to –1 or +1 are very strong correlations. A correlation coefficient equal to zero indicates there is no correlation between the two variables. This test is a good indicator of whether or not the equation for the line of best fit is accurate. The formula for the correlation coefficient is:

$$r = \frac{\sum_{i=1}^{n}(x_i - \bar{x})(y_i - \bar{y})}{\sqrt{\sum_{i=1}^{n}(x_i - \bar{x})^2}\sqrt{\sum_{i=1}^{n}(y_i - \bar{y})^2}}$$

where r is the correlation coefficient, n is the number of data values in the set, (x_i, y_i) is a point in the set, and $\bar{x}$ and $\bar{y}$ are the means.

Z-SCORE

A **z-score** is an indication of how many standard deviations a given value falls from the mean. To calculate a z-score, use the formula $\frac{x-\mu}{\sigma}$, where x is the data value, μ is the mean of the data set, and σ is the standard deviation of the population. If the z-score is positive, the data value lies above the mean. If the z-score is negative, the data value falls below the mean. These scores are useful in interpreting data such as standardized test scores, where every piece of data in the set has been counted, rather than just a small random sample. In cases where standard deviations are calculated from a random sample of the set, the z-scores will not be as accurate.

AREA UNDER A NORMAL CURVE

The area under a normal curve can be represented using one or two z-scores or a mean and a z-score. A z-score represents the number of standard deviations a score falls above, or below, the mean. A normal distribution table (z-table) shows the mean to z area, small portion area, and larger portion area, for any z-score from 0 to 4. The area between a mean and z-score is simply equal to the mean to z area. The area under the normal curve, between two z-scores, may be calculated by adding or subtracting the mean to z areas. An area above, or below, a z-score is equal to the smaller or larger portion area. The area may also be calculated by subtracting the mean to z area from 0.5, when looking at the smaller area, or adding the mean to z area to 0.5, when looking at the larger area.

CENTRAL LIMIT THEOREM

According to the **central limit theorem**, regardless of what the original distribution of a sample is, the distribution of the means tends to get closer and closer to a normal distribution as the sample size gets larger and larger (this is necessary because the sample is becoming more all-encompassing of the elements of the population). As the sample size gets larger, the distribution of the sample mean will approach a normal distribution with a mean of the population mean and a variance of the population variance divided by the sample size.

DISPLAYING INFORMATION

FREQUENCY TABLES

Frequency tables show how frequently each unique value appears in the set. A **relative frequency table** is one that shows the proportions of each unique value compared to the entire set. Relative frequencies are given as percentages; however, the total percent for a relative frequency table will not necessarily equal 100 percent due to rounding. An example of a frequency table with relative frequencies is below.

Favorite Color	Frequency	Relative Frequency
Blue	4	13%
Red	7	22%
Green	3	9%
Purple	6	19%
Cyan	12	38%

A **two-way frequency table** quickly shows intersections and total frequencies. These values would have to be calculated from a manual list. The conditional probability, $P(B|A)$, read as "The probability of B, given A," is equal to $P(B \cap A)/A$. A two-way frequency table can quickly show these frequencies. Consider the table below:

	Cat	Dog	Bird	Total
Male	24	16	26	66
Female	32	12	20	64
Total	56	28	46	130

Find $P(Cat|Female)$. The two-way frequency table shows $C \cap F$ to be 32, while the total for female is 64. Thus, $P(Cat \mid Female) = \frac{32}{64} = \frac{1}{2}$.

PICTOGRAPHS

A **pictograph** is a graph, generally in the horizontal orientation, that uses pictures or symbols to represent the data. Each pictograph must have a key that defines the picture or symbol and gives the quantity each picture or symbol represents. Pictures or symbols on a pictograph are not always shown as whole elements. In this case, the fraction of the picture or symbol shown represents the same fraction of the quantity a whole picture or symbol stands for. For example, a row with $3\frac{1}{2}$ ears of corn, where each ear of corn represents 100 stalks of corn in a field, would equal $3\frac{1}{2} \times 100 = 350$ stalks of corn in the field.

CIRCLE GRAPHS

Circle graphs, also known as *pie charts*, provide a visual depiction of the relationship of each type of data compared to the whole set of data. The circle graph is divided into sections by drawing radii to create central angles whose percentage of the circle is equal to the individual data's percentage of the whole set. Each 1% of data is equal to 3.6° in the circle graph. Therefore, data represented by a 90° section of the circle graph makes up 25% of the whole. When complete, a circle graph often looks like a pie cut into uneven wedges. The pie chart below shows the data from the frequency table referenced earlier where people were asked their favorite color.

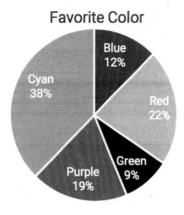

LINE GRAPHS

Line graphs have one or more lines of varying styles (solid or broken) to show the different values for a set of data. The individual data are represented as ordered pairs, much like on a Cartesian plane. In this case, the *x*- and *y*-axes are defined in terms of their units, such as dollars or time. The individual plotted points are joined by line segments to show whether the value of the data is increasing (line sloping upward), decreasing (line sloping downward) or staying the same (horizontal line). Multiple sets of data can be graphed on the same line graph to give an easy visual comparison. An example of this would be graphing achievement test scores for different groups of students over the same time period to see which group had the greatest increase or decrease in performance from year-to-year (as shown below).

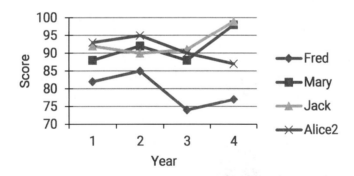

Review Video: **How to Create a Line Graph**
Visit mometrix.com/academy and enter code: 480147

LINE PLOTS

A **line plot**, also known as a *dot plot*, has plotted points that are not connected by line segments. In this graph, the horizontal axis lists the different possible values for the data, and the vertical axis lists the number of times the individual value occurs. A single dot is graphed for each value to show the number of times it occurs. This graph is more closely related to a bar graph than a line graph. Do not connect the dots in a line plot or it will misrepresent the data.

Review Video: **Line Plot**
Visit mometrix.com/academy and enter code: 754610

STEM AND LEAF PLOTS

A **stem and leaf plot** is useful for depicting groups of data that fall into a range of values. Each piece of data is separated into two parts: the first, or left, part is called the stem; the second, or right, part is called the leaf. Each stem is listed in a column from smallest to largest. Each leaf that has the common stem is listed in that stem's row from smallest to largest. For example, in a set of two-digit numbers, the digit in the tens place is the stem, and the digit in the ones place is the leaf. With a stem and leaf plot, you can easily see which subset of numbers (10s, 20s, 30s, etc.) is the largest. This information is also readily available by looking at a histogram, but a stem and leaf plot also allows you to look closer and see exactly which values fall in that range. Using a sample set of test scores (82, 88, 92, 93, 85, 90, 92, 95, 74, 88, 90, 91, 78, 87, 98, 99), we can assemble a stem and leaf plot like the one below.

Test Scores

7	4	8						
8	2	5	7	8	8			
9	0	0	1	2	2	3	5	8	9

> **Review Video: Stem-and-Leaf Plots**
> Visit mometrix.com/academy and enter code: 302339

BAR GRAPHS

A **bar graph** is one of the few graphs that can be drawn correctly in two different configurations – both horizontally and vertically. A bar graph is similar to a line plot in the way the data is organized on the graph. Both axes must have their categories defined for the graph to be useful. Rather than placing a single dot to mark the point of the data's value, a bar, or thick line, is drawn from zero to the exact value of the data, whether it is a number, percentage, or other numerical value. Longer bar lengths correspond to greater data values. To read a bar graph, read the labels for the axes to find the units being reported. Then look where the bars end in relation to the scale given on the corresponding axis and determine the associated value.

The bar chart below represents the responses from our favorite color survey.

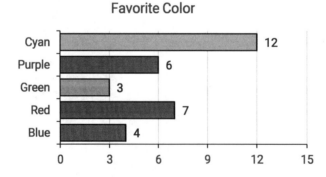

HISTOGRAMS

At first glance, a **histogram** looks like a vertical bar graph. The difference is that a bar graph has a separate bar for each piece of data and a histogram has one continuous bar for each *range* of data. For example, a histogram may have one bar for the range 0–9, one bar for 10–19, etc. While a bar graph has numerical values on one axis, a histogram has numerical values on both axes. Each range is of equal size, and they are ordered left to right from lowest to highest. The height of each column on a histogram represents the number of data values within that range. Like a stem and leaf plot, a histogram makes it easy to glance at the graph and quickly determine which range has the greatest quantity of values. A simple example of a histogram is below.

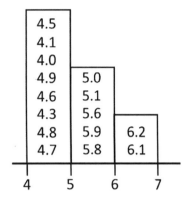

BIVARIATE DATA

Bivariate data is simply data from two different variables. (The prefix *bi-* means *two*.) In a *scatter plot*, each value in the set of data is plotted on a grid similar to a Cartesian plane, where each axis represents one of the two variables. By looking at the pattern formed by the points on the grid, you can often determine whether or not there is a relationship between the two variables, and what that relationship is, if it exists. The variables may be directly proportionate, inversely proportionate, or show no proportion at all. It may also be possible to determine if the data is linear, and if so, to find an equation to relate the two variables. The following scatter plot shows the relationship between preference for brand "A" and the age of the consumers surveyed.

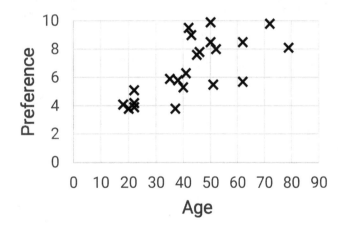

SCATTER PLOTS

Scatter plots are also useful in determining the type of function represented by the data and finding the simple regression. Linear scatter plots may be positive or negative. Nonlinear scatter plots are generally exponential or quadratic. Below are some common types of scatter plots:

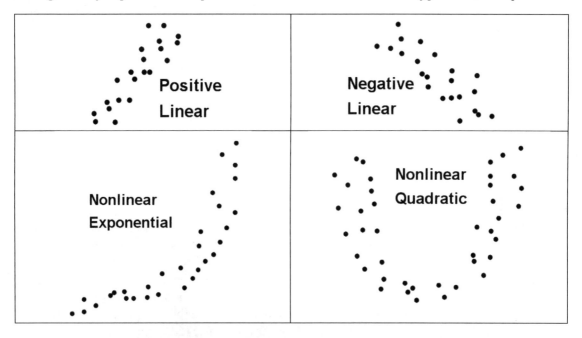

> **Review Video: What is a Scatter Plot?**
> Visit mometrix.com/academy and enter code: 596526

PRACTICE

P1. Given the following graph, determine the range of patient ages:

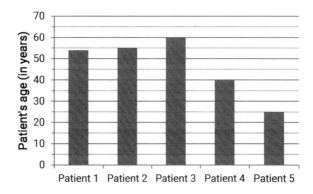

96

P2. Today, there were two food options for lunch at a local college cafeteria. Given the following survey data, what is the probability that a junior selected at random from the sample had a sandwich?

	Freshman	Sophomore	Junior	Senior
Salad	15	12	27	36
Sandwich	24	40	43	35
Nothing	42	23	23	30

PRACTICE SOLUTIONS

P1. Patient 1 is 54 years old; Patient 2 is 55 years old; Patient 3 is 60 years old; Patient 4 is 40 years old; and Patient 5 is 25 years old. The range of patient ages is the age of the oldest patient minus the age of the youngest patient. In other words, $60 - 25 = 35$. The range of ages is 35 years.

P2. With two-way tables it is often most helpful to start by totaling the rows and columns:

	Freshman	Sophomore	Junior	Senior	Total
Salad	15	12	27	36	90
Sandwich	24	40	43	35	142
Nothing	42	23	23	30	118
Total	81	75	93	101	350

Since the question is focused on juniors, we can focus on that column. There was a total of 93 juniors surveyed and 43 of them had a sandwich for lunch. Thus, the probability that a junior selected at random had a sandwich would be $\frac{43}{93} \cong 0.462 \cong 46.2\%$.

Probability

Probability is the likelihood of a certain outcome occurring for a given event. An **event** is a situation that produces a result; that could be something as simple as flipping a coin or as complex as launching a rocket. Determining the probability of an outcome for an event can be equally simple or complex. As such there are specific terms used in the study of probability that need to be understood:

- **Compound event**—an event that involves two or more independent events (rolling a pair of dice and taking the sum)
- **Desired outcome** (or success)—an outcome that meets a particular set of criteria (a roll of 1 or 2 if we are looking for numbers less than 3)
- **Independent events**—two or more events whose outcomes do not affect one another (two coins tossed at the same time)
- **Dependent events**—two or more events whose outcomes affect one another (two cards drawn consecutively from the same deck)
- **Certain outcome**—probability of outcome is 100% or 1

- **Impossible outcome**—probability of outcome is 0% or 0
- **Mutually exclusive outcomes**—two or more outcomes whose criteria cannot all be satisfied in a single event (a coin coming up heads and tails on the same toss)
- **Random variable**—refers to all possible outcomes of a single event which may be discrete or continuous.

Review Video: Intro to Probability
Visit mometrix.com/academy and enter code: 212374

THEORETICAL AND EXPERIMENTAL PROBABILITY

Theoretical probability can usually be determined without actually performing the event. The likelihood of a outcome occurring, or the probability of an outcome occurring, is given by the formula:

$$P(A) = \frac{\text{Number of acceptable outcomes}}{\text{Number of possible outcomes}}$$

Note that $P(A)$ is the probability of an outcome A occurring, and each outcome is just as likely to occur as any other outcome. If each outcome has the same probability of occurring as every other possible outcome, the outcomes are said to be equally likely to occur. The total number of acceptable outcomes must be less than or equal to the total number of possible outcomes. If the two are equal, then the outcome is certain to occur and the probability is 1. If the number of acceptable outcomes is zero, then the outcome is impossible and the probability is 0. For example, if there are 20 marbles in a bag and 5 are red, then the theoretical probability of randomly selecting a red marble is 5 out of 20, ($\frac{5}{20} = \frac{1}{4}$, 0.25, or 25%).

If the theoretical probability is unknown or too complicated to calculate, it can be estimated by an experimental probability. **Experimental probability**, also called empirical probability, is an estimate of the likelihood of a certain outcome based on repeated experiments or collected data. In other words, while theoretical probability is based on what *should* happen, experimental probability is based on what *has* happened. Experimental probability is calculated in the same way as theoretical probability, except that actual outcomes are used instead of possible outcomes. The more experiments performed or datapoints gathered, the better the estimate should be.

Theoretical and experimental probability do not always line up with one another. Theoretical probability says that out of 20 coin-tosses, 10 should be heads. However, if we were actually to toss 20 coins, we might record just 5 heads. This doesn't mean that our theoretical probability is incorrect; it just means that this particular experiment had results that were different from what was predicted. A practical application of empirical probability is the insurance industry. There are no set functions that define lifespan, health, or safety. Insurance companies look at factors from hundreds of thousands of individuals to find patterns that they then use to set the formulas for insurance premiums.

Review Video: Empirical Probability
Visit mometrix.com/academy and enter code: 513468

OBJECTIVE AND SUBJECTIVE PROBABILITY

Objective probability is based on mathematical formulas and documented evidence. Examples of objective probability include raffles or lottery drawings where there is a pre-determined number of possible outcomes and a predetermined number of outcomes that correspond to an event. Other cases of objective probability include probabilities of rolling dice, flipping coins, or drawing cards. Most gambling games are based on objective probability.

In contrast, **subjective probability** is based on personal or professional feelings and judgments. Often, there is a lot of guesswork following extensive research. Areas where subjective probability is applicable include sales trends and business expenses. Attractions set admission prices based on subjective probabilities of attendance based on varying admission rates in an effort to maximize their profit.

SAMPLE SPACE

The total set of all possible results of a test or experiment is called a **sample space**, or sometimes a universal sample space. The sample space, represented by one of the variables S, Ω, or U (for universal sample space) has individual elements called outcomes. Other terms for outcome that may be used interchangeably include elementary outcome, simple event, or sample point. The number of outcomes in a given sample space could be infinite or finite, and some tests may yield multiple unique sample sets. For example, tests conducted by drawing playing cards from a standard deck would have one sample space of the card values, another sample space of the card suits, and a third sample space of suit-denomination combinations. For most tests, the sample spaces considered will be finite.

An **event**, represented by the variable E, is a portion of a sample space. It may be one outcome or a group of outcomes from the same sample space. If an event occurs, then the test or experiment will generate an outcome that satisfies the requirement of that event. For example, given a standard deck of 52 playing cards as the sample space, and defining the event as the collection of face cards, then the event will occur if the card drawn is a J, Q, or K. If any other card is drawn, the event is said to have not occurred.

For every sample space, each possible outcome has a specific likelihood, or probability, that it will occur. The probability measure, also called the **distribution**, is a function that assigns a real number probability, from zero to one, to each outcome. For a probability measure to be accurate, every outcome must have a real number probability measure that is greater than or equal to zero and less than or equal to one. Also, the probability measure of the sample space must equal one, and the probability measure of the union of multiple outcomes must equal the sum of the individual probability measures.

Probabilities of events are expressed as real numbers from zero to one. They give a numerical value to the chance that a particular event will occur. The probability of an event occurring is the sum of the probabilities of the individual elements of that event. For example, in a standard deck of 52 playing cards as the sample space and the collection of face cards as the event, the probability of drawing a specific face card is $\frac{1}{52} = 0.019$, but the probability of drawing any one of the twelve face cards is $12(0.019) = 0.228$. Note that rounding of numbers can generate different results. If you multiplied 12 by the fraction $\frac{1}{52}$ before converting to a decimal, you would get the answer $\frac{12}{52} = 0.231$.

TREE DIAGRAM

For a simple sample space, possible outcomes may be determined by using a **tree diagram** or an organized chart. In either case, you can easily draw or list out the possible outcomes. For example, to determine all the possible ways three objects can be ordered, you can draw a tree diagram:

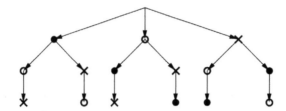

You can also make a chart to list all the possibilities:

First object	Second object	Third object
●	X	O
●	O	X
O	●	X
O	X	●
X	●	O
X	O	●

Either way, you can easily see there are six possible ways the three objects can be ordered.

If two events have no outcomes in common, they are said to be **mutually exclusive**. For example, in a standard deck of 52 playing cards, the event of all card suits is mutually exclusive to the event of all card values. If two events have no bearing on each other so that one event occurring has no influence on the probability of another event occurring, the two events are said to be independent. For example, rolling a standard six-sided die multiple times does not change that probability that a particular number will be rolled from one roll to the next. If the outcome of one event does affect the probability of the second event, the two events are said to be dependent. For example, if cards are drawn from a deck, the probability of drawing an ace after an ace has been drawn is different than the probability of drawing an ace if no ace (or no other card, for that matter) has been drawn.

In probability, the **odds in favor of an event** are the number of times the event will occur compared to the number of times the event will not occur. To calculate the odds in favor of an event, use the formula $\frac{P(A)}{1-P(A)}$, where $P(A)$ is the probability that the event will occur. Many times, odds in favor is given as a ratio in the form $\frac{a}{b}$ or $a{:}b$, where a is the probability of the event occurring and b is the complement of the event, the probability of the event not occurring. If the odds in favor are given as 2:5, that means that you can expect the event to occur two times for every 5 times that it does not occur. In other words, the probability that the event will occur is $\frac{2}{2+5} = \frac{2}{7}$.

In probability, the **odds against an event** are the number of times the event will not occur compared to the number of times the event will occur. To calculate the odds against an event, use the formula $\frac{1-P(A)}{P(A)}$, where $P(A)$ is the probability that the event will occur. Many times, odds against is given as a ratio in the form $\frac{b}{a}$ or $b{:}a$, where b is the probability the event will not occur (the complement of the event) and a is the probability the event will occur. If the odds against an event

100

are given as 3:1, that means that you can expect the event to not occur 3 times for every one time it does occur. In other words, 3 out of every 4 trials will fail.

PERMUTATIONS AND COMBINATIONS

When trying to calculate the probability of an event using the $\frac{\text{desired outcomes}}{\text{total outcomes}}$ formula, you may frequently find that there are too many outcomes to individually count them. **Permutation** and **combination formulas** offer a shortcut to counting outcomes. A permutation is an arrangement of a specific number of a set of objects in a specific order. The number of **permutations** of r items given a set of n items can be calculated as $_nP_r = \frac{n!}{(n-r)!}$. Combinations are similar to permutations, except there are no restrictions regarding the order of the elements. While ABC is considered a different permutation than BCA, ABC and BCA are considered the same combination. The number of **combinations** of r items given a set of n items can be calculated as $_nC_r = \frac{n!}{r!(n-r)!}$ or $_nC_r = \frac{_nP_r}{r!}$.

Suppose you want to calculate how many different 5-card hands can be drawn from a deck of 52 cards. This is a combination since the order of the cards in a hand does not matter. There are 52 cards available, and 5 to be selected. Thus, the number of different hands is $_{52}C_5 = \frac{52!}{5! \times 47!} = 2,598,960$.

COMPLEMENT OF AN EVENT

Sometimes it may be easier to calculate the possibility of something not happening, or the **complement of an event**. Represented by the symbol $\bar{A}$, the complement of A is the probability that event A does not happen. When you know the probability of event A occurring, you can use the formula $P(\bar{A}) = 1 - P(A)$, where $P(\bar{A})$ is the probability of event A not occurring, and $P(A)$ is the probability of event A occurring.

ADDITION RULE

The **addition rule** for probability is used for finding the probability of a compound event. Use the formula $P(A \text{ or } B) = P(A) + P(B) - P(A \text{ and } B)$, where $P(A \text{ and } B)$ is the probability of both events occurring to find the probability of a compound event. The probability of both events occurring at the same time must be subtracted to eliminate any overlap in the first two probabilities.

CONDITIONAL PROBABILITY

Conditional probability is the probability of an event occurring once another event has already occurred. Given event A and dependent event B, the probability of event B occurring when event A has already occurred is represented by the notation $P(A|B)$. To find the probability of event B occurring, take into account the fact that event A has already occurred and adjust the total number of possible outcomes. For example, suppose you have ten balls numbered 1–10 and you want ball number 7 to be pulled in two pulls. On the first pull, the probability of getting the 7 is $\frac{1}{10}$ because there is one ball with a 7 on it and 10 balls to choose from. Assuming the first pull did not yield a 7, the probability of pulling a 7 on the second pull is now $\frac{1}{9}$ because there are only 9 balls remaining for the second pull.

MULTIPLICATION RULE

The **multiplication rule** can be used to find the probability of two independent events occurring using the formula $P(A \text{ and } B) = P(A) \times P(B)$, where $P(A \text{ and } B)$ is the probability of two independent events occurring, $P(A)$ is the probability of the first event occurring, and $P(B)$ is the probability of the second event occurring.

The multiplication rule can also be used to find the probability of two dependent events occurring using the formula $P(A \text{ and } B) = P(A) \times P(B|A)$, where $P(A \text{ and } B)$ is the probability of two dependent events occurring and $P(B|A)$ is the probability of the second event occurring after the first event has already occurred. Before using the multiplication rule, you MUST first determine whether the two events are *dependent* or *independent*.

Use a **combination of the multiplication** rule and the rule of complements to find the probability that at least one outcome of the element will occur. This given by the general formula $P(\text{at least one event occurring}) = 1 - P(\text{no outcomes occurring})$. For example, to find the probability that at least one even number will show when a pair of dice is rolled, find the probability that two odd numbers will be rolled (no even numbers) and subtract from one. You can always use a tree diagram or make a chart to list the possible outcomes when the sample space is small, such as in the dice-rolling example, but in most cases, it will be much faster to use the multiplication and complement formulas.

> **Review Video: Multiplication Rule**
> Visit mometrix.com/academy and enter code: 782598

EXPECTED VALUE

Expected value is a method of determining the expected outcome in a random situation. It is a sum of the weighted probabilities of the possible outcomes. Multiply the probability of an event occurring by the weight assigned to that probability (such as the amount of money won or lost). A practical application of the expected value is to determine whether a game of chance is really fair. If the sum of the weighted probabilities is equal to zero, the game is generally considered fair because the player has a fair chance to at least break even. If the expected value is less than zero, then players are expected to lose more than they win. For example, a lottery drawing might allow the player to choose any three-digit number, 000–999. The probability of choosing the winning number is 1:1000. If it costs \$1 to play, and a winning number receives \$500, the expected value is $\left(-\$1 \times \frac{999}{1,000}\right) + \left(\$499 \times \frac{1}{1,000}\right) = -\$0.50$. You can expect to lose on average 50 cents for every dollar you spend.

> **Review Video: Expected Value**
> Visit mometrix.com/academy and enter code: 643554

EXPECTED VALUE AND SIMULATORS

A die roll simulator will show the results of *n* rolls of a die. The result of each die roll may be recorded. For example, suppose a die is rolled 100 times. All results may be recorded. The numbers of 1s, 2s, 3s, 4s, 5s, and 6s, may be counted. The experimental probability of rolling each number will equal the ratio of the frequency of the rolled number to the total number of rolls. As the number of rolls increases, or approaches infinity, the experimental probability will approach the theoretical probability of 1/6. Thus, the expected value for the roll of a die is shown to be $(1 \times \frac{1}{6}) + (2 \times \frac{1}{6}) + (3 \times \frac{1}{6}) + (4 \times \frac{1}{6}) + (5 \times \frac{1}{6}) + (6 \times \frac{1}{6})$, or 3.5.

Mometrix

PRACTICE

P1. Determine the theoretical probability of the following events:

(a) Rolling an even number on a regular 6-sided die.

(b) Not getting a red ball when selecting one from a bag of 3 red balls, 4 black balls, and 2 green balls.

(c) Rolling a standard die and then selecting a card from a standard deck that is less than the value rolled.

P2. There is a game of chance involving a standard deck of cards that has been shuffled and then laid on a table. The player wins $10 if they can turn over 2 cards of matching color (black or red), $50 for 2 cards with matching value (A-K), and $100 for 2 cards with both matching color and value. What is the expected value of playing this game?

PRACTICE SOLUTIONS

P1. (a). The values on the faces of a regular die are 1, 2, 3, 4, 5, and 6. Since three of these are even numbers (2, 4, 6), The probability of rolling an even number is $\frac{3}{6} = \frac{1}{2} = 0.5 = 50\%$.

(b) The bag contains a total of 9 balls, 6 of which are not red, so the probability of selecting one non-red ball would be $\frac{6}{9} = \frac{2}{3} \cong 0.667 \cong 66.7\%$.

(c) In this scenario, we need to determine how many cards could satisfy the condition for each possible value of the die roll. If a one is rolled, there is no way to achieve the desired outcome, since no cards in a standard deck are less than 1. If a two is rolled, then any of the four aces would achieve the desired result. If a three is rolled, then either an ace or a two would satisfy the condition, and so on. Note that any value on the die is equally likely to occur, meaning that the probability of each roll is $\frac{1}{6}$. Putting all this in a table can help:

Roll	Cards < Roll	Probability of Card	Probability of Event
1	-	$\frac{0}{52} = 0$	$\frac{1}{6} \times 0 = 0$
2	1	$\frac{4}{52} = \frac{1}{13}$	$\frac{1}{6} \times \frac{1}{13} = \frac{1}{78}$
3	1,2	$\frac{8}{52} = \frac{2}{13}$	$\frac{1}{6} \times \frac{2}{13} = \frac{2}{78}$
4	1,2,3	$\frac{12}{52} = \frac{3}{13}$	$\frac{1}{6} \times \frac{3}{13} = \frac{3}{78}$
5	1,2,3,4	$\frac{16}{52} = \frac{4}{13}$	$\frac{1}{6} \times \frac{4}{13} = \frac{4}{78}$
6	1,2,3,4,5	$\frac{20}{52} = \frac{5}{13}$	$\frac{1}{6} \times \frac{5}{13} = \frac{5}{78}$

Assuming that each value of the die is equally likely, then the probability of selecting a card less than the value of the die is the sum of the probabilities of each way to achieve the desired outcome: $\frac{0+1+2+3+4+5}{78} = \frac{15}{78} = \frac{5}{26} \cong 0.192 \cong 19.2\%$.

P2. First, determine the probability of each way of winning each way. In each case, the first card simply determines which of the remaining 51 cards in the deck correspond to a win. For the color of the cards to match, there are 25 cards of those remaining in the deck that match the color of the first, but one of the 25 also matches the value, so only 24 are left in this category. For the value of the cards to match, there are 3 cards of the remaining cards in the deck that match the value of the first, but one of the three also matches the color, so only 2 are left in this category. For the cards to match both color and value, there is only one card in the deck that will work. Finally, there are 24 cards left that don't match at all.

Now we can find the expected value of playing the game, where we multiply the value of each event by the probability it will occur and sum over all of them:

$$\$10 \times \frac{24}{51} = \$4.71$$
$$\$50 \times \frac{2}{51} = \$1.96$$
$$\$100 \times \frac{1}{51} = \$1.96$$
$$\$0 \times \frac{24}{51} = \$0$$

$$\$4.71 + \$1.96 + \$1.96 = \$8.63$$

This game therefore has an expected value of $8.63 each time you play, which means if the cost to play is less than $8.63 then you would, on average, *gain* money. However, if the cost to play is more than $8.63, then you would, on average, *lose* money.

Reading Comprehension

Reading and Reasoning

TYPES OF PASSAGES

A **narrative** passage is a story that can be fiction or nonfiction. However, there are a few elements that a text must have in order to be classified as a narrative. First, the text must have a plot (i.e., a series of events). Narratives often proceed in a clear sequence, but this is not a requirement. If the narrative is good, then these events will be interesting to readers.

Second, a narrative has characters. These characters could be people, animals, or even inanimate objects--so long as they participate in the plot. Third, a narrative passage often contains figurative language which is meant to stimulate the imagination of readers by making comparisons and observations. For instance, a metaphor, a common piece of figurative language, is a description of one thing in terms of another. *The moon was a frosty snowball* is an example of a metaphor. In the literal sense this is obviously untrue, but the comparison suggests a certain mood for the reader.

> **Review Video: Figurative Language**
> Visit mometrix.com/academy and enter code: 584902
>
> **Review Video: Narratives**
> Visit mometrix.com/academy and enter code: 280100

An **expository** passage aims to inform and enlighten readers. The passage is nonfiction and usually centers around a simple, easily defined topic. Since the goal of exposition is to teach, such a passage should be as clear as possible. Often, an expository passage contains helpful organizing words, like *first*, *next*, *for example*, and *therefore*. These words keep the reader oriented in the text. Although expository passages do not need to feature colorful language and artful writing, they are often more effective with these features.

For a reader, the challenge of expository passages is to maintain steady attention. Expository passages are not always about subjects that will naturally interest a reader, and the writer is often more concerned with clarity and comprehensibility than with engaging the reader. By reading actively, you will ensure a good habit of focus when reading an expository passage.

> **Review Video: Expository Passages**
> Visit mometrix.com/academy and enter code: 256515

A **technical** passage is written to describe a complex object or process. Technical writing is common in medical and technological fields, in which complex ideas of mathematics, science, and engineering need to be explained simply and clearly. To ease comprehension, a technical passage usually proceeds in a very logical order. Technical passages often have clear headings and subheadings, which are used to keep the reader oriented in the text. Additionally, you will find that these passages divide sections up with numbers or letters. Many technical passages look more like an outline than a piece of prose. The amount of jargon or difficult vocabulary will vary in a technical passage depending on the intended audience. As much as possible, technical passages try to avoid

105

language that the reader will have to research in order to understand the message, yet readers will find that jargon cannot always be avoided.

Review Video: Technical Passages
Visit mometrix.com/academy and enter code: 478923

A **persuasive** passage is meant to change the mind of readers and lead them into agreement with the author. The persuasive intent may be very obvious or quite difficult to discern. In some cases, a persuasive passage will be indistinguishable from one that is informative. Both passages make an assertion and offer supporting details. However, a persuasive passage is more likely to appeal to the reader's emotions and to make claims based on opinion. Persuasive passages may not describe alternate positions, but--when they do--they often display significant bias. Readers may find that a persuasive passage is giving the author's viewpoint, or the passage may adopt a seemingly objective tone. A persuasive passage is successful if it can make a convincing argument and win the trust of the reader.

Persuasive passages tend to focus on one central argument while making many smaller claims along the way. These smaller claims are subordinate arguments that readers must accept if they are going to agree with the central argument. Thus, the central argument will only be as strong as the subordinate claims. These claims should be rooted in fact and observation, rather than subjective judgment. The best persuasive essays provide enough supporting detail to justify claims without overwhelming readers. Remember that a fact must be susceptible to independent verification (i.e., the fact must be something that readers could confirm). Also, statistics are only effective when they take into account possible objections. For instance, a statistic on the number of foreclosed houses would only be useful if it was taken over a defined interval and in a defined area. Most readers are wary of statistics because they can be misleading. The writers of your test are aware that their work will be met by inquiring readers, and your ability to maintain doubt with persuasive passages will be a benefit in your exam.

Review Video: Persuasive Essay
Visit mometrix.com/academy and enter code: 621428

Opinions are formed by emotion as well as reason, and persuasive writers often appeal to the feelings of readers. Although readers should always be skeptical of this technique, these appeals are often used in a proper and ethical manner. For instance, there are many subjects that have an obvious emotional component and therefore cannot be completely treated without an appeal to the emotions. Consider an article on drunk driving: specific examples that will alarm or sadden readers are likely to be included as an appeal to emotions. After all, drunk driving can have serious and tragic consequences. On the other hand, emotional appeals are not appropriate when they attempt to mislead readers. For instance, in political advertisements, one will observe the emphasis on the patriotism of the preferred candidate because this will encourage the audience to link their own positive feelings about the country with their opinion of the candidate. However, these advertisements often imply that the other candidate is unpatriotic which--in most cases--is far from the truth. Another common and improper emotional appeal is the use of loaded language. Referring to an avidly religious person as a "fanatic" or a passionate environmentalist as a "tree hugger" are examples of this. These terms introduce an emotional component that detracts from the argument.

Review Video: Logical Fallacies
Visit mometrix.com/academy and enter code: 644845

ORGANIZATION OF THE TEXT

The way a text is organized can help readers to understand the author's intent and his or her conclusions. There are various ways to organize a text, and each one has a purpose and use.

Some nonfiction texts are organized to **present a problem** followed by a solution. For this type of text, the problem is often explained before the solution is offered. In some cases, as when the problem is well known, the solution may be introduced briefly at the beginning. Other passages may focus on the solution, and the problem will be referenced only occasionally. Some texts will outline multiple solutions to a problem, leaving readers to choose among them. If the author has an interest or an allegiance to one solution, he or she may fail to mention or describe accurately some of the other solutions. Readers should be careful of the author's agenda when reading a problem-solution text. Only by understanding the author's perspective and interests can one develop a proper judgment of the proposed solution.

Occasionally, authors will organize information logically in a passage so the reader can follow and locate the information within the text. Since this is not always the case with passages in an exam, you need to be familiar with other examples of provided information. Two common organizational structures are cause and effect and chronological order. When using **chronological order**, the author presents information in the order that it happened. For example, biographies are written in chronological order. The subject's birth and childhood are presented first, followed by their adult life, and lastly by the events leading up to the person's death.

In **cause and effect**, an author presents one thing that makes something else happen. For example, if one were to go to bed very late and awake very early, then they would be tired in the morning. The cause is lack of sleep, with the effect of being tired the next day.

Identifying the cause-and-effect relationships in a text can be tricky, but there are a few ways to approach this task. Often, these relationships are signaled with certain terms. When an author uses words like *because*, *since*, *in order*, and *so*, he or she is likely describing a cause-and-effect relationship. Consider the sentence: *He called her because he needed the homework.* This is a simple causal relationship in which the cause was his need for the homework, and the effect was his phone call. Yet, not all cause-and-effect relationships are marked in this way. Consider the sentences: *He called her. He needed the homework.* When the cause-and-effect relationship is not indicated with a keyword, the relationship can be discovered by asking why something happened. He called her: why? The answer is in the next sentence: He needed the homework.

Persuasive essays, in which an author tries to make a convincing argument and change the minds of readers, usually include cause-and-effect relationships. However, these relationships should not always be taken at face value. Frequently, an author will assume a cause or take an effect for granted. To read a persuasive essay effectively, readers need to judge the cause-and-effect relationships that the author is presenting. For instance, imagine an author wrote the following: *The parking deck has been unprofitable because people would prefer to ride their bikes.* The relationship is clear: the cause is that people prefer to ride their bikes, and the effect is that the parking deck has been unprofitable. However, readers should consider whether this argument is conclusive. Perhaps there are other reasons for the failure of the parking deck: a down economy, excessive fees, etc. Too often, authors present causal relationships as if they are fact rather than opinion. Readers should be on the alert for these dubious claims.

Many texts follow the **compare-and-contrast** model in which the similarities and differences between two ideas or things are explored. Analysis of the similarities between ideas is called comparison. In an ideal comparison, the author places ideas or things in an equivalent structure

107

(i.e., the author presents the ideas in the same way). If an author wants to show the similarities between cricket and baseball, then he or she may do so by summarizing the equipment and rules for each game. Be mindful of the similarities as they appear in the passage and take note of any differences that are mentioned. Often, these small differences will only reinforce the more general similarity.

Thinking critically about ideas and conclusions can seem like a daunting task. One way to ease this task is to understand the basic elements of ideas and writing techniques. Looking at the way different ideas relate to each other can be a good way for readers to begin their analysis. For instance, sometimes authors will write about two ideas that are in opposition to each other. Or one author will provide his or her ideas on a topic, and another author may respond in opposition. The analysis of these opposing ideas is known as **contrast**. Contrast is often marred by the author's obvious partiality to one of the ideas. A discerning reader will be put off by an author who does not engage in a fair fight. In an analysis of opposing ideas, both ideas should be presented in clear and reasonable terms. If the author does prefer a side, you need to read carefully to determine the areas where the author shows or avoids this preference. In an analysis of opposing ideas, you should proceed through the passage by marking the major differences point by point with an eye that is looking for an explanation of each side's view. For instance, in an analysis of capitalism and communism, there is an importance in outlining each side's view on labor, markets, prices, personal responsibility, etc. Additionally, as you read through the passages, you should note whether the opposing views present each side in a similar manner.

> **Review Video: Compare and Contrast**
> Visit mometrix.com/academy and enter code: 171799

PURPOSES FOR WRITING

In order to be an effective reader, one must pay attention to the author's **position** and purpose. Even those texts that seem objective and impartial, like textbooks, have a position and bias. Readers need to take these positions into account when considering the author's message. When an author uses emotional language or clearly favors one side of an argument, his or her position is clear. However, the author's position may be evident not only in what he or she writes, but also in what he or she doesn't write. In a normal setting, a reader would want to review some other texts on the same topic in order to develop a view of the author's position. If this was not possible, then you would want to acquire some background about the author. However, since you are in the middle of an exam and the only source of information is the text, you should look for language and argumentation that seems to indicate a particular stance on the subject.

> **Review Video: Author's Position**
> Visit mometrix.com/academy and enter code: 827954

Usually, identifying the **purpose** of an author is easier than identifying his or her position. In most cases, the author has no interest in hiding his or her purpose. A text that is meant to entertain, for instance, should be written to please the reader. Most narratives, or stories, are written to entertain, though they may also inform or persuade. Informative texts are easy to identify, while the most difficult purpose of a text to identify is persuasion because the author has an interest in making this purpose hard to detect. When a reader discovers that the author is trying to persuade, he or she should be skeptical of the argument. For this reason, persuasive texts often try to establish an entertaining tone and hope to amuse the reader into agreement. On the other hand, an informative tone may be implemented to create an appearance of authority and objectivity.

An author's purpose is evident often in the organization of the text (e.g., section headings in bold font points to an informative text). However, you may not have such organization available to you in your exam. Instead, if the author makes his or her main idea clear from the beginning, then the likely purpose of the text is to inform. If the author begins by making a claim and provides various arguments to support that claim, then the purpose is probably to persuade. If the author tells a story or seems to want the attention of the reader more than to push a particular point or deliver information, then his or her purpose is most likely to entertain. As a reader, you must judge authors on how well they accomplish their purpose. In other words, you need to consider the type of passage (e.g., technical, persuasive, etc.) that the author has written and whether the author has followed the requirements of the passage type.

> **Review Video: <u>Understanding the Author's Intent</u>**
> Visit mometrix.com/academy and enter code: 511819

The author's purpose for writing will affect his or her writing style and the response of the reader. In a **persuasive essay**, the author is attempting to change the reader's mind or convince him or her of something that he or she did not believe previously. There are several identifying characteristics of persuasive writing. One is opinion presented as fact. When authors attempt to persuade readers, they often present their opinions as if they were fact. Readers must be on guard for statements that sound factual but which cannot be subjected to research, observation, or experiment. Another characteristic of persuasive writing is emotional language. An author will often try to play on the emotions of readers by appealing to their sympathy or sense of morality. When an author uses colorful or evocative language with the intent of arousing the reader's passions, then the author may be attempting to persuade. Finally, in many cases, a persuasive text will give an unfair explanation of opposing positions, if these positions are mentioned at all.

An **informative text** is written to educate and enlighten readers. Informative texts are almost always nonfiction and are rarely structured as a story. The intention of an informative text is to deliver information in the most comprehensible way. So, look for the structure of the text to be very clear. In an informative text, the thesis statement is one or two sentences that normally appears at the end of the first paragraph. The author may use some colorful language, but he or she is likely to put more emphasis on clarity and precision. Informative essays do not typically appeal to the emotions. They often contain facts and figures and rarely include the opinion of the author; however, readers should remain aware of the possibility for a bias as those facts are presented. Sometimes a persuasive essay can resemble an informative essay, especially if the author maintains an even tone and presents his or her views as if they were established fact.

The success or failure of an author's intent to **entertain** is determined by those who read the author's work. Entertaining texts may be either fiction or nonfiction, and they may describe real or imagined people, places, and events. Entertaining texts are often narratives or poems. A text that is written to entertain is likely to contain colorful language that engages the imagination and the emotions. Such writing often features a great deal of figurative language, which typically enlivens the subject matter with images and analogies.

Though an entertaining text is not usually written to persuade or inform, authors may accomplish both of these tasks in their work. An entertaining text may appeal to the reader's emotions and cause him or her to think differently about a particular subject. In any case, entertaining texts tend to showcase the personality of the author more than other types of writing.

When an author intends to **express feelings,** he or she may use expressive and bold language. An author may write with emotion for any number of reasons. Sometimes, authors will express feelings because they are describing a personal situation of great pain or happiness. In other situations, authors will attempt to persuade the reader and will use emotion to stir up the passions. This kind of expression is easy to identify when the writer uses phrases like *I felt* and *I sense*. However, readers may find that the author will simply describe feelings without introducing them. As a reader, you must know the importance of recognizing when an author is expressing emotion and not to become overwhelmed by sympathy or passion. Readers should maintain some detachment so that they can still evaluate the strength of the author's argument or the quality of the writing.

> **Review Video: Emotional Language in Literature**
> Visit mometrix.com/academy and enter code: 759390

In a sense, almost all writing is descriptive, insofar as an author seeks to describe events, ideas, or people to the reader. Some texts, however, are primarily concerned with **description**. A descriptive text focuses on a particular subject and attempts to depict the subject in a way that will be clear to readers. Descriptive texts contain many adjectives and adverbs (i.e., words that give shades of meaning and create a more detailed mental picture for the reader). A descriptive text fails when it is unclear to the reader. A descriptive text will certainly be informative and may be persuasive and entertaining as well.

WRITING DEVICES

Authors will use different stylistic and writing devices to make their meaning clear for readers. One of those devices is comparison and contrast. As mentioned previously, when an author describes the ways in which two things are alike, he or she is **comparing** them. When the author describes the ways in which two things are different, he or she is **contrasting** them. The "compare and contrast" essay is one of the most common forms in nonfiction. These passages are often signaled with certain words: a comparison may have indicating terms such as *both, same, like, too*, and *as well*; while a contrast may have terms like *but, however, on the other hand, instead*, and *yet*. Of course, comparisons and contrasts may be implicit without using any such signaling language. A single sentence may both compare and contrast. Consider the sentence *Brian and Sheila love ice cream, but Brian prefers vanilla and Sheila prefers strawberry*. In one sentence, the author has described both a similarity (love of ice cream) and a difference (favorite flavor).

> **Review Video: Compare and Contrast**
> Visit mometrix.com/academy and enter code: 798319

One of the most common text structures is **cause and effect**. A **cause** is an act or event that makes something happen, and an **effect** is the thing that happens as a result of the cause. A cause-and-effect relationship is not always explicit, but there are some terms in English that signal causes, such as *since, because*, and *due to*. Furthermore, terms that signal effects include *consequently, therefore, this leads to*. As an example, consider the sentence *Because the sky was clear, Ron did not bring an umbrella*. The cause is the clear sky, and the effect is that Ron did not bring an umbrella. However, readers may find that sometimes the cause-and-effect relationship will not be clearly noted. For instance, the sentence *He was late and missed the meeting* does not contain any signaling words, but the sentence still contains a cause (he was late) and an effect (he missed the meeting).

Be aware of the possibility for a single cause to have multiple effects (e.g., *Single cause*: Because you left your homework on the table, your dog engulfs the assignment. *Multiple effects*: As a result, you receive a failing grade; your parents do not allow you to visit your friends; you miss out on the new movie and holding the hand of a potential significant other).

Also, the possibility of a single effect to have multiple causes (e.g.. *Single effect*: Alan has a fever. *Multiple causes*: An unexpected cold front came through the area, and Alan forgot to take his multi-vitamin to avoid being sick.)

Additionally, an effect can in turn be the cause of another effect, in what is known as a cause-and-effect chain. (e.g., As a result of her disdain for procrastination, Lynn prepared for her exam. This led to her passing her test with high marks. Hence, her resume was accepted and her application was approved.)

> **Review Video: Cause and Effect**
> Visit mometrix.com/academy and enter code: 868099
>
> **Review Video: Rhetorical Strategy of Cause and Effect Analysis**
> Visit mometrix.com/academy and enter code: 725944

Another element that impacts a text is the author's point-of-view. The **point of view** of a text is the perspective from which a passage is told. An author will always have a point of view about a story before he or she draws up a plot line. The author will know what events they want to take place, how they want the characters to interact, and how they want the story to resolve. An author will also have an opinion on the topic or series of events which is presented in the story that is based on their prior experience and beliefs.

The two main points of view that authors use--especially in a work of fiction--are first person and third person. If the narrator of the story is also the main character, or *protagonist*, the text is written in first-person point of view. In first person, the author writes from the perspective of *I*. Third-person point of view is probably the most common that authors use in their passages. Using third person, authors refer to each character by using *he* or *she*. In third-person omniscient, the narrator is not a character in the story and tells the story of all of the characters at the same time.

> **Review Video: Point of View**
> Visit mometrix.com/academy and enter code: 383336

Transitional words and phrases are devices that guide readers through a text. You are no doubt familiar with the common transitions, though you may never have considered how they operate. Some transitional phrases (*after, before, during, in the middle of*) give information about time. Some indicate that an example is about to be given (*for example, in fact, for instance*). Writers use them to compare (*also, likewise*) and contrast (*however, but, yet*). Transitional words and phrases can suggest addition (*and, also, furthermore, moreover*) and logical relationships (*if, then, therefore, as a result, since*). Finally, transitional words and phrases can separate the steps in a process (*first, second, last*).

> **Review Video: Transitional Words and Phrases**
> Visit mometrix.com/academy and enter code: 197796

UNDERSTANDING A PASSAGE

One of the most important skills in reading comprehension is the identification of **topics** and **main ideas.** There is a subtle difference between these two features. The topic is the **subject** of a text (i.e., what the text is all about). The main idea, on the other hand, is the **most important point** being made by the author. The topic is usually expressed in a few words at the most while the main idea often needs a full sentence to be completely defined. As an example, a short passage might have the topic of penguins and the main idea could be written as *Penguins are different from other birds in* *many ways*. In most nonfiction writing, the topic and the main idea will be stated directly and often appear in a sentence at the very beginning or end of the text. When being tested on an understanding of the author's topic, you may be able to skim the passage for the general idea, by reading only the first sentence of each paragraph. A body paragraph's first sentence is often—but not always—the main topic sentence which gives you a summary of the content in the paragraph.

However, there are cases in which the reader must figure out an unstated topic or main idea. In these instances, you must read every sentence of the text and try to come up with an overarching idea that is supported by each of those sentences.

Note: A thesis statement should not be confused with the main idea of the passage. While the main idea gives a brief, general summary of a text, the thesis statement provides a specific perspective on an issue that the author supports with evidence.

> **Review Video: Topics and Main Ideas**
> Visit mometrix.com/academy and enter code: 407801

Supporting details provide evidence and backing for the main point. In order to show that a main idea is correct, or valid, authors add details that prove their point. All texts contain details, but they are only classified as supporting details when they serve to reinforce some larger point. Supporting details are most commonly found in informative and persuasive texts. In some cases, they will be clearly indicated with terms like *for example* or *for instance*, or they will be enumerated with terms like *first*, *second*, and *last*. However, you need to be prepared for texts that do not contain those indicators. As a reader, you should consider whether the author's supporting details really back up his or her main point. Supporting details can be factual and correct, yet they may not be relevant to the author's point. Conversely, supporting details can seem pertinent, but they can be ineffective because they are based on opinion or assertions that cannot be proven.

> **Review Video: Supporting Details**
> Visit mometrix.com/academy and enter code: 396297

An example of a **main idea** is: *Giraffes live in the Serengeti of Africa.* A **supporting detail** about giraffes could be: *A giraffe in this region benefits from a long neck by reaching twigs and leaves on tall trees.* The main idea expresses that the text is about giraffes in general. The supporting detail gives a specific fact about how the giraffes eat.

As opposed to a main idea, themes are seldom expressed directly in a text and can be difficult to identify. A **theme** is an issue, an idea, or a question raised by the text. For instance, a theme of *Cinderella* (the Charles Perrault version) is perseverance as the title character serves her step-sisters and step-mother, and the prince seeks to find the girl with the missing slipper. A passage may have many themes, and a dedicated reader must take care to identify only themes that you are asked to find. One common characteristic of themes is that they raise more questions than they answer. In a good piece of fiction, authors are trying to elevate the reader's perspective and encourage him or her to consider the themes in a deeper way. In the process of reading, one can identify themes by constantly asking about the general issues that the text is addressing. A good way to evaluate an author's approach to a theme is to begin reading with a question in mind (e.g., How does this text approach the theme of love?) and to look for evidence in the text that addresses that question.

> **Review Video: Themes in Literature**
> Visit mometrix.com/academy and enter code: 732074

112

Mometrix

Evaluating a Passage

When reading informational texts, there is importance in understanding the logical conclusion of the author's ideas. **Identifying a logical conclusion** can help you determine whether you agree with the writer or not. Coming to this conclusion is much like making an inference: the approach requires you to combine the information given by the text with what you already know in order to make a logical conclusion. If the author intended the reader to draw a certain conclusion, then you can expect the author's argumentation and detail to be leading in that direction.

One way to approach the task of drawing conclusions is to make brief notes of all the points made by the author. When the notes are arranged on paper, they may clarify the logical conclusion. Another way to approach conclusions is to consider whether the reasoning of the author raises any pertinent questions. Sometimes you will be able to draw several conclusions from a passage. On occasion these will be conclusions that were never imagined by the author. Therefore, be aware that these conclusions must be supported directly by the text.

> **Review Video: How to Support a Conclusion**
> Visit mometrix.com/academy and enter code: 281653

The term **text evidence** refers to information that supports a main point or minor points and can help lead the reader to a conclusion. Information used as text evidence is precise, descriptive, and factual. A main point is often followed by supporting details that provide evidence to back-up a claim. For example, a passage may include the claim that winter occurs during opposite months in the Northern and Southern hemispheres. Text evidence based on this claim may include countries where winter occurs in opposite months along with reasons that winter occurs at different times of the year in separate hemispheres (due to the tilt of the earth as it rotates around the sun).

> **Review Video: Textual Evidence**
> Visit mometrix.com/academy and enter code: 486236

The text used to support an argument can be the argument's downfall if the text is not credible. A text is **credible**, or believable, when the author is knowledgeable and objective, or unbiased. The author's motivations for writing the text play a critical role in determining the credibility of the text and must be evaluated when assessing that credibility. Reports written about the ozone layer by an environmental scientist and a hairdresser will have a different level of credibility.

A reader should always be drawing conclusions from the text. Sometimes conclusions are implied from written information, and other times the information is **stated directly** within the passage. One should always aim to draw conclusions from information stated within a passage, rather than to draw them from mere implications. At times an author may provide some information and then describe a counterargument. Readers should be alert for direct statements that are subsequently rejected or weakened by the author. Furthermore, you should always read through the entire passage before drawing conclusions. Many readers are trained to expect the author's conclusions at either the beginning or the end of the passage, but many texts do not adhere to this format.

Drawing conclusions from information implied within a passage requires confidence on the part of the reader. **Implications** are things that the author does not state directly, but readers can assume based on what the author does say. Consider the following passage: *I stepped outside and opened my umbrella. By the time I got to work, the cuffs of my pants were soaked.* The author never states that it is raining, but this fact is clearly implied. Conclusions based on implication must be well supported by the text. In order to draw a solid conclusion, readers should have multiple pieces of evidence. If readers have only one piece, they must be assured that there is no other possible explanation than

113

their conclusion. A good reader will be able to draw many conclusions from information implied by the text which will be a great help in the exam.

As an aid to drawing conclusions, **outlining** the information contained in the passage should be a familiar skill to readers. An effective outline will reveal the structure of the passage and will lead to solid conclusions. An effective outline will have a title that refers to the basic subject of the text though the title needs not recapitulate the main idea. In most outlines, the main idea will be the first major section. Each major idea of the passage will be established as the head of a category. For instance, the most common outline format calls for the main ideas of the passage to be indicated with Roman numerals. In an effective outline of this kind, each of the main ideas will be represented by a Roman numeral and none of the Roman numerals will designate minor details or secondary ideas. Moreover, all supporting ideas and details should be placed in the appropriate place on the outline. An outline does not need to include every detail listed in the text, but the outline should feature all of those that are central to the argument or message. Each of these details should be listed under the appropriate main idea.

Ideas from a text can also be organized using **graphic organizers**. A graphic organizer is a way to simplify information and take key points from the text. A graphic organizer such as a timeline may have an event listed for a corresponding date on the timeline while an outline may have an event listed under a key point that occurs in the text. Each reader needs to create the type of graphic organizer that works the best for him or her in terms of being able to recall information from a story. Examples include a *spider-map,* which takes a main idea from the story and places it in a bubble with supporting points branching off the main idea. An *outline* is useful for diagramming the main and supporting points of the entire story, and a *Venn diagram* classifies information as separate or overlapping.

> **Review Video: Graphic Organizers**
> Visit mometrix.com/academy and enter code: 665513

A helpful tool is the ability to **summarize** the information that you have read in a paragraph or passage format. This process is similar to creating an effective outline. First, a summary should accurately define the main idea of the passage though the summary does not need to explain this main idea in exhaustive detail. The summary should continue by laying out the most important supporting details or arguments from the passage. All of the significant supporting details should be included, and none of the details included should be irrelevant or insignificant. Also, the summary should accurately report all of these details. Too often, the desire for brevity in a summary leads to the sacrifice of clarity or accuracy. Summaries are often difficult to read because they omit all of the graceful language, digressions, and asides that distinguish great writing. However, an effective summary should contain much the same message as the original text.

Paraphrasing is another method that the reader can use to aid in comprehension. When paraphrasing, one puts what they have read into their words by rephrasing what the author has written, or one "translates" all of what the author shared into their words by including as many details as they can.

RESPONDING TO A PASSAGE

When reading a good passage, readers are moved to engage actively in the text. One part of being an active reader involves making predictions. A **prediction** is a guess about what will happen next. Readers constantly make predictions based on what they have read and what they already know. Consider the following sentence: *Staring at the computer screen in shock, Kim blindly reached over for the brimming glass of water on the shelf to her side.* The sentence suggests that Kim is agitated, and that she is not looking at the glass that she is going to pick up. So, a reader might predict that Kim is going to knock over the glass. Of course, not every prediction will be accurate: perhaps Kim will pick the glass up cleanly. Nevertheless, the author has certainly created the expectation that the water might be spilled. Predictions are always subject to revision as the reader acquires more information.

Review Video: Predictive Reading
Visit mometrix.com/academy and enter code: 437248

Test-taking tip: To respond to questions requiring future predictions, your answers should be based on evidence of past or present behavior.

Readers are often required to understand a text that claims and suggests ideas without stating them directly. An **inference** is a piece of information that is implied but not written outright by the author. For instance, consider the following sentence: *After the final out of the inning, the fans were filled with joy and rushed the field*. From this sentence, a reader can infer that the fans were watching a baseball game and their team won the game. Readers should take great care to avoid using information beyond the provided passage before making inferences. As you practice drawing inferences, you will find that they require concentration and attention.

Review Video: Inference
Visit mometrix.com/academy and enter code: 379203

Test-taking tip: While being tested on your ability to make correct inferences, you must look for contextual clues. An answer can be *true* but not *correct*. The contextual clues will help you find the answer that is the best answer out of the given choices. Be careful in your reading to understand the context in which a phrase is stated. When asked for the implied meaning of a statement made in the passage, you should immediately locate the statement and read the context in which the statement was made. Also, look for an answer choice that has a similar phrase to the statement in question.

Readers must be able to identify a text's **sequence**, or the order in which things happen. Often, when the sequence is very important to the author, the text is indicated with signal words like *first*, *then*, *next*, and *last*. However, a sequence can be merely implied and must be noted by the reader. Consider the sentence *He walked through the garden and gave water and fertilizer to the plants*. Clearly, the man did not walk through the garden before he collected water and fertilizer for the plants. So, the implied sequence is that he first collected water, then he collected fertilizer, next he walked through the garden, and last he gave water or fertilizer as necessary to the plants. Texts do not always proceed in an orderly sequence from first to last. Sometimes they begin at the end and start over at the beginning. As a reader, you can enhance your understanding of the passage by taking brief notes to clarify the sequence.

Review Video: Sequence
Visit mometrix.com/academy and enter code: 489027

In addition to inference and prediction, readers must often **draw conclusions** about the information they have read. When asked for a *conclusion* that may be drawn, look for critical "hedge" phrases, such as *likely*, *may*, *can*, *will often*, among many others. When you are being tested on this knowledge, remember the question that writers insert into these hedge phrases to cover every possibility. Often an answer will be wrong simply because there is no room for exception. Extreme positive or negative answers (such as always or never) are usually not correct. The reader should <u>not</u> use any outside knowledge that is not gathered from the passage to answer the related questions. Correct answers can be derived straight from the passage.

Building a Vocabulary

The **denotative** meaning of a word is the literal meaning. The **connotative** meaning goes beyond the denotative meaning to include the emotional reaction that a word may invoke. The connotative meaning often takes the denotative meaning a step further due to associations which the reader makes with the denotative meaning. Readers can differentiate between the denotative and connotative meanings by first recognizing how authors use each meaning. Most nonfiction, for example, is fact-based, and nonfiction authors rarely use flowery, figurative language. The reader can assume that the writer is using the denotative meaning of words. In fiction, the author may use the connotative meaning. Readers can determine whether the author is using the denotative or connotative meaning of a word by implementing context clues.

> **Review Video: Connotation and Denotation**
> Visit mometrix.com/academy and enter code: 310092

Readers of all levels will encounter words that they either have never seen or have only encountered on a limited basis. The best way to define a word in **context** is to look for nearby words that can assist in learning the meaning of the word. For instance, unfamiliar nouns are often accompanied by examples that provide a definition. Consider the following sentence: *Dave arrived at the party in hilarious garb: a leopard-print shirt, buckskin trousers, and high heels.* If a reader was unfamiliar with the meaning of garb, he or she could read the examples (i.e., a leopard-print shirt, buckskin trousers, and high heels) and quickly determine that the word means *clothing*. Examples will not always be this obvious. Consider this sentence: *Parsley, lemon, and flowers were just a few of items he used as garnishes.* Here, the word *garnishes* is exemplified by parsley, lemon, and flowers. Readers who have eaten in a few restaurants will probably be able to identify a garnish as something used to decorate a plate.

> **Review Video: Context Clues**
> Visit mometrix.com/academy and enter code: 613660

In addition to looking at the context of a passage, readers can use contrasts to define an unfamiliar word in context. In many sentences, the author will not describe the unfamiliar word directly; instead, he or she will describe the opposite of the unfamiliar word. Thus, you are provided with some information that will bring you closer to defining the word. Consider the following example: *Despite his intelligence, Hector's low brow and bad posture made him look obtuse.* The author writes that Hector's appearance does not convey intelligence. Therefore, *obtuse* must mean unintelligent. Here is another example: *Despite the horrible weather, we were beatific about our trip to Alaska.* The word *despite* indicates that the speaker's feelings were at odds with the weather. Since the weather is described as *horrible*, then *beatific* must mean something positive.

In some cases, there will be very few contextual clues to help a reader define the meaning of an unfamiliar word. When this happens, one strategy that readers may employ is **substitution**. A good reader will brainstorm some possible synonyms for the given word, and he or she will substitute these words into the sentence. If the sentence and the surrounding passage continue to make sense, then the substitution has revealed at least some information about the unfamiliar word. Consider the sentence: *Frank's admonition rang in her ears as she climbed the mountain.* A reader unfamiliar with *admonition* might come up with some substitutions like *vow, promise, advice, complaint,* or *compliment*. All of these words make general sense of the sentence though their meanings are diverse. The process has suggested; however, that an admonition is some sort of message. The substitution strategy is rarely able to pinpoint a precise definition, but this process can be effective as a last resort.

Occasionally, you will be able to define an unfamiliar word by looking at the descriptive words in the context. Consider the following sentence: *Fred dragged the recalcitrant boy kicking and screaming up the stairs.* The words *dragged*, *kicking*, and *screaming* all suggest that the boy does not want to go up the stairs. The reader may assume that *recalcitrant* means something like unwilling or protesting. In this example, an unfamiliar adjective was identified.

Additionally, using description to define an unfamiliar noun is a common practice compared to unfamiliar adjectives, as in this sentence: *Don's wrinkled frown and constantly shaking fist identified him as a curmudgeon of the first order.* Don is described as having a *wrinkled frown and constantly shaking fist* suggesting that a *curmudgeon* must be a grumpy person. Contrasts do not always provide detailed information about the unfamiliar word, but they at least give the reader some clues.

When a word has more than one meaning, readers can have difficulty with determining how the word is being used in a given sentence. For instance, the verb *cleave*, can mean either *join* or *separate*. When readers come upon this word, they will have to select the definition that makes the most sense. Consider the following sentence: *Hermione's knife cleaved the bread cleanly.* Since, a knife cannot join bread together, the word must indicate separation. A slightly more difficult example would be the sentence: *The birds cleaved together as they flew from the oak tree.* Immediately, the presence of the word *together* should suggest that in this sentence *cleave* is being used to mean *join.* Discovering the intent of a word with multiple meanings requires the same tricks as defining an unknown word: look for contextual clues and evaluate the substituted words.

Critical Thinking Skills

OPINIONS, FACTS, AND FALLACIES

Critical thinking skills are mastered through understanding various types of writing and the different purposes of authors in writing their passages. Every author writes for a purpose. When you understand their purpose and how they accomplish their goal, you will be able to analyze their writing and determine whether or not you agree with their conclusions.

Readers must always be conscious of the distinction between fact and opinion. A **fact** can be subjected to analysis and can be either proved or disproved. An **opinion**, on the other hand, is the author's personal thoughts or feelings which may not be alterable by research or evidence. If the author writes that the distance from New York to Boston is about two hundred miles, then he or she is stating a fact. If an author writes that New York is too crowded, then he or she is giving an opinion because there is no objective standard for overpopulation. An opinion may be indicated by words like *believe*, *think*, or *feel*. Readers must be aware that an opinion may be supported by facts. For instance, the author might give the population density of New York as a reason for an overcrowded population. An opinion supported by fact tends to be more convincing. On the other hand, when authors support their opinions with other opinions, readers should not be persuaded by the argument to any degree.

When you have an argumentative passage, you need to be sure that facts are presented to the reader from reliable sources. An opinion is what the author thinks about a given topic. An opinion is not common knowledge or proven by expert sources, instead the information is the personal beliefs and thoughts of the author. To distinguish between fact and opinion, a reader needs to consider the type of source that is presenting information, the information that backs-up a claim, and the author's motivation to have a certain point-of-view on a given topic. For example, if a panel of scientists has conducted multiple studies on the effectiveness of taking a certain vitamin, then the results are more likely to be factual than a company that is selling a vitamin and claims that taking the vitamin can produce positive effects. The company is motivated to sell their product, and the scientists are using the scientific method to prove a theory. Remember: if you find sentences that contain phrases such as "I think...", then the statement is an opinion.

> **Review Video: Fact or Opinion**
> Visit mometrix.com/academy and enter code: 870899

In their attempts to persuade, writers often make mistakes in their thinking patterns and writing choices. These patterns and choices are important to understand so you can make an informed decision. Every author has a point-of-view, but authors demonstrate a bias when they ignore reasonable counterarguments or distort opposing viewpoints. A bias is evident whenever the author is unfair or inaccurate in his or her presentation. Bias may be intentional or unintentional, and readers should be skeptical of the author's argument. Remember that a biased author may still be correct; however, the author will be correct in spite of his or her bias, not because of the bias.

A **stereotype** is like a bias, yet a stereotype is applied specifically to a group or place. Stereotyping is considered to be particularly abhorrent because the practice promotes negative generalizations about people. Readers should be very cautious of authors who stereotype in their writing. These faulty assumptions typically reveal the author's ignorance and lack of curiosity.

> **Review Video: Bias and Stereotype**
> Visit mometrix.com/academy and enter code: 644829

Literature

LITERARY GENRES

The purpose of literary genres is to classify and analyze literature that separates texts into the basic generic types of poetry, drama, fiction, and nonfiction. There are numerous subdivisions within a genre, including such categories as novels, novellas, and short stories in fiction. Drama may also be divided into the main categories of comedy and tragedy. Genres can have overlap, and the distinctions among them are blurred. Examples include the *nonfiction novel* and *docudrama*, as well as many others.

> **Review Video: Literary Genres**
> Visit mometrix.com/academy and enter code: 587617

Fiction is a general term for any form of literary narrative that is invented or imagined as opposed to a true event. A work of fiction on your exam will include a passage that has been written for your exam, or one that has been taken from a published work. There is a good chance that you will encounter a fictional work on your exam that you will recognize as the writers of your exam are aware of the literary canon. During your exam, if you recognize an excerpted piece from a published work, then you still need to read the text thoroughly once before going to the test questions. That applies to the other genres (i.e., poetry and drama) as well. Now, let's start with the genre of fiction.

Prose is derived from Latin and means "straightforward discourse." Prose fiction, although having many categories, may be divided into three main groups:

- **Short stories**: a fictional narrative that usually contains fewer than 20,000 words. Short stories have only a few characters and generally describe one major event or insight. The short story began in magazines in the late 1800s and has found an audience ever since.
- **Novels**: a longer work of fiction that may contain a large cast of characters and an extensive plot. The emphasis may be on an event, action, social problem, or an experience. An addition to the genre came in 1966 when Truman Capote's *In Cold Blood* was published and created the nonfiction novel category. Note: novels may be written in verse.
- **Novellas**: a work of narrative fiction that is longer than a short story but not as long as a novel. Novellas may also be called short novels or novelettes. They originated from the German tradition and have become a common form in literature throughout the world.

Many elements influence a work of prose fiction. Some important ones are:

- Speech and dialogue: Characters may speak for themselves or through the narrator. Depending on the author's aim, dialogue may be realistic or fantastic.
- Thoughts and mental processes: There may be internal dialogue used as a device for plot development or character understanding.
- Dramatic involvement: Some narrators encourage readers to become involved in the events of the story, whereas other authors attempt to distance readers through literary devices.
- Action: The information that advances the plot or involves new interactions between the characters.
- Duration: The time frame of the work may be long or short, and the relationship between described time and narrative time may vary.
- Setting and description: Is the setting critical to the plot or characters? How are the action scenes described?
- Themes: This is any perspective or topic that is given sustained attention.
- Symbolism: Authors often veil meanings through imagery and other literary constructions.

Fiction extends beyond the realm of prose fiction. Songs, ballads, epics, and narrative poems are examples of non-prose fiction. A full definition of fiction must include not only the work itself but also the framework in which the work is read. Literary fiction includes many works of historical fiction that refer to real people, places, and events that are treated as if they were true. These imaginary elements enrich and broaden literary expression.

When analyzing fiction, you need to read slowly and carefully throughout the passage. The plot of a narrative can become so entertaining that the language of the work is ignored. The language of an author's work (i.e., the author's choice of vocabulary) should not simply be a way to relate a plot—the language should yield many insights to the judicious reader. Some prose fiction is based on the reader's engagement with the language rather than the story. A studious reader will analyze the mode of expression as well as the narrative. A reward of reading in this manner is to discover how the author uses different language to describe familiar objects, events, or emotions. Some works have the reader focus on an author's unorthodox use of language, whereas others may emphasize characters or storylines. The events of a story are not always the critical element in the work. You may find this approach to reading to be a struggle at first, but the rewards overshadow the initial difficulty.

Plot lines are one way to visualize the information given in a story. Every plot line follows the same stages. One can identify each of these stages in every story that they read. These stages include the introduction, rising action, conflict, climax, falling action, and resolution. The introduction tells readers the point of the story and sets up the plot. The rising action is the events that lead up to the conflict (e.g., a problem that arises) with the climax at the peak. The falling action is what happens after the climax of the conflict. The resolution is the conclusion and often has the final solution to the problem in the conflict. A plot line looks like this:

Most texts place events in chronological order. However, some authors may employ an unorthodox structure in order to achieve a certain effect. For instance, many of the Greek epics begin *in medias res* (i.e., in the middle of things). The text begins with an account of a climactic moment. Then, the author goes back to the beginning to describe how events led up to that climax. This technique is found in mystery novels: a crime is committed, and the detective must reconstruct the events that led to the crime. For the reader, you may want to keep in mind the cause-and-effect relationships that shape the story. By definition, a cause must precede an effect. Therefore, an outline of the various causes and effects in a text will mimic the chronological sequence. Readers should remember that the order in which events are described in a text is not necessarily the order in which they occurred.

The **narrator** is a central part of any work of fiction and can give insight about the purpose of the work and the main themes and ideas. The following are important questions to address in order to understand the voice and role of the narrator and incorporate that voice into an overall understanding of the passage:

- Who is the narrator of the passage? What is the narrator's perspective: first person or third person? What is the role of the narrator in the plot? Are there changes in narrators or the perspective of narrators?

- Does the narrator explain things in the passage or does meaning emerge from the plot and events? The personality of the narrator is important. The narrator may have a vested interest in the description of a character or an event. Some narratives follow the time sequence of the plot, whereas others do not follow the sequence. A narrator may express approval or disapproval about a character or events in the work.
- Tone is the attitude expressed by a character through his or her words. Who is actually being addressed by the narrator? Is the tone familiar or formal, intimate or impersonal? Does the vocabulary suggest clues about the narrator?

> **Review Video: <u>The Narrator</u>**
> Visit mometrix.com/academy and enter code: 742528

A **character** is a person intimately involved with the plot and development of the passage. Development of the passage's characters not only moves the story along but also tells the reader about the passage itself. There is usually a physical description of the character, but this may be omitted in modern and postmodern passages as these works focus often on the psychological state or motivation of the character. The choice of a character's name may give valuable clues to his or her role in the work.

Characters can be identified as flat, round, or stock. Flat characters tend to be minor figures that may undergo some change or none at all. Round characters (those understood from a well-rounded view) are central to the story and tend to change at the unfolding of the plot. Stock characters--like flat characters--fill out the story without influencing the story.

Modern literature has been affected greatly by Freudian psychology and given rise to such devices as interior monologue and magical realism as methods of understanding characters in a work. These give readers a complex understanding of the inner lives of the characters and enrich the understanding of relationships between characters.

> **Review Video: <u>What is the Definition of a Character in a Story</u>**
> Visit mometrix.com/academy and enter code: 429493

Prose is ordinary spoken language as opposed to verse (i.e., language with metric patterns). The everyday, normal communication is known as prose and can be found in textbooks, memos, reports, articles, short stories, and novels. Distinguishing characteristics of prose include:

- Some sort of rhythm may be present, but there is no formal arrangement.
- The common unit of organization is the sentence which may include literary devices of repetition and balance.
- There must be coherent relationships among sentences.

Poetry, or verse, is the manipulation of language with respect to meaning, meter, sound, and rhythm. Lines of poetry vary in length and scope, and they may or may not rhyme. Related groups of lines are called stanzas and may be any length. Some poems are as short as a few lines, and some are as long as a book.

A line of poetry can be any length and can have any metrical pattern. A line is determined by the physical position of the words on a page. A line is one group of words that follows the next group in a stanza. Lines may or may not have punctuation at the end depending on the need for punctuation. Consider the following example from John Milton:

"When I consider how my light is spent,

E're half my days, in this dark world and wide,"

A stanza is a group of lines. The grouping denotes a relationship among the lines. A stanza can be any length, but the separation of lines into different stanzas indicates an intentional pattern created by the poet. The breaks between stanzas indicate a change of subject or thought. As a group of lines, the stanza is a melodic unit that can be analyzed for metrical patterns and rhyme patterns. Stanzas of a certain length have been named to indicate an author's purpose with a form of poetry. A few examples include the couplet (two lines), the tercet (three lines), and the quatrain (four lines).

> **Review Video: Structural Elements of Poetry**
> Visit mometrix.com/academy and enter code: 265216

Another important genre is **drama**: a play written to be spoken aloud. The drama is in many ways inseparable from performance. Ideally, reading drama involves using imagination to visualize and re-create the play with characters and settings. Readers stage the play in their imagination and watch characters interact and developments unfold. Sometimes this involves simulating a theatrical presentation, while other times you need to imagine the events. In either case, you are imagining the unwritten to recreate the dramatic experience. Novels present some of the same problems, but a narrator will provide much more information about the setting, characters, inner dialogues, and many other supporting details. In drama, much of this is missing, and you are required to use your powers of projection and imagination to understand the dramatic work. There are many empty spaces in dramatic texts that must be filled by the reader to appreciate the work.

> **Review Video: Dramas**
> Visit mometrix.com/academy and enter code: 216060

Figurative Language

There are many types of language devices that authors use to convey their meaning in a descriptive way. Understanding these concepts will help you understand what you read. These types of devices are called *figurative language* – language that goes beyond the literal meaning of a word or phrase. **Descriptive language** that evokes imagery in the reader's mind is one type of figurative language. **Exaggeration** is another type of figurative language. Also, when you compare two things, you are using figurative language. **Similes** and **metaphors** are ways of comparing things, and both are types of figurative language commonly found in poetry. An example of figurative language (a simile in this case): *The child howled like a coyote when her mother told her to pick up the toys*. In this example, the child's howling is compared to that of a coyote and helps the reader understand the sound being made by the child.

A **figure-of-speech**, sometimes termed a rhetorical figure or device is a word or phrase that departs from straightforward, literal language. Figures-of-speech are often used and crafted for emphasis, freshness of expression, or clarity. However, clarity of a passage may suffer from use of these devices.

As an example of the figurative use of a word, consider the sentence: *I am going to crown you.* The author may mean:

- I am going to place a literal crown on your head.
- I am going to symbolically exalt you to the place of kingship.
- I am going to punch you in the head with my clenched fist.
- I am going to put a second checker's piece on top of your checker piece to signify that it has become a king.

> **Review Video: Figures of Speech**
> Visit mometrix.com/academy and enter code: 111295

An **allusion** is a comparison of someone or something to a person or event in history or literature. Allusions that refer to people or events that are more or less contemporary are called topical allusions. Those referring to specific persons are called personal allusions. For example, *His desire for power was his Achilles' heel.* This example refers to Achilles, a notable hero in Greek mythology who was known to be invincible with the exception of his heels. Today, the term *Achilles' heel* refers to an individual's weakness.

> **Review Video: Allusions**
> Visit mometrix.com/academy and enter code: 294065

Alliteration is a stylistic device, or literary technique, in which successive words (more strictly, stressed syllables) begin with the same sound or letter. Alliteration is a frequent tool in poetry and is common in prose--particularly to highlight short phrases. An example of alliteration could be "thundering through the thickets," in which the initial th sound is used in four consecutive words. Especially in poetry, alliteration contributes to the euphony (i.e., a pleasing or harmonious sound) of the passage. For instance, *We thrashed through the thick forest with our blades.* In this example, a *th* sound is somewhat difficult to make quickly in four consecutive words. Thus, the phrase conveys the difficulty of moving through tall grass. If the author is trying to suggest this difficulty, then the alliteration is a success. Now, consider the description of eyes as *glassy globes of glitter.* This is alliteration since the initial *gl* sound is used three times. However, one might question whether this awkward sound is appropriate for a description of pretty eyes. The phrase is not especially pleasant to the ear and is not a very good implementation of alliteration. Related to alliteration is *assonance*, the repetition of vowel sounds, and *consonance*, the repetition of consonant sounds. Assonance is the repetition of vowel sounds in a phrase as in: *Low and slow, he rolled the coal.* Assonance functions in much the same way as alliteration.

> **Review Video: Alliterations Are All Around**
> Visit mometrix.com/academy and enter code: 462837

A **metaphor** is a type of figurative language in which the writer equates one thing with a different thing. For instance: *The bird was an arrow arcing through the sky.* In this sentence, the arrow is serving as a metaphor for the bird. The point of a metaphor is to encourage the reader to consider the item being described in a different way. Let's continue with this metaphor for a bird: you are asked to envision the bird's flight as being similar to the arc of an arrow. So, you imagine the flight to be swift and bending.

Metaphors are a way for the author to describe an item without being direct and obvious. This literary device is a lyrical and suggestive way of providing information. Note that the reference for a metaphor will not always be mentioned explicitly by the author. Consider the following description of a forest in winter: *Swaying skeletons reached for the sky and groaned as the wind blew through them.* In this example, the author is using *skeletons* as a metaphor for leafless trees. This metaphor creates a spooky tone while inspiring the reader's imagination.

> **Review Video: Metaphors in Writing**
> Visit mometrix.com/academy and enter code: 133295

Metonymy is referring to one thing in terms of a closely related thing. This is similar to metaphor, but there is not as much distance between the description and the thing being described. An example of metonymy is referring to the news media as *the press*, when of course *the press* is the device that prints newspapers. Metonymy is a way of referring to something without having to repeat the name constantly. **Synecdoche**, on the other hand, refers to a whole by one of the parts. An example of synecdoche would be calling a police officer a *badge*. Synecdoche, like metonymy, is an easy way of referring without having to overuse certain words. The device also allows writers to emphasize aspects of the thing being described. For instance, referring to businessmen as *suits* suggests professionalism, conformity, and blandness.

Hyperbole is overstatement for effect. For example: *He jumped ten feet in the air when he heard the good news.* Obviously, no person has the natural ability to jump ten feet in the air. The author exaggerates because the hyperbole conveys the extremity of emotion. If the author simply said: *He jumped when he heard the good news*, then readers would be led to think that the character is not experiencing an extreme emotion. Hyperbole can be dangerous if the author does not exaggerate enough. For instance, if the author wrote, *He jumped two feet in the air when he heard the good news*, then readers may assume that the author is writing a factual statement, not an exaggeration. Readers should be cautious with confusing or vague hyperboles as some test questions may have a hyperbole and a factual statement listed in the answer options.

Understatement is the opposite of hyperbole. The device minimizes or downplays something for effect. Consider a person who climbs Mount Everest and then describes the journey as *a little stroll*. As with other types of figurative language, understatement has a range of uses. The device may convey self-deprecation or modesty as in the above example. Of course, some people might interpret understatement as false modesty (i.e., a deliberate attempt to call attention to oneself or a situation). For example, a woman is complimented on her enormous diamond engagement ring and says, *Oh, this little thing?* Her understatement might be viewed as snobby or insensitive.

> **Review Video: Hyperbole and Understatement**
> Visit mometrix.com/academy and enter code: 308470

A **simile** is a figurative expression that is similar to a metaphor, yet the expression requires the use of the distancing words *like* or *as*. Some examples: *The sun was like an orange, eager as a beaver*, and *nimble as a mountain goat*. Because a simile includes *like* or *as*, the device creates a space between the description and the thing being described. If an author says that *a house was like a shoebox*, then the tone is different than the author saying that the house *was* a shoebox. In a simile, authors indicate an awareness that the description is not the same thing as the thing being described. In a metaphor, there is no such distinction. Authors will use metaphors and similes depending on their intended tone.

> **Review Video: Similes**
> Visit mometrix.com/academy and enter code: 642949

Copyright © Mometrix Media. You have been licensed one copy of this document for personal use only. Any other reproduction or redistribution is strictly prohibited. All rights reserved. This content is provided for test preparation purposes only and does not imply an endorsement by Mometrix of any particular political, scientific, or religious point of view.

Another type of figurative language is **personification.** This is the description of a nonhuman thing as if the item were human. Literally, the word means the process of making something into a person. The general intent of personification is to describe things in a manner that will be comprehensible to readers. When an author states that a tree *groans* in the wind, he or she does not mean that the tree is emitting a low, pained sound from a mouth. Instead, the author means that the tree is making a noise similar to a human groan. Of course, this personification establishes a tone of sadness or suffering. A different tone would be established if the author said that the tree was *swaying* or *dancing*.

> **Review Video: <u>Personification</u>**
> Visit mometrix.com/academy and enter code: 260066

Irony is a statement that suggests the opposite of what one expects to occur. In other words, the device is used when an author or character says one thing but means another. For example, imagine a man who is covered in mud and dressed in tattered clothes and walks in his front door to meet his wife. Then, his wife asks him, "How was your day?", and he says, "Great!" The man's response to his wife is an example of irony. As in this example, irony often depends on information that the reader obtains elsewhere. There is a fine distinction between irony and sarcasm. Irony is any statement in which the literal meaning is opposite from the intended meaning. Sarcasm is similar, yet the statement is insulting to the person at whom the words are directed. A sarcastic statement suggests that the other person is foolish to believe that an obviously false statement is true.

> **Review Video: <u>What is the Definition of Irony?</u>**
> Visit mometrix.com/academy and enter code: 374204

As a person is exposed to more words, the extent of their vocabulary will expand. By reading on a regular basis, a person can increase the number of ways that they have seen a word in context. Based on experience, a person can recall how a word was used in the past and apply that knowledge to a new context. For example, a person may have seen the word *gull* used to mean a bird that is found near the seashore. However, a *gull* can be a person who is tricked easily. If the word in context is used in reference to a character, the reader can recognize the insult since gulls are not seen as extremely intelligent. When you use your knowledge about a word, you can find comparisons or figure out the meaning for a new use of a word.

Verbal

The Verbal test of the SSAT consists of a total of 60 questions (30 Synonyms and 30 Analogies).

Synonyms

As part of your exam, you need to understand how words connect to each other. When you understand how words relate to each other, you will discover more in a passage. This is explained by understanding **synonyms** (e.g., words that mean the same thing) and **antonyms** (e.g., words that mean the opposite of one another). As an example, *dry* and *arid* are synonyms, and *dry* and *wet* are antonyms. There are many pairs of words in English that can be considered synonyms, despite having slightly different definitions. For instance, the words *friendly* and *collegial* can both be used to describe a warm interpersonal relationship, and one would be correct to call them **synonyms**. However, *collegial* (kin to *colleague*) is often used in reference to professional or academic relationships, and *friendly* has no such connotation. If the difference between two words is too great, then they should not be called synonyms. *Hot* and *warm* are not synonyms because their meanings are too distinct. A good way to determine whether two words are synonyms is to substitute one word for the other word and verify that the meaning of the sentence has not changed. Substituting *warm* for *hot* in a sentence would convey a different meaning. Although warm and hot may seem close in meaning, warm generally means that the temperature is moderate, and hot generally means that the temperature is excessively high.

> **Review Video: <u>Synonyms</u>**
> Visit mometrix.com/academy and enter code: 355036
>
> **Review Video: <u>What are Synonyms and Antonyms?</u>**
> Visit mometrix.com/academy and enter code: 105612

SYNONYM EXAMPLES

For the Synonyms section, you will have one word and four choices for a synonym of that word. Before you look at the choices, try to think of a few words that could be a synonym for your question. Then, check the choices for a synonym of the question. Some words may seem close to the question, but you are looking for the best choice of a synonym. So, don't let your first reaction be your final decision.

Example 1

Insatiable:

> A. Compensated
> B. Content
> C. Fulfilled
> D. Quenched
> E. Unsatisfied

Example 2

Adherent:

>A. Antagonist
>B. Disciple
>C. Piquant
>D. Submissive
>E. Zealot

Example 3

Protrude:

>A. Contract
>B. Evocative
>C. Secede
>D. Swell
>E. Tumult

Example 4

Unkempt:

>A. Disorder
>B. Flaunt
>C. Volatile
>D. Unblemished
>E. Writhe

Answers

Example 1: E, Unsatisfied

Example 2: B, Disciple

Example 3: D, Swell

Example 4: A, Disorder

Analogies

DETERMINE THE RELATIONSHIP

As you try to decide on how the words in question are connected, don't jump to understand the meaning of the words. Instead, see if you can find the relationship between the two words. To understand the relationship, you can start by creating a sentence that links the two words and puts them into perspective. At first, try to use a simple sentence to find a connection.

Then, go through each answer choice and replace the words in the answer choices with the parts of your simple sentence. Depending on the question, you may need to make changes to your sentence to make it more specific.

EXAMPLE:

Wood is to fire as

Simple Sentence: *Wood* feeds a *fire* as

Wood is to fire as

> A. Farmer is to cow
> B. Gasoline is to engine

Using the simple sentence, you would state "Farmer feeds a cow" which is correct. Yet, the next answer choice "Gasoline feeds an engine" is also true. So which is the correct answer? With this simple sentence, we need to be more specific.

Specific Sentences: "Wood feeds a fire and is consumed" / "Wood is burned in a fire"

These specific sentences show that answer choice (A) is incorrect and answer choice (B) is clearly correct. With the specific sentences, you have "Gasoline feeds an engine and is consumed" is correct. Also, "Farmer feeds a cow and is consumed" is clearly incorrect.

If your simple sentence seems correct with more than one answer choice, then keep making changes until only one answer choice makes sense.

ELIMINATING SIMILARITIES

This method works well in the Analogies section and the Synonyms section. You can start by looking over the answer choices and see what clues they provide. If there are any common relationships between the pairs of terms, then those answer choices have to be wrong.

Example:

Tough is to rugged as

> A. Soft is to hard
> B. Clear is to foggy
> C. Inhale is to exhale
> D. Throw is to catch
> E. Rigid is to taut

In this example, tough and rugged are synonyms. Also, the first four answer choices are antonyms. You may not realize that taut and rigid are synonyms. However, it has to be correct. The reason is that you know the other four answer choices all had the same relationship of being antonyms.

WORD TYPES

Example:

Gardener is to hedge as

>   A. Wind is to rock
>   B. Woodcarver is to stick

In this example, you could start with a simple sentence of "Gardener cuts away at hedges." Now, both answer choices seem correct with this sentence. For choice (A), you can say that "Wind cuts away at rocks" due to erosion. For choice (B), you can say that a "Woodcarver cuts away at sticks." The difference is that a gardener is a person, and a woodcarver is a person. However, the wind is a thing which makes answer choice (B) correct.

FACE VALUE

When you are not sure about an answer, you should try to accept the problem at face value. Don't read too much into it. These problems will not ask you to make impossible comparisons. Truly, the SSAT test writers are not trying to throw you off with cheap tricks. If you have to make a stretch of the question to make a connection between the two terms, then you should start over and find another relationship. Don't make the problem more difficult. These are normal questions with differences in difficulty. Sometimes the terms that go together and their relationships may not be very clear. So, you will want to read over the question and answer choices carefully.

EXAMPLE:

Odor is to smell as flavor is to

>   A. believe
>   B. know
>   C. feel
>   D. taste
>   E. punish

Would a flavor be "punished," "known", "felt", "tasted", or "believed"? The analogy is about a synonym. So, answer choice D which is "taste" is a synonym of flavor and is the best answer.

READ CAREFULLY

To understand the analogies, you need to read the terms and answer choices carefully. You can miss the question because you misread the terms. Each question here has only a few words, so you can spend time reading them carefully. Yet, you cannot forget your time limit of the section. So, don't spend too much time on one question. Just focus on reading carefully and be sure to read all of the choices. You may find an answer choice that seems correct. Yet, when you finish reading over the choices, you may find a better choice.

Essay

PRACTICE MAKES PREPARED WRITERS

Writing is a skill that continues to need development throughout a person's life. For some people, writing seems to be a natural gift. They rarely struggle with writer's block. When you read their papers, they have persuasive ideas. For others, writing is an intimidating task that they endure. As you practice, you can improve your skills and be better prepared for writing a time-sensitive essay.

Remember that you are practicing for more than an exam. Two of the most valuable skills in life are the abilities to **read critically** and to **write clearly**. When you work on evaluating the arguments of a passage and explain your thoughts well, you are developing skills that you will use for a lifetime. In this overview of essay writing, you will find strategies and tools that will prepare you to write better essays.

CREATIVE WRITING

Take time to read a story or hear stories read aloud and use those opportunities to learn more about how stories are put together. This offers a frame for you to talk about a story with others and will help you to write better stories. With each new story that you read, try to predict what could happen in the story. Try to understand the setting by picturing the scenes and sounds that are described and the behaviors of characters. Then, try to summarize the events to understand more of the story.

If you need more help with understanding a story, you can try to relate narrative characters and events to your own life. For example, when reading a story, you can ask the following: Who is the main character in the story? What happened first? What happened next? What happened at the end of the story? Where does this story take place? And what is the theme or point of this story?

ESTABLISH A CONTEXT

When writing a narrative, a context for the story has to be introduced. The context could consist of a description of a situation or a setting. A point of view also has to be established. It could be introduced by a narrator and may or may not be the same as the author's. The points of view can be shown through dialogue or how the narrator reacts to or describes what characters do in the story. The characters will need to be drawn very clearly through their descriptions (i.e., what they do and what they say). You may hide his point of view in the characters' thoughts or actions. The narrator's point of view is usually more overtly seen in what is said in the narrative by the narrator.

Decide the character and point of view in the following passage.

> Alma Way stared straight ahead. Her long delicate face was pale. Her gloved hands, clutching the hymn book, trembled as she sang. The time for her solo was near. She felt panic rising within her but she took a deep breath. Then her voice rang out, clear as a bell. The congregation nodded admiringly.

The author has chosen to tell the narrative from the third-person omniscient viewpoint which means the narrator is all-knowing. Readers are introduced to the character of Alma Way by the author's description of Alma. Readers can learn a lot about her from the description of how she is staring: that her face is pale and that her gloved hands clutched a hymn book. The narrator also shares that she feels panic.

POINT OF VIEW

Point of view is the perspective from which writing occurs. There are several possibilities:

- *First person* is written so that the *I* of the story is a participant or observer. First-person narratives let narrators express inner feelings and thoughts. The narrator may be a close friend of the protagonist, or the narrator can be less involved with the main characters and plot.
- *Second person* is a device to draw the reader in more closely. It is really a variation or refinement of the first-person narrative. In some cases, a narrative combines both second-person and first-person voices, speaking of "you" and "I." When the narrator is also a character in the story, the narrative is better defined as first-person even though it also has addresses of "you."
- *Third person* may be either objective or subjective, and either omniscient or limited. Objective third-person narration does not include what the characters are thinking or feeling, while subjective third-person narration does include this information. The third-person omniscient narrator knows everything about all characters, including their thoughts and emotions; and all related places, times, and events. The third-person limited narrator may know everything about a particular character of focus, but is limited to that character. In other words, the narrator cannot speak about anything that character does not know.

SEQUENCE OF EVENTS

The sequence of events in a narrative should follow naturally out of the action and the plot. Rather than being forced, the sequence should follow the natural flow of a dialogue or plot and enhance what happens in the story. The only time that the sequence is not in the order that events naturally happen is when an author decides to use the literary device called flashback. In this case the action does not flow in sequence; instead, the action jumps back and forth in time. Events in a narrative are extremely important in helping the reader understand the intent or message of a narrative, which is why it is important to take note of the way in which the plot unfolds.

> **Review Video: <u>Sequence of Events in a Story</u>**
> Visit mometrix.com/academy and enter code: 807512

Remember from the Reading section that a plot shows the order of a story. The introduction is the beginning of the story. Next, the rising action, conflict, climax, and falling action are the middle. Then, the resolution or conclusion is the ending. So, stay focused on the goal of writing a story that needs those main parts: a beginning, a middle, and an ending.

AUTHOR TECHNIQUES

You can employ many techniques to make your narrative essay come alive in a fresh and interesting way. Dialogue is an important one. Often, dialogue is the means that helps readers understand what is happening and what a character is like. Equally important are the descriptions that you can use to help readers visualize a setting and what a character looks or acts like. Remember that you have limited time to write a whole story. So, don't be concerned with providing description for everything that you put in your story.

TRANSITIONS WORDS

Transition words can be helpful when writing a narrative so that readers can follow the events in a seamless manner. Sequence words such as *first*, *second*, and *last* assist readers in understanding the order in which events occur. Words such as *then* or *next* also show the order in which events occur. *After a while* and *before this* are other sequence expressions.

Additionally, transition words can indicate a change from one time frame or setting to another: "We were sitting on a rock near the lake when we heard a strange sound."At this point we decided to look to see where the noise was coming from by going further into the woods." In this excerpt the phrase *at this point* signals a shift in setting between what was happening and what came next.

PRECISE LANGUAGE

Your use of precise language, phrases, and sensory language (i.e., language that appeals to the five senses), helps readers imagine a place, situation, or person in the way that you intended. Details of character's actions, the setting, and the events in a narrative help create a lively and thought-provoking story. Sensory language helps convey the mood and feeling of the setting and characters and can highlight the theme of your story.

Read the excerpt and analyze its language.

> All through his boyhood, George Willard had been in the habit of walking on Trunion Pike. He had been there on winter nights when it was covered with snow and only the moon looked down at him; he had been there in the fall when bleak winds blew and on summer evenings when the air vibrated with the song of insects.

This excerpt is filled with precise and sensory language. The descriptions of walking on Turnion Pike *when it was covered with snow and only the moon looked down*, of the *bleak winds* that blew, and times that *the air vibrated with the song of insects* all contribute to bring the words to life and allows readers to see what the author envisioned by creating images through vivid and precise language. The description of the setting uses relevant details that readers can use to understand something about George Willard.

ROLE OF A CONCLUSION

The conclusion of a narrative is extremely important because it shapes the entire story and is the resolution of the characters' conflict(s). Some conclusions may be tragic (e.g., classic tragedies), and other endings may be lighthearted (e.g., classic comedies). Modern stories tend to have endings that are more complex than the clear-cut endings of classic literature. They often leave readers without a clear sense of how a character fares at the end. Nonetheless, this element can show how life is not always clear in its conclusions.

A student is writing a story about a girl who wants to be on the basketball team and works out every day to get in shape. The student has written about the girl's feelings and the obstacles she has had to overcome. Now, a conclusion is needed for the story. Describe what needs to be done to develop a good conclusion.

The student should think about the character as though the girl were a real person because this seems to be a realistic story. The student should think about what he or she wants to have as the story's theme. Does the student want to show that hard work pays off? Or is the goal to show that you cannot always get what you want even with hard work? In other words, the student has to decide whether the story will have a happy ending or not. Whatever kind of an ending the student decides upon, the conclusion should bring the entire story to a fitting and appropriate end so that readers have a sense of closure.

TRADITIONAL ESSAY OVERVIEW

A traditional way to prepare for the writing section is to read. When you read newspapers, magazines, and books, you learn about new ideas. You can read newspapers and magazines to become informed about issues that affect many people.

As you think about those issues and ideas, you can take a position and form opinions. Try to develop these ideas and your opinions by sharing them with friends. After you develop your opinions, try writing them down as if you were going to spread your ideas beyond your friends.

For your exam you need to write an essay that shows your ability to understand and respond to an assignment. When you talk with others, you give beliefs, opinions, and ideas about the world around you. As you talk, you have the opportunity to share information with spoken words, facial expressions, or hand motions. If your audience seems confused about your ideas, you can stop and explain. However, when you write, you have a different assignment. As you write, you need to share information in a clear, precise way. Your readers will not have the chance to ask questions about your ideas. So, before you write your essay, you need to understand the assignment. As you write, you should be clear and precise about your ideas.

BRAINSTORM

Spend the first three to five minutes brainstorming for ideas. Write down any ideas that you might have on the topic. The purpose is to pull any helpful information from the depths of your memory. In this stage, anything goes down on note paper regardless of how good or bad the idea may seem at first glance. You may not bring your own paper for these notes. Instead, you will be provided with paper at the time of your test.

STRENGTH THROUGH DIFFERENT VIEWPOINTS

The best papers will contain several examples and mature reasoning. As you brainstorm, you should consider different perspectives. There are more than two sides to every topic. In an argument, there are countless perspectives that can be considered. On any topic, different groups are impacted and many reach the same conclusion or position. Yet, they reach the same conclusion through different paths. Before writing your essay, try to *see* the topic through as many different *eyes* as you can.

Once you have finished with your creative flow, you need to stop and review what you brainstormed. *Which idea allowed you to come up with the most supporting information?* Be sure to pick an angle that will allow you to have a thorough coverage of the prompt.

Every garden of ideas has weeds. The ideas that you brainstormed are going to be random pieces of information of different values. Go through the pieces carefully and pick out the ones that are the best. The best ideas are strong points that will be easy to write a paragraph in response.

Now, you have your main ideas that you will focus on. So, align them in a sequence that will flow in a smooth, sensible path from point to point. With this approach, readers will go smoothly from one idea to the next in a reasonable order. Readers want an essay that has a sense of continuity (i.e., Point 1 to Point 2 to Point 3 and so on).

START YOUR ENGINES

Now, you have a logical flow of the main ideas for the start of your essay. Begin by expanding on the first point, then move to your second point. Pace yourself. Don't spend too much time on any one of the ideas that you are expanding on. You want to have time for all of them. *Make sure that you watch your time.* If you have twenty minutes left to write out your ideas and you have four ideas, then you can only use five minutes per idea. Writing so much information in so little time can be an intimidating task. Yet, when you pace yourself, you can get through all of your points. If you find that you are falling behind, then you can remove one of your weaker arguments. This will allow you to give enough support to your remaining paragraphs.

Once you finish expanding on an idea, go back to your brainstorming session where you wrote out your ideas. You can scratch through the ideas as you write about them. This will let you see what you need to write about next and what you have left to cover.

Your introductory paragraph should have several easily identifiable features.

- First, the paragraph should have a quick description or paraphrasing of the topic. Use your own words to briefly explain what the topic is about.
- Second, you should list your writing points. What are the main ideas that you came up with earlier? If someone was to read only your introduction, they should be able to get a good summary of the entire paper.
- Third, you should explain your opinion of the topic and give an explanation for why you feel that way. What is your decision or conclusion on the topic?

Each of your following paragraphs should develop one of the points listed in the main paragraph. Use your personal experience and knowledge to support each of your points. Examples should back up everything.

Once you have finished expanding on each of your main points, you need to conclude your essay. Summarize what you written in a conclusion paragraph. Explain once more your argument on the prompt and review why you feel that way in a few sentences. At this stage, you have already backed up your statements. So, there is no need to do that again. You just need to refresh your readers on the main points that you made in your essay.

DON'T PANIC

Whatever you do during the essay, do not panic. When you panic, you will put fewer words on the page and your ideas will be weak. Therefore, panicking is not helpful. If your mind goes blank when you see the prompt, then you need to take a deep breath. Remember to brainstorm and put anything on scratch paper that comes to mind.

Also, don't get clock fever. You may be overwhelmed when you're looking at a page that is mostly blank. Your mind is full of random thoughts and feeling confused, and the clock is ticking down faster. You have already brainstormed for ideas. Therefore, you don't have to keep coming up with ideas. If you're running out of time and you have a lot of ideas that you haven't written down, then don't be afraid to make some cuts. Start picking the best ideas that you have left and expand on them. Don't feel like you have to write on all of your ideas.

A short paper that is well written and well organized is better than a long paper that is poorly written and poorly organized. Don't keep writing about a subject just to add sentences and avoid repeating a statement or idea that you have explained already. The goal is 1 to 2 pages of quality writing. That is your target, but you should not mess up your paper by trying to get there. You want to have a natural end to your work without having to cut something short. If your essay is a little long, then that isn't a problem as long as your ideas are clear and flow well from paragraph to paragraph. Remember to expand on the ideas that you identified in the brainstorming session.

Leave time at the end (at least three minutes) to go back and check over your work. Reread and make sure that everything you've written makes sense and flows well. Clean up any spelling or grammar mistakes. Also, go ahead and erase any brainstorming ideas that you weren't able to include. Then, clean up any extra information that you might have written that doesn't fit into your paper.

As you proofread, make sure that there aren't any fragments or run-ons. Check for sentences that are too short or too long. If the sentence is too short, then look to see if you have a specific subject and an active verb. If it is too long, then break up the long sentence into two sentences. Watch out for any "big words" that you may have used. Be sure that you are using difficult words correctly. Don't misunderstand; you should try to increase your vocabulary and use difficult words in your essay. However, your focus should be on developing and expressing ideas in a clear and precise way.

THE SHORT OVERVIEW

Depending on your preferences and personality, the essay may be your hardest or your easiest section. You are required to go through the entire process of writing a paper in a limited amount of time which is very challenging.

Stay focused on each of the steps for brainstorming. Go through the process of creative flow first. You can start by generating ideas about the prompt. Next, organize those ideas into a smooth flow. Then, pick out the ideas that are the best from your list.

Create a recognizable essay structure in your paper. Start with an introduction that explains what you have decided to argue. Then, choose your main points. Use the body paragraphs to touch on those main points and have a conclusion that wraps up the topic.

Save a few moments to go back and review what you have written. Clean up any minor mistakes that you might have made and make those last few critical touches that can make a huge difference. Finally, be proud and confident of what you have written!

Practice Test #1

Want to take this practice test in an online interactive format?
Check out the bonus page, which includes interactive practice questions and much more: **https://www.mometrix.com/bonus948/ssatupper**

Writing

Review the following prompts and choose to write a creative story or a traditional essay. You have 25 minutes to write a creative story or respond to the traditional essay prompt.

Creative Writing

"Never throughout history has a man who lived a life of ease left a name worth remembering."

-Theodore Roosevelt

Think carefully about this quote and some of the great things that have been accomplished by living a life of difficulty. Then, write a creative story that covers the importance of working hard to accomplish great things.

Traditional Essay

Prompt: Some people feel that video games actually promote intelligence. They say that strategy games force players to make strategic choices, plan ahead, and react in appropriate ways to challenges. Others feel that video games are simply a mindless pastime, and that time would be better spent doing something constructive like reading or participating in sports.

Write an essay to a parent who is deciding whether they should allow their child to play video games. Take a position on whether video games are a valuable activity or simply a waste of time. Use arguments and examples to support your position.

Section 1: Quantitative

1. Jerry needs to load four pieces of equipment onto a factory elevator that has a weight limit of 800 pounds. Jerry weighs 200 pounds. What would the average weight of each item have to be so that the elevator's weight limit is not exceeded?

    a. 128 pounds
    b. 150 pounds
    c. 175 pounds
    d. 180 pounds
    e. 185 pounds

2. Chan receives a bonus from his job. He pays 30% in taxes, gives 20% to charity, uses another 20% to pay off an old debt, and sets aside 10% in a savings account. He has $600 remaining from his bonus. What was the total amount of Chan's bonus?

    a. $2,400
    b. $2,800
    c. $3,000
    d. $3,600
    e. $3,800

3. A jar contains pennies and nickels. The ratio of nickels to pennies is 6:2. What percent of the coins are pennies?

    a. 25%
    b. 33.3%
    c. 40%
    d. 50%
    e. 75%

4. Given the equation, $ax + b = c$, what is the value of x?

    a. $(c + b)/a$
    b. ca/b
    c. $c - ba$
    d. $(c - b)/a$
    e. cb/a

5. If c is to be chosen at random from the set {1, 2, 3, 4} and d is to be chosen at random from the set {1, 2, 3, 4}, what is the probability cd will be odd?

    a. $\frac{1}{4}$
    b. $\frac{1}{3}$
    c. $\frac{3}{4}$
    d. 2
    e. 4

137

6. If $x = 2y - 3$ and $2x + \frac{1}{2}y = 3$, then $y = ?$

    a. $-\frac{2}{3}$

    b. 1

    c. 2

    d. $\frac{18}{7}$

    e. 3

7. A bag contains 14 blue, 6 red, 12 green and 8 purple buttons. 25 buttons are removed from the bag randomly. How many of the removed buttons were red if the chance of drawing a red button from the bag is now $\frac{1}{3}$?

    a. 0

    b. 1

    c. 3

    d. 5

    e. 6

8. The sides of a triangle are equal to integral numbers of units. Two sides are 4 and 6 units long, respectively; what is the minimum value for the triangle's perimeter?

    a. 9 units

    b. 10 units

    c. 11 units

    d. 12 units

    e. 13 units

9. The average of six numbers is 4. If the average of two of those numbers is 2, what is the average of the other four numbers?

    a. 3

    b. 4

    c. 5

    d. 7

    e. 8

10. There are 64 squares on a checkerboard. Bobby puts one penny on the first square, two on the second square, four on the third, eight on the fourth. He continues to double the number of coins at each square until he has covered all 64 squares. How many coins must he place on the last square?

    a. 2^{63}

    b. $2^{63} + 1$

    c. $2^{63} - 1$

    d. $2^{64} - 1$

    e. 2^{64}

11. The length of Square A is 3 feet longer than the length of Square B. If the difference between their areas is 75 ft^2, what is the length of Square B?

    a. 6 feet
    b. 9 feet
    c. 10 feet
    d. 11 feet
    e. 12 feet

12. The cost, in dollars, of shipping x computers to California for sale is $3000 + 100x$. The amount received when selling these computers is $400x$ dollars. What is the least number of computers that must be shipped and sold so that the amount received is at least equal to the shipping cost?

    a. 10
    b. 15
    c. 20
    d. 25
    e. 30

13. If $\frac{x}{8} = \frac{y}{4} = 4$, what is the value of $x - y$?

    a. 8
    b. 16
    c. 24
    d. 32
    e. 48

14. The scientific notation for the diameter of a red blood cell is approximately 7.4×10^{-4} centimeters. What is that amount in standard form?

    a. 0.00074
    b. 0.0074
    c. 7.40000
    d. 296
    e. 7,400

15. What is the area of the shaded region? (Each square represents one unit.)

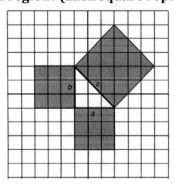

    a. 4.5
    b. 18
    c. 24
    d. 32
    e. 36

16. 5 more than 6 times a number is 77. What is the number?

    a. 12
    b. 17
    c. 19
    d. 24
    e. 72

17. Simplify $\left(3 \times 10^4\right) \times \left(2 \times 10^5\right)$.

    a. 5×10^9
    b. 5×10^{20}
    c. 6×10^9
    d. 6×10^{12}
    e. 6×10^{20}

18. Which of the following is the factored form of the expression, $x^2 + 3x - 28$?

    a. $(x - 14)(x + 2)$
    b. $(x + 6)(x - 3)$
    c. $(x + 4)(x - 1)$
    d. $(x - 4)(x + 7)$
    e. $(x - 14)(x + 7)$

19. Given $x^2 - 7x + 10 \geq 0$, what is the solution set for x?

    a. $2 \leq x \leq 5$
    b. $x \leq 2$ or $x \geq 5$
    c. $7 \leq x \leq 10$
    d. $x \leq 7$ or $x \geq 10$
    e. $7 \leq x \leq 5$

20. The equation for line A is $5y - 100x = 25$. What are the slope and *y*-intercept of line A?

    a.   The slope is 100, and the *y*-intercept is 5.
    b.   The slope is 5, and the *y*-intercept is 100.
    c.   The slope is 20, and the *y*-intercept is 5.
    d.   The slope is 25, and the *y*-intercept is 5.
    e.   The slope is 5, and the *y*-intercept is 20.

21. The Charleston Recycling Company collects 50,000 tons of recyclable material every month. The chart shows the kinds of materials that are collected by the company's five trucks.

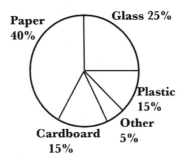

About how much paper is recycled every month?

    a.   15,000 tons
    b.   20,000 tons
    c.   25,000 tons
    d.   40,000 tons
    e.   50,000 tons

22. The volume of a rectangular box is found by multiplying its length, width, and height. If the dimensions of a box are $\sqrt{3}$, $2\sqrt{5}$, and 4, what is its volume?

    a. $2\sqrt{60}$
    b. $4\sqrt{15}$
    c. $8\sqrt{15}$
    d. $24\sqrt{5}$
    e. $8\sqrt{5}$

23. Simplify $\left(8 \times 10^3\right) + \left(1 \times 10^3\right)$.

    a. 8×10^3
    b. 8×10^6
    c. 9×10^3
    d. 9×10^6
    e. 9×10^9

24. Which function represents the graph?

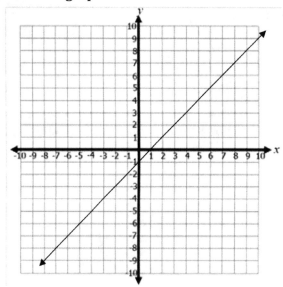

a. $y = x + 1$
b. $y = x - 1$
c. $y = -x + 1$
d. $y = -x - 1$
e. $y = 1$

25. A dress is marked down by 20% and placed on a clearance rack, on which is posted a sign reading, "Take an extra 25% off already reduced merchandise." What fraction of the original price is the final sale price of the dress?

a. $\dfrac{1}{4}$

b. $\dfrac{2}{5}$

c. $\dfrac{3}{5}$

d. $\dfrac{8}{20}$

e. $\dfrac{11}{20}$

Section 2: Reading Comprehension

Excerpt from *Pride and Prejudice* by Jane Austen:

It is a truth universally acknowledged, that a single man in possession of a good fortune, must be in want of a wife.

However little known the feelings or views of such a man may be on his first entering a neighbourhood, this truth is so well fixed in the minds of the surrounding families, that he is considered the rightful property of some one or other of their daughters.

"My dear Mr. Bennet," said his lady to him one day, "have you heard that Netherfield Park is let at last?"

Mr. Bennet replied that he had not.

"But it is," returned she; "for Mrs. Long has just been here, and she told me all about it."

Mr. Bennet made no answer.

"Do you not want to know who has taken it?" cried his wife impatiently.

"You want to tell me, and I have no objection to hearing it."

This was invitation enough.

"Why, my dear, you must know, Mrs. Long says that Netherfield is taken by a young man of large fortune from the north of England; that he came down on Monday in a chaise and four to see the place, and was so much delighted with it, that he agreed with Mr. Morris immediately; that he is to take possession before Michaelmas, and some of his servants are to be in the house by the end of next week."

"What is his name?"

"Bingley."

"Is he married or single?"

"Oh! Single, my dear, to be sure! A single man of large fortune; four or five thousand a year. What a fine thing for our girls!"

"How so? How can it affect them?"

"My dear Mr. Bennet," replied his wife, "how can you be so tiresome!" You must know that I am thinking of his marrying one of them."

"Is that his design in settling here?"

"Design! Nonsense, how can you talk so! But it is very likely that he may fall in love with one of them, and therefore you must visit him as soon as he comes."

"I see no occasion for that. You and the girls may go, or you may send them by themselves, which perhaps will be still better, for as you are as handsome as any of them, Mr. Bingley may like you the best of the party."

1. What is the central idea of this selection?

a. A new neighbor is due to arrive who may become good friends with Mr. and Mrs. Bennet.
b. A new neighbor is due to arrive who may be a prospective husband for one of the Bennet daughters.
c. A new neighbor is due to arrive who may be a good business connection for Mr. Bennet.
d. A new neighbor is due to arrive who has expressed an interest in marrying one of the Bennet daughters.
e. A new neighbor is due to arrive who has expressed an interest in purchasing more property.

2. How does Mrs. Bennet feel about the arrival of Mr. Bingley?

a. Mrs. Bennet is excited about the arrival of Mr. Bingley.
b. Mrs. Bennet is nervous about the arrival of Mr. Bingley.
c. Mrs. Bennet is afraid the arrival of Mr. Bingley will upset Mr. Bennet.
d. Mrs. Bennet is indifferent to the arrival of Mr. Bingley.
e. Mrs. Bennet is skeptical about the arrival of Mr. Bingley.

3. Which of the following statements best describes Mrs. Bennet's feelings about her husband as indicated by this selection?

a. Mrs. Bennet is tired of her husband.
b. Mrs. Bennet is exasperated by her husband.
c. Mrs. Bennet is afraid of her husband.
d. Mrs. Bennet is indifferent toward her husband.
e. Mrs. Bennet is bored with her husband.

4. "It is a truth universally acknowledged, that a single man in possession of a good fortune, must be in want of a wife."

Which of the following most nearly matches the meaning of the underlined phrase?

a. Everyone knows
b. The universe has decided
c. It is a documented fact
d. It is best to tell the truth
e. Some may not recall

5. "Is that his design in settling here?"

What does the word design mean in the context of this selection?

a. Policy
b. Drawing
c. Creation
d. Improvisation
e. Intention

Helen Keller

Helen Keller was born on June 27, 1880. She was a happy and healthy child until the age of 19 months when she fell ill with a terrible fever. Although Helen recovered from the fever, it left her both deaf and blind.

Helen was loved and cared for by her doting parents, but her behavior became erratic after she Lost her hearing and sight, with Unpredictable outbursts of temper. Her parents were at a loss how to reach her and teach her how to behave. Helen herself was Frustrated and lonely in her dark, silent world. All of that began to change in March 1887 when Anne Sullivan came to live with the Kellers and be Helen's teacher.

Anne taught Helen to communicate by forming letters with her fingers held in another person's hand. In this way, Teacher, as Helen called her, taught her pupil to spell cake, doll, and milk. However, it was not until Anne spelled w-a-t-e-r in Helen's hands as cold water gushed over both of them that Helen made the exciting connection between the words and the world around her. This connection engendered an insatiable curiosity within Helen. After that day, Helen learned at an incredible rate with Teacher by her side.

Helen went on to graduate from Radcliffe College. She became a famous writer, speaker, and advocate. The story of Helen's remarkable life is known worldwide. Anne Sullivan and Helen Keller were inseparable until Anne's death in 1936. Teacher shined a light in Helen's dark world and showed her the way.

6. Which organizational pattern does the author use?
   a. Comparison and contrast
   b. Chronological order
   c. Cause and effect
   d. Problem/solution
   e. No apparent pattern

7. What is the author's primary purpose in writing this passage?
   a. To inform people about Helen Keller's college career
   b. To inform people about Anne Sullivan's life
   c. To inform people about services available for the deaf and blind
   d. To inform people about overcoming incredible obstacles
   e. To inform people about Helen Keller's life

8. How does the author make a connection between the second and third paragraphs?
   a. The author begins the third paragraph by continuing to talk about Helen's parents who were introduced in the second paragraph.
   b. The author organizes the second and third paragraphs the same way.
   c. The author ends the second paragraph with the advent of Anne Sullivan in Helen's life, and begins the third paragraph with the most important contribution Anne made to Helen's education.
   d. The author uses the third paragraph to elaborate on Helen's frustration and resulting temper tantrums introduced in the second paragraph.
   e. The author continues to use the theme of teamwork throughout both paragraphs.

9. What is the author's tone in this passage?

a. Indifferent
b. Censorious
c. Admiring
d. Impartial
e. Informational

10. What was the turning point in Helen's life?

a. When Helen learned to connect feeling water on her hands with the word "water."
b. When Helen graduated from Radcliffe College.
c. When Helen contracted the fever that took away her hearing and sight.
d. When Anne Sullivan came to live with the Kellers and be Helen's teacher.
e. When Anne Sullivan taught Helen to spell cake, doll, and milk.

11. Which of the following can you infer was true about Helen's parents?

a. Helen's parents were frustrated that they were unable to help Helen communicate.
b. Helen's parents were jealous that Anne Sullivan was closer to Helen than they were.
c. Helen's parents were glad to give Anne Sullivan full responsibility for Helen.
d. Helen's parents wanted their daughter to graduate from Radcliffe College.
e. Helen's parents wished that they had contacted Anne Sullivan sooner.

Annelids

The phylum Annelida, named for the Latin word *anellus*, meaning "ring", includes earthworms, leeches, and other similar organisms. In their typical form, these animals exhibit bilateral symmetry, a cylindrical cross section, and an elongate body divided externally into segments (*metameres*) by a series of rings (*annuli*). They are segmented internally as well, with most of the internal organs repeated in series in each segment. This organization is termed *metamerism*. Metameric segmentation is the distinguishing feature of this phylum, and provides it with a degree of evolutionary plasticity in that certain segments can be modified and specialized to perform specific functions. For example, in some species certain of the locomotor *parapodia*, or feet, may be modified for grasping, and some portions of the gut may evolve digestive specializations.

The gut is a straight, muscular tube that functions independently of the muscular activity in the body wall. The Annelida resemble the nematodes, another worm phylum, in possessing a fluid-filled internal cavity separating the gut from the body wall. In both phyla, this cavity is involved in locomotion. However, in the annelids, this space is formed at a much later time during the development of the embryo, and presumably evolved much later as well. This fluid-filled internal space is called a true *coelom*.

The annelid excretory and circulatory systems are well developed, and some members of the phylum have evolved respiratory organs. The nervous system offers a particular example of metameric specialization. It is concentrated anteriorly into enlarged cerebral ganglia connected to a ventral nerve cord that extends posteriorly and is organized into repeating segmental ganglia.

This phylum includes members bearing adaptations required for aquatic (marine or freshwater) or terrestrial habitats. They may be free-living entities or exist as parasites. Among the best known are the earthworm *Lumbricus*, the water leech *Hirudo*, and the marine worm *Nereis*.

12 What is the purpose of this passage?

    a. To describe the annelid nervous system.

    b. To describe the annelid digestive system.

    c. To introduce distinctive features of annelid anatomy.

    d. To define metamerism.

    e. To review the evolution of annelids

13. Which of the following is one evolutionary advantage of segmentation?

    a. segmented animals have many feet.

    b. segmented animals have a fluid-filled coelom.

    c. these animals are able to move at a faster rate than previous annelids.

    d. these animals are now able to have aquatic or terrestrial habitats.

    e. parts of some segments can become specialized to perform certain functions.

14. The main difference between the Annelida and all other animal phyla is that

    a. the Annelida are worms.

    b. the Annelida include the leeches.

    c. the Annelida are metameric.

    d. the Annelida are aquatic.

    e. the Annelida's excretory and circulatory systems.

15. The purpose of the last paragraph in the passage is to

    a. give familiar examples of members of the annelid phylum.

    b. show that annelids may be parasites.

    c. tell the reader that annelids may be adapted to aquatic environments.

    d. show that there are many annelids in nature and that they are adapted to a wide variety of habitats.

    e. None of the above

16. The second paragraph discusses annelids and nematodes. Which relationship(s) between these two phyla does the author establish by describing their respective characteristics?

    a. Comparison

    b. Contrast

    c. Cause and Effect

    d. Comparison and Contrast

    e. None of the above

17. After the first sentence, which of the following describes the structure of this passage relative to the paragraph content sequence?

    a. Body parts; body systems; types, habitats, names; distinctive feature

    b. Distinctive feature; body parts; body systems; types, habitats, names

    c. Body systems; distinctive feature; types, habitats, names; body parts

    d. Types, habitats, names; distinctive feature; body parts; body systems

    e. Types, habitats, names; body parts; body systems; distinctive feature

"The Thought-Fox" by Ted Hughes

I imagine this midnight moment's forest:
Something else is alive
Beside the clock's loneliness
And this blank page where my fingers move.

Through the window I see no star:
Something more near
Though deeper within darkness
Is entering the loneliness:

Cold, delicately as the dark snow
A fox's nose touches twig, leaf;
Two eyes serve a movement, that now
And again now, and now, and now

Sets neat prints into the snow
Between trees, and warily a lame
Shadow lags by stump and in hollow
Of a body that is bold to come

Across clearings, an eye,
A widening deepening greenness,
Brilliantly, concentratedly,
Coming about its own business

Till, with a sudden sharp hot stink of fox,
It enters the dark hole of the head.
The window is starless still; the clock ticks,
The page is printed.

18. The primary literary device used by the poet here is

    a. foreshadowing.
    b. irony.
    c. cliché.
    d. metaphor.
    e. allusion.

19. Which of these does this poem really describe?

    a. The process of a fox's natural actions
    b. The process of being inspired by nature
    c. The process of being inspired to write
    d. The process of being attacked by a fox
    e. The process of working in a print shop

20. Which of the following best characterizes how this poem portrays the creative process?
  a. The poet exercises tight control of a thought.
  b. The poet finds his best writing when visiting forests.
  c. The poet carefully guides the thought to him.
  d. The poet imagines a fox to help him to write.
  e. The poet is a passive recipient of the thought.

<u>"The Gettysburg Address" by Abraham Lincoln</u>

Four score and seven years ago our fathers brought forth, upon this continent, a new nation, conceived in Liberty, and dedicated to the proposition that all men are created equal.

Now we are engaged in a great civil war, testing whether that nation, or any nation so conceived, and so dedicated, can long endure. We are met here on a great battlefield of that war. We have come to dedicate a portion of it as a final resting place for those who here gave their lives that that nation might live. It is altogether fitting and proper that we should do this.

But in a larger sense we cannot dedicate - we cannot consecrate - we cannot hallow this ground. The brave men, living and dead, who struggled here, have consecrated it far above our poor power to add or detract. The world will little note, nor long remember, what we say here, but can never forget what they did here.

It is for us, the living, rather to be dedicated here to the unfinished work which they have, thus far, so nobly carried on. It is rather for us to be here dedicated to the great task remaining before us - that from these honored dead we take increased devotion to that cause for which they here gave the last full measure of devotion - that we here highly resolve that these dead shall not have died in vain; that this nation shall have a new birth of freedom; and that this government of the people, by the people, for the people, shall not perish from the earth.

21. What is the main message of this speech?
  a. Those who died in this battle honor this land we are dedicating today better than anyone else.
  b. As we honor those who died in this battle, we should move forward with renewed dedication to ensuring the nation our founding fathers created continues to function the way they intended.
  c. We need to put the regrets of the past aside, without remembering the sacrifices of those who gave their lives for our country.
  d. The war we are fighting is far from over, as evidenced by the number of lives lost in this battle.
  e. The struggle to make this battle a historic one will be a long fight. We must ensure that the people who paid the ultimate price are remembered.

22. The phrase "the world will little note" means what?
  a. The world will not soon forget.
  b. The world will record what we say here.
  c. The world will not spread this information to distant places.
  d. The world will recall what we do with perfect accuracy.
  e. The world will not pay much attention.

23. There were nearly 100 years between the American Revolution and the Civil War. The speech connects ideas about these two conflicts by saying that the ideas of the Civil War

  a. threaten those of the Revolution.
  b. are similar to those of the Revolution.
  c. are newer than those of the Revolution.
  d. are better than those of the Revolution.
  e. are incomparable to those of the Revolution.

24. Why does Lincoln most likely talk about the past before he talks about the present?

  a. To incite listeners of his message to protest
  b. To remember what has been lost in the past
  c. To establish context for his main message
  d. To try to get listeners to side with his position
  e. To appeal to the audience's patriotism and loyalty

25. What is the following sentence addressing?

  Now we are engaged in a great civil war, testing whether that nation, or any nation so conceived, and so dedicated, can long endure.

  a. whether or not a nation based on ideas of freedom and equality can survive for any significant length of time
  b. whether or not the Union will be able to preserve the existing structure of the United States by preventing the Confederacy from seceding
  c. whether or not the Confederacy will be successful in seceding from the United States and surviving on its own
  d. whether or not Lincoln should continue dedicating troops to the war
  e. None of the above

26. In line 15, the word "vain" most nearly means:

  a. decisive
  b. frivolous
  c. momentous
  d. practical
  e. important

Close Relationships in the 21st Century

We all know the drill: the consequences of urban sprawl, Americans' long work hours, and devotion to television and the internet are doing nothing good for American communities.

A new study by sociologists at Duke University and the University of Arizona adds more grist to this mill, noting that Americans in 2004 had smaller networks of people with whom they talk about matters important to them than they did in 1985. (*Social Isolation in America: Changes in Core Discussion Networks Over Two Decades*, American Sociological Review, June 2006.) In 1985, Americans had three confidants, in 2004, we averaged two. The number of Americans who had no one with whom to talk about important matters almost doubled in 2004 to over 25%. Increasingly, most confidants are family: in 2004, 80% of people talked only to family about important matters and about 9% of people depended totally on their spouse.

This decrease in confidants is part (a result) of the same trend that's leaving fewer people knowing their neighbors or participating in social clubs or public affairs than in the past (phenomena noted in the book *Better Together: Restoring the American Community* by Robert Putnam and Lewis Feldstein). We know a lot of people but not necessarily very well.

Left to our own devices and cultural trends then, we seem to be moving in an unpleasant direction. Communities are formed ad hoc around specific shared individual interests. This wouldn't be bad, of course, except that those communities seem to exist only within the constraints of those shared interests and don't develop into close and meaningful relationships. The transient and specific nature of many of our relationships today can keep us socially busy without building the lasting relationships and communities that we want.

So what do we do about it if we want to change things? Harvard University's School of Government put together 150 ways to increase what they call "social capital" (i.e., the value of our social networks). Among their suggestions are: support local merchants; audition for community theater or volunteer to usher; participate in political campaigns; start or join a carpool; eat breakfast at a local gathering spot on Saturdays; and stop and make sure the person on the side of the highway is OK.

27. According to the author, which of the following was true in 2004:
   a. The average American had three confidants and 9% of people depended totally on their spouse for discussion of important matters.
   b. The average American had two confidants, and 80% of people discussed important matters only with their spouses.
   c. The average American had two confidants, and 9% of people discussed important matters only with family members.
   d. The average American had two confidants, and 80% of people discussed important matters only with family members.
   e. The average American had three confidants, and 80% of people depended totally on their spouse for discussion of important matters.

28. The author argues that the transient nature of many of today's relationships is problematic for what reason?
   a. we don't share specific interests
   b. we don't know many people
   c. it prevents us building lasting relationships and communities
   d. we have too much social capital
   e. we are overcommitted in our personal and professional lives

29. Which of the following are some of the causes to which the author attributes problems in American communities:
   a. too much homework and devotion to television
   b. urban sprawl and long work hours
   c. long work hours and growth of exercise
   d. urban sprawl and decline of sports team membership
   e. long work hours and too much homework

30. Which of the following is not something the author states was suggested by Harvard University as a way to increase social capital:

a. eat breakfast at a local gathering spot
b. join a bowling team
c. support local merchants
d. join a carpool
e. audition for community theater

31. How many ways did Harvard University's School of Government suggest to increase social capital?

a. 25
b. 50
c. 80
d. 100
e. 150

An Excerpt from "To Build a Fire" by Jack London

But all this—the mysterious, far-reaching hair-line trail, the absence of sun from the sky, the tremendous cold, and the strangeness and weirdness of it all—made no impression on the man. It was not because he was long used to it. He was a newcomer in the land, a chechaquo, and this was his first winter. The trouble with him was that he was without imagination. He was quick and alert in the things of life, but only in the things, and not in the significances. Fifty degrees below zero meant eighty-odd degrees of frost. Such fact impressed him as being cold and uncomfortable, and that was all. It did not lead him to meditate upon his frailty as a creature of temperature, and upon man's frailty in general, able only to live within certain narrow limits of heat and cold; and from there on it did not lead him to the conjectural field of immortality and man's place in the universe. Fifty degrees below zero stood for a bite of frost that hurt and that must be guarded against by the use of mittens, ear-flaps, warm moccasins, and thick socks. Fifty degrees below zero was to him just precisely fifty degrees below zero. That there should be anything more to it than that was a thought that never entered his head.

. . . .

At the man's heels trotted a dog, a big native husky, the proper wolf-dog, gray-coated and without any visible or temperamental difference from its brother, the wild wolf. The animal was depressed by the tremendous cold. It knew that it was no time for travelling. Its instinct told it a truer tale than was told to the man by the man's judgment. In reality, it was not merely colder than fifty below zero; it was colder than sixty below, than seventy below. It was seventy-five below zero. Since the freezing-point is thirty-two above zero, it meant that one hundred and seven degrees of frost obtained. The dog did not know anything about thermometers. Possibly in its brain there was no sharp consciousness of a condition of very cold such as was in the man's brain. But the brute had its instinct. It experienced a vague but menacing apprehension that subdued it and made it slink along at the man's heels, and that made it question eagerly every unwonted movement of the man as if expecting him to go into camp or to seek shelter somewhere and build a fire. The dog had learned fire, and it wanted fire, or else to burrow under the snow and cuddle its warmth away from the air.

32. In the story that this passage comes from, the main character struggles against the cold and eventually freezes to death. Given this information, which of the following devices is the author using in the first paragraph?

a. First person point of view
b. Hyperbole
c. Onomatopoeia
d. Foreshadowing
e. Symbolism

33. What is the point of view used in this passage?

a. First person
b. First person plural
c. Unreliable narrator
d. Third person omniscient
e. Third person limited

34. In what sense should the passage be taken when it mentions immortality and man's place in the universe?

a. Humans are frail
b. Humans are stronger than nature
c. Humans will one day attain immortality
d. Humans are smarter than animals
e. Human inventions will always protect mankind from nature

35. In what way does the narrator say the dog is better off than the man?

a. The dog is better equipped for the cold because of its fur.
b. The dog has a better conscious idea of what the cold means.
c. The dog's instinct guides it, while the man's intellect fails him.
d. The dog understands mankind's place in the universe.
e. The dog is humble before nature.

Comets

Comets are bodies that orbit the sun. They are distinguishable from asteroids by the presence of comas or tails. In the outer solar system, comets remain frozen and are so small that they are difficult to detect from Earth. As a comet approaches the inner solar system, solar radiation causes the materials within the comet to vaporize and trail off the nuclei. The released dust and gas form a fuzzy atmosphere called the coma, and the force exerted on the coma causes a tail to form, pointing away from the sun.

Comet nuclei are made of ice, dust, rock and frozen gases and vary widely in size: from 100 meters or so to tens of kilometers across. The comas may be even larger than the sun. Because of their low mass, they do not become spherical and have irregular shapes.

There are over 3,500 known comets, and the number is steadily increasing. This represents only a small portion of the total comets existing, however. Most comets are too faint to be visible without the aid of a telescope; the number of comets visible to the naked eye is around one a year.

Comets leave a trail of solid debris behind them. If a comet's path crosses Earth's path, there will likely be meteor showers as Earth passes through the trail of debris.

Many comets and asteroids have collided into Earth. Some scientists believe that comets hitting Earth about 4 billion years ago brought a significant portion of the water in Earth's oceans. There are still many near-Earth comets.

Most comets have oval shaped orbits that take them close to the sun for part of their orbit and then out further into the solar system for the remainder of the orbit. Comets are often classified according to the length of their orbital period: short period comets have orbital periods of less than 200 years, long period comets have orbital periods of more than 200 years, single apparition comets have trajectories which cause them to permanently leave the solar system after passing the sun once.

36. What does the passage claim distinguishes comets from asteroids?
   a. The make-up of their nuclei
   b. The presence of comas or tails
   c. Their orbital periods
   d. Their irregular shapes
   e. Their classification system

37. According to the passage, which of the following is true?
   a. There are 350 known comets, and the number is steadily increasing.
   b. There are 3,500 known comets, and the number is staying the same.
   c. There are 3,500 known comets, and many more comets that aren't known.
   d. Most comets are visible to the naked eye.
   e. None of the above

38. According to the passage, why do comets have irregular shapes?
   a. because they are not spherical
   b. because they have orbital periods
   c. because of their low mass
   d. because of their tails
   e. because they are made of ice and frozen gases

39. What does the passage claim about the size of comets?
   a. Some are tens of kilometers across and can be seen without the use of a telescope
   b. Some are tens of kilometers across, and the coma is never larger than the Sun.
   c. Some are 100 meters across, and the coma is never larger than the Sun.
   d. The smallest comet is at least a kilometer, and the coma can be larger than the Sun.
   e. Some are tens of kilometers across, and the coma can be larger than the Sun.

40. According to the passage, what does the name "single apparition comets" mean?
   a. They only appear during the part of their orbit that is nearest to the sun.
   b. They stay in the solar system even though they are only apparent once.
   c. Their orbital periods are so long they only appear once across millennia.
   d. They only remain in the solar system long enough to pass the sun once.
   e. They only appear once every 200 years.

Section 3: Verbal

Synonyms

Directions: Select the one word whose meaning is closest to the word in capital letters.

1. ENTHRALL
   a. bizarre
   b. devote
   c. extreme
   d. fascinate
   e. weary

2. COWARD
   a. boor
   b. brave
   c. gutless
   d. judge
   e. hero

3. NOVICE
   a. beginner
   b. expert
   c. naught
   d. nurse
   e. veteran

4. TEMPERATE
   a. extreme
   b. lenient
   c. moderate
   d. taut
   e. disagreeable

5. AUTHENTIC
   a. colorful
   b. flimsy
   c. genuine
   d. laughable
   e. invalid

6. SALVAGE
   a. bless
   b. recover
   c. slobber
   d. swagger
   e. injure

7. VERNACULAR

    a. ballad
    b. language
    c. poison
    d. silence
    e. formal

8. ATTEST

    a. accommodate
    b. bewitch
    c. heed
    d. vouch
    e. disprove

9. DERELICT

    a. abandoned
    b. corrupted
    c. depressed
    d. dispirited
    e. improved

10. ORDAIN

    a. adorn
    b. arrange
    c. command
    d. create
    e. neglect

11. HAUGHTY

    a. arrogant
    b. bitter
    c. obscure
    d. perilous
    e. humble

12. LAPSE

    a. award
    b. error
    c. margin
    d. prank
    e. accurate

13. NAUSEATE

    a. annoy
    b. crave
    c. repulse
    d. rival
    e. attract

14. PALTRY

   a. cheap
   b. valuable
   c. peaceful
   d. severely
   e. plenty

15. REFINED

   a. aromatic
   b. blatant
   c. cultured
   d. frightened
   e. rough

16. VIRTUAL

   a. potent
   b. real
   c. simulated
   d. visible
   e. authentic

17. LOATHE

   a. charge
   b. exist
   c. fear
   d. hate
   e. commend

18. MIMIC

   a. curtail
   b. delve
   c. imitate
   d. recall
   e. deviate

19. BRITTLE

   a. broad
   b. fragile
   c. radical
   d. smooth
   e. flexible

20. WRETCHED

   a. absorbed
   b. awry
   c. miserable
   d. wicked
   e. lively

21. FALLIBLE
a. certain
b. infallible
c. precise
d. careful
e. imperfect

22. ANGUISH
a. loneliness
b. confusion
c. anger
d. sorrow
e. relief

23. VOLATILE
a. firm
b. calm
c. predictable
d. masked
e. unstable

24. PALLID
a. healthy
b. sickly
c. rosy
d. deep
e. glowing

25. DEMURE
a. forward
b. outgoing
c. modest
d. sociable
e. bold

26. ADHERE
a. unfasten
b. revere
c. loose
d. convince
e. unite

27. SOILED
a. dirty
b. sullen
c. sultry
d. dainty
e. rich

28. PLIABLE

- a. fragile
- b. contrary
- c. rigid
- d. light
- e. spongy

29. DISDAIN

- a. favor
- b. fancy
- c. calculate
- d. scorn
- e. respect

30. STOIC

- a. bored
- b. tolerant
- c. grumble
- d. stammer
- e. impatient

Analogies

Directions: For each of the following questions, you will find terms and five answer choices designated a, b, c, d, and e. Select the one answer choice that best completes the analogy.

31. Punishment is to reprimand as impetuous is to

- a. cautious
- b. considerate
- c. hasty
- d. meticulous
- e. poor

32. Cue is to queue as

- a. incessant is to relentless
- b. joule is to jewel
- c. penultimate is to ultimate
- d. redress is to transgress
- e. solve is to revolve

33. Frog is to amphibian as hydrogen is to

- a. aerospace
- b. element
- c. galaxy
- d. instrumental
- e. seismograph

34. Light is to hologram as film is to

a. aesthetic
b. panoramic
c. photographer
d. transistor
e. video camera

35. Superficial is to mature as

a. approach is to reproach
b. beguile is to deceive
c. exorbitant is to excess
d. noxious is to toxic
e. submissive is to defiant

36. Innovation is to prodigy as

a. editorial is to epic
b. extract is to illusionist
c. manuscript is to composer
d. office is to faculty
e. painting is to narrator

37. Rubber is to pliable as

a. dream is to reality
b. legacy is to immutable
c. luck is to serendipity
d. psychopath is to medicine
e. rift is to solid

38. Kayak is to quest as

a. antibiotic is to sneeze
b. cloister is to party
c. intercom is to communication
d. memoir is to personal
e. prudence is to foresight

39. Particle is to remnant as

a. ameliorate is to alleviate
b. irreverent is to religious
c. indifference is to remorse
d. sanguine is to pessimistic
e. sedentary is to energetic

40. Cardiologist is to specialist as

a. artifact is to journey
b. crusade is to amoral
c. kiwi is to vitamin
d. parable is to fiction
e. tribulation is to adversity

41. Politician is to policy as

   a. coach is to extrovert
   b. critic is to synopsis
   c. emissary is to dramatization
   d. police is to illegal
   e. spendthrift is to discipline

42. Error is to iniquity as

   a. cliché is to frivolous
   b. compassion is to forgiveness
   c. fragment is to whole
   d. lengthy is to transient
   e. wave is to tsunami

43. Gorilla is to guerilla as

   a. adroit is to incompetent
   b. enigma is to mystery
   c. lurch is to perch
   d. pseudonym is to prestige
   e. sign is to sine

44. Apathy is to persistence as

   a. anecdote is to narrative
   b. fatuous is to dense
   c. pervasive is to ubiquitous
   d. profuse is to sparse
   e. vale is to veil

45. Index is to book as elegy is to

   a. artifact
   b. audition
   c. equinox
   d. funeral
   e. penance

46. Tenet is to professor as

   a. exposition is to silence
   b. facsimile is to replica
   c. parody is to comedian
   d. pollen is to bee
   e. terrarium is to athlete

47. Underdog is to audacious as conspirator is to

   a. altruistic
   b. elusive
   c. illegible
   d. passive
   e. relic

48. Marshal is to martial as

   a. delude is to mislead
   b. earn is to urn
   c. lithe is to tithe
   d. ornate is to plain
   e. repel is to impel

49. Dollar is to salary as

   a. antihero is to prodigious
   b. festival is to decadence
   c. sprinter is to speedster
   d. tear is to melancholy
   e. wheel is to vehicle

50. Intermission is to drama as plant is to

   a. compliment
   b. constellation
   c. habitat
   d. memorabilia
   e. metropolitan

51. Copious is to extensive as

   a. amiss is to proper
   b. dubious is to undoubted
   c. epitome is to felicity
   d. resilient is to supple
   e. supreme is to paramount

52. Antagonist is to fiction as

   a. admonition is to forewarning
   b. marriage is to fidelity
   c. journal is to database
   d. mural is to iconic
   e. protagonist is to hero

53. Novella is to brief as

   a. computer is to microscopic
   b. dorm is to resilient
   c. infant is to naïve
   d. master is to unkempt
   e. star is to monitor

54. Jog is to marathon as hypothesis is to

   a. discovery
   b. forgery
   c. irate
   d. punishment
   e. surreal

55. Opinion is to connoisseur as

- a. hybrid is to innovator
- b. itinerary is to plan
- c. montage is to scientist
- d. riot is to heat
- e. season is to farmer

56. Insight is to decision as

- a. advocate is to defend
- b. conjecture is to truth
- c. guide is to misled
- d. ignition is to fuel
- e. neighbor is to fence

57. Antipathy is to sympathy as convivial is to

- a. avarice
- b. gloomy
- c. harmonious
- d. sociable
- e. wary

58. Espionage is to discreet as kindling is to

- a. grotesque
- b. majestic
- c. novelty
- d. ominous
- e. suave

59. Benediction is to ceremony as

- a. aroma is to odor
- b. landmark is to city
- c. introvert is to friend
- d. milestone is to suburb
- e. relationship is to personality

60. Interjection is to attorney as

- a. claim is to rejection
- b. insinuation is to judge
- c. money is to auction
- d. veil is to wedding
- e. voucher is to redeemer

Section 4: Quantitative

1. On his last math test, Sam got 2 questions correct for every 3 questions he missed. If the test had a total of 60 questions, how many questions did Sam answer correctly?

    a. 12
    b. 24
    c. 36
    d. 40
    e. 60

2. Expand $(3x + 1)(7x + 10)$.

    a. $12x^2 + 17x + 10$
    b. $21x^2 + 37x + 10$
    c. $21x^2 + 23x + 10$
    d. $21x^2 + 37x + 9$
    e. $10x^2 + 21x + 11$

3. In the figure below, lines a and b are parallel. Find the value of x.

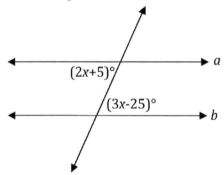

    a. $x = 22$
    b. $x = 30$
    c. $x = 40$
    d. $x = 55$
    e. $x = 65$

4. Joseph purchased 12 pounds of peaches at 80 cents per pound. He calculated the total amount as $12 \times \$0.80 = \$9.60$. Another method Joseph could have used to calculate the total cost of the peaches is:

    a. $(10 \times \$0.80) + (2 \times \$0.80)$
    b. $(12 \times \$0.40) + (2 \times \$0.80)$
    c. $(12 \times \$0.20) + (12 \times \$0.20)$
    d. $(2 \times \$0.80) + (10 \times \$0.40)$
    e. $(10 \times \$0.80) + (2 \times \$0.40)$

5. Joshua has to earn more than 92 points on the state test in order to qualify for an academic scholarship. Each question is worth 4 points, and the test has a total of 30 questions. Let x represent the number of test questions.

Which of the following inequalities can be solved to determine the number of questions Joshua must answer correctly?

   a. $4x < 30$
   b. $4x < 92$
   c. $4x > 30$
   d. $x > 30$
   e. $4x > 92$

6. If $\frac{4}{x-3} - \frac{2}{x} = 1$, then $x = ?$

   a. -6
   b. -1
   c. -6 or -1
   d. -1 or 6
   e. 6 or 1

7. The histogram below represents the overall GRE scores for a sample of college students. Which of the following is a true statement?

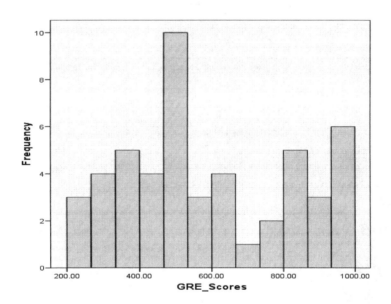

   a. The range of GRE scores is approximately 600.
   b. The average GRE score is 750.
   c. The median GRE score is approximately 500.
   d. The fewest number of college students had an approximate score of 800.
   e. The median GRE score is approximately 300.

8. If $a \neq 0$, then $12a^2b \div 3a = ?$

    a. $4a$
    b. $4b$
    c. $4ab$
    d. $9b^2$
    e. $9ab$

9. If the square of twice the sum of x and three is equal to the product of twenty-four and x, which of these is a possible value of x?

    a. $6 + 3\sqrt{2}$
    b. $\dfrac{3}{2}$
    c. $-3i$
    d. -3
    e. -9

10. What statement best describes the rate of change?

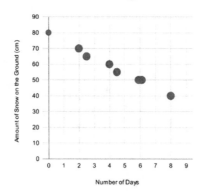

    a. Every day, the snow melts 10 centimeters.
    b. Every day, the snow melts 5 centimeters.
    c. Every day, the snow increases by 10 centimeters.
    d. Every day, the snow increases by 5 centimeters.
    e. None of the above

11. What is the expected value of drawing a card from a deck when the cards are labeled 1-5?

    a. 1.5
    b. 2
    c. 2.5
    d. 3
    e. 3.5

12. Which of the following represents the expected value of the number of tails Adam will get after tossing a coin 6 times?

    a. 2
    b. 3
    c. 6
    d. 9
    e. 12

13. Based on the figure below, if $\overline{BG} = 6x - 4$ and $\overline{GD} = 2x + 8$, what is the length of $\overline{GD}$?

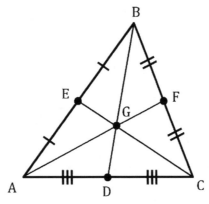

  a. 10
  b. 14
  c. 28
  d. 34
  e. 56

14. Matthew has to earn more than 96 points on his high school entrance exam in order to be eligible for varsity sports. Each question is worth 3 points, and the test has a total of 40 questions. Let x represent the number of test questions. How many questions can Matthew answer incorrectly and still qualify for varsity sports?

  a. $x < 8$
  b. $x > 8$
  c. $x > 32$
  d. $0 < x \leq 8$
  e. $0 \leq x < 8$

15. A box in the form of a rectangular solid has a square base of 5 feet in length, a width of 5 feet, and a height of h feet. If the volume of the rectangular solid is 200 cubic feet, which of the following equations may be used to find h?

  a. $5h = 200$
  b. $5h^2 = 200$
  c. $25h = 200$
  d. $h = 200 \div 5$
  e. $10h = 200$

16. Robert is planning to drive 1,800 miles on a cross-country trip. If his car gets 30 miles to the gallon, and his tank holds 12 gallons of gas, how many tanks of gas will he need to complete the trip?

  a. 3 tanks of gas
  b. 5 tanks of gas
  c. 10 tanks of gas
  d. 30 tanks of gas
  e. 60 tanks of gas

17. Which line appears to have a slope of 2?

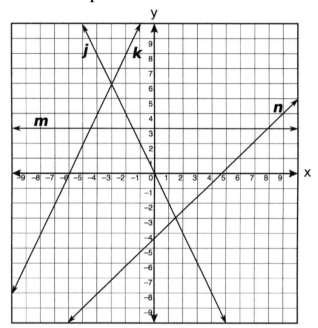

- a. Line j
- b. Line k
- c. Line m
- d. Line n
- e. None of the lines

18. Three quarters of the students running a 100-yard race finished with an average time of 16 seconds. The remaining 25% of students finished with an average time of 12 seconds. What was the average time overall?

- a. 13 seconds
- b. 14 seconds
- c. 15 seconds
- d. 16 seconds
- e. 20 seconds

19. A bag contains 8 red marbles, 3 blue marbles, and 4 green marbles. What is the probability Carlos draws a red marble, does not replace it, and then draws another red marble?

- a. $\dfrac{2}{15}$
- b. $\dfrac{4}{15}$
- c. $\dfrac{64}{225}$
- d. $\dfrac{32}{105}$
- e. $\dfrac{15}{29}$

20. If $\sqrt{3x-2} = x-2$, then $x = ?$

    a. 1
    b. 6
    c. −1 or 6
    d. 1 or 6
    e. None of the above

21. If $7\sqrt{x} + 16 = 79$, what is the value of x?

    a. 6
    b. 9
    c. 27
    d. 46
    e. 81

22. Which of the following is equivalent to $27x^3 + y^3$?

    a. $(3x+y)(3x+y)(3x+y)$
    b. $(3x+y)(9x^2 - 3xy + y^2)$
    c. $(3x-y)(9x^2 + 3xy + y^2)$
    d. $(3x-y)(9x^2 + 9xy + y^2)$
    e. $(3x+y)(9x^2 - 3xy - y^2)$

23. On a road map, $\frac{1}{4}$ inch represents 8 miles of actual road distance. The towns of Dinuba and Clovis are measured to be $2\frac{1}{8}$ inches apart on the map. What is the actual distance, in miles, between the two towns?

    a. 32
    b. 40
    c. 60
    d. 68
    e. 76

24. In the figure below, ΔJKL is dilated to the image $\Delta J'K'L'$.

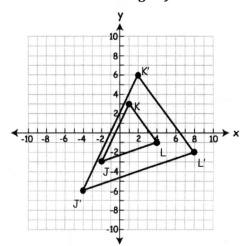

What is the scale factor of the dilation?

a. $\dfrac{1}{3}$

b. $\dfrac{1}{2}$

c. $\dfrac{3}{4}$

d. 2

e. 3

25. In the figure shown here, the arc $\widehat{AB}$ is 4 meters long, and the total perimeter of the circle is 48 meters. Which of the following best represents the measure of $\angle AOB$, which subtends arc $\widehat{AB}$?

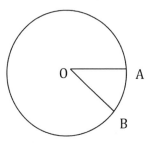

a. 15 degrees

b. 30 degrees

c. 45 degrees

d. 55 degrees

e. 60 degrees

Answer Key and Explanations for Test #1

Section 1: Quantitative

1. B: To solve, first subtract Jerry's weight from the total permitted: 800-200 = 600. Divide 600 by 4 (the four pieces of equipment) to get 150, the average weight.

2. C: The correct answer is $3000. Besides the $600 he has remaining, Chan has paid out a total of 30% + 20% + 20% + 10% = 80% of his bonus for the expenses described in the question. Therefore, the $600 represents the remaining 20%. To determine his total bonus, solve $\frac{100}{20} \times 600 = 3000$.

3. A: If the ratio of pennies to nickels is 2:6, the ratio of the pennies to the combined coins is 2:2+6, or 2:8. This is $\frac{1}{4}$ or, expressed as a percentage, 25%.

4. D: The literal equation may be solved for x by first subtracting b from both sides of the equation. Doing so gives $ax = c - b$. Dividing both sides of the equation by a gives $x = \frac{c-b}{a}$.

5. A: There are 4 members of the first set and 4 members of the second set, so there are $4(4) = 16$ possible products for cd. cd is odd only when both c and d are odd. There are 2 odd numbers in the first set and two in the second set, so $2(2) = 4$ products are odd and the probability cd is odd is 4/16 or 1/4.

6. C: The given equations form a system of linear equations. Since the first equation is already given in terms of x, it will be easier to solve the system using the substitution method. Start by substituting $2y - 3$ for x in the second equation:

$$2x + \frac{1}{2}y = 3$$
$$2(2y - 3) + \frac{1}{2}y = 3$$

Next, solve the resulting equation for y. Distribute the 2 and then combine like y-terms in the result:

$$4y - 6 + \frac{1}{2}y = 3$$
$$\frac{9}{2}y - 6 = 3$$

Finally, isolate the variable y by adding 6 to both sides and then dividing both sides by the coefficient of y, which is $\frac{9}{2}$ (or, equivalently, multiply by 2 and divide by 9):

$$\frac{9}{2}y = 9$$
$$y = 2$$

7. B: Add the 14 blue, 6 red, 12 green and 8 purple buttons to get a total of 40 buttons. If 25 buttons are removed, there are 15 buttons remaining in the bag. The chance of drawing a red button is now

$\frac{1}{3}$. So, you divide 15 into thirds to get 5 red buttons remaining in the bag. The original total of red buttons was 6; so $6 - 5 = 1$: one red button was removed, choice (B).

8. E: The sides of a triangle must all be greater than zero. The sum of the lengths of the two shorter sides must be greater than the length of the third side. Since we are looking for the minimum value of the perimeter, assume the longer of the two given sides, which is 6, is the longest side of the triangle. Then the third side must be greater than $6 - 4 = 2$. Since we are told the sides are all integral numbers, the last side must be 3 units in length. Thus, the minimum length for the perimeter is $4 + 6 + 3 = 13$ units.

9. C: A set of six numbers with an average of 4 must have a collective sum of 24. The two numbers that average 2 will add up to 4, so the remaining numbers must add up to 20. The average of these four numbers can be calculated: $20/4 = 5$.

10. A: This table shows the numbers of coins added to the first few squares and the equivalent powers of 2:

Square	1	2	3	4
Coins	1	2	4	8
Power of 2	2^0	2^1	2^2	2^3

In this series, the number of coins on each is the consecutive powers of 2. The reason is that the number doubles with each consecutive square. However, the series of powers begins with 0 for the first square. For the 64th square, the number of coins will be 2^{63}.

11. D: First establish a variable, s, for the length of the smaller square. Since the larger square is 3 feet longer than the smaller one, its length is $s + 3$. Given that the difference between the areas of the two squares is 75, and the area of any square is equal to its side lengths squared, the following equation can be established and solved:

$$(s + 3)^2 - s^2 = 75$$
$$(s + 3)(s + 3) - s^2 = 75$$
$$s^2 + 6s + 9 - s^2 = 75$$
$$6s + 9 = 75$$

Isolate the variable and divide both sides by its coefficient to solve for s:

$$6s = 66$$
$$s = 11$$

12. A: Setting the cost of shipping equal to the amount received gives us the equation $3{,}000 + 100x = 400x$. Subtract $100x$ from both sides to get $3{,}000 = 300x$, then divide both sides by 300 to see that $x = 10$.

13. B: $\frac{x}{8}$ and $\frac{y}{4}$ both equal 4. Now, $\frac{x}{8} = 4$, and $x = 8 \times 4 = 32$.

Then, $\frac{y}{4} = 4$. So, $y = 4 \times 4 = 16$

$$x - y = 32 - 16 = 16$$

14. A: To solve, you will need to move the decimal 4 places. Since the scientific notation had a negative power of 10, move the decimal left. If the power of 10 had been positive, you would have needed to move it to the right. In this problem, solve as follows:

$$7.4 \times 10^{-4} = 7.4 \times 0.0001 = 0.00074$$

15. E: The area of the squares whose side lengths are the legs of the triangles, a and b, are each 9 squares. If the whole squares, and half squares, in the grid are summed, the area of the square with side length c is 18 squares. Add the area of all three squares together to get the total: $9 + 9 + 18 = 36$ units.

16. A: Set up an equation and then solve.

$$
\begin{aligned}
5 + 6x &= 77 && \text{Subtract 5 from both sides of the equation} \\
6x &= 72 && \text{Divide both sides by 6} \\
x &= 12
\end{aligned}
$$

17. C: Multiply the first numbers in each of the parentheses to get 6, and add the exponents of the tens. $(2 \times 10^5) \times (3 \times 10^4) = 2 \times 3 \times 10^{5+4} = 6 \times 10^9$.

18. D: When the factors, $(x - 4)$ and $(x + 7)$ are multiplied, the x-terms sum to $3x$ and the constants produce a product of -28.

19. B: Solve the inequality by changing the inequality sign to an equal sign and solve the resulting equation by factoring the left side:

$$
\begin{aligned}
x^2 - 7x + 10 &= 0 \\
(x - 2)(x - 5) &= 0 \\
x - 2 = 0 \qquad & x - 5 = 0 \\
x = 2 \qquad\quad & x = 5
\end{aligned}
$$

Since the original inequality sign was a greater-than-or-equal-to sign (rather than just a greater-than sign), the solution set will include $x = 2$ and $x = 5$.

These two solutions divide the number line into three distinct regions: $x < 2$, $2 < x < 5$, and $x > 5$. To see which regions are in the solution set, pick one test value from each region and substitute it in the original inequality. If the result is a true inequality, then the whole region is part of the solution set. Otherwise, the whole region is not part in the solution set:

Region	Test Value	$x^2 - 7x + 10 \geq 0$	Conclusion
$x < 2$	0	$(0)^2 - 7(0) + 10 \geq 0$ $7 \geq 0$	Part of the solution set
$2 < x < 5$	3	$(3)^2 - 7(3) + 10 \geq 0$ $9 - 21 + 10 \geq 0$ $-2 \geq 0$	Not part of the solution set
$x > 5$	6	$(6)^2 - 7(6) + 10 \geq 0$ $36 - 42 + 10 \geq 0$ $4 \geq 0$	Part of the solution set

Therefore, the solution set is $x \leq 2$ or $x \geq 5$.

20. C: First write the equation for line A in slope-intercept form: $y = mx + b$ where m is the slope and b is the y-intercept.

$$5y - 100x = 25$$
$$5y = 100x + 25$$
$$y = 20x + 5$$

Based on the slope-intercept form of Equation A, the slope, $m = 20$ and the y-intercept, $b = 5$.

21. B: The chart indicates that 40% of the total recycled material is paper. Since 50,000 tons of material are recycled every month, the total amount of paper will be 40% of 50,000 tons, or $\frac{40}{100} \times 50,000 = 20,000$ tons.

22. C: The volume of the box is the product of $\sqrt{3}$, $2\sqrt{5}$, and 4. To multiply two or more square root radicals, multiply the coefficients and then multiply the radicands:

$$\sqrt{3} \times 2\sqrt{5} \times 4 = 2\sqrt{15} \times 4$$
$$= 8\sqrt{15}$$

23. C: Because both expressions share the factor 10^3, we can simply factor and add the ones places. $(8 \times 10^3) + (1 \times 10^3) = (1 + 8)(10^3) = 9 \times 10^3$.

24. B: The y-intercept of the line is $(0, -1)$. Another point on the line is $(1,0)$. Slope is the vertical change over horizontal change which is $\frac{1}{1} = 1$. Plugging this information into the slope-intercept form $y = mx + b$, the equation is $y = x - 1$.

25. C: When the dress is marked down by 20%, the cost of the dress is 80% of its original price. Since a percentage can be written as a fraction by placing the percentage over 100, the reduced price of the dress can be written as $\frac{80}{100}x$, or $\frac{4}{5}x$, where x is the original price. When discounted an extra 25%, the dress costs 75% of the reduced price. This results in the expression $\frac{75}{100}\left(\frac{4}{5}x\right)$, which can be simplified to $\frac{3}{4}\left(\frac{4}{5}x\right)$, or $\frac{3}{5}x$. So the final price of the dress is three-fifths of the original price.

Section 2: Reading Comprehension

1. B: There is no indication in the passage that the Bennets are interested in becoming friends with Mr. Bingley (choice A), that Mr. Bingley would be a valuable business connection (choice C), that Mr. Bingley has any prior knowledge of the Bennet daughters (choice D), or that Mr. Bingley has an interest in acquiring more property beyond Netherfiled Park (choice E). Mrs. Bennet tells her husband that a new neighbor is moving in: "Mrs. Long says that Netherfield is taken by a young man of large fortune." Mrs. Bennet is sure he will make an excellent husband for one of her daughters: "You must know that I am thinking of his marrying one of them."

2. A: Mrs. Bennet is quite excited and feels that Mr. Bingley is likely to marry one of her daughters. She tells her husband that Mr. Bingley is a "single man of large fortune; four or five thousand a year. What a fine thing for our girls!"

3. B: Mrs. Bennet is annoyed and fed up with her husband's seeming indifference to Mr. Bingley: "'My dear Mr. Bennet,' replied his wife, 'how can you be so tiresome!'"

4. A: "It is a truth universally acknowledged" means that something is understood to be true by the general public.

5. E: Mr. Bennet is facetiously asking if the idea of marriage (particularly to one of his own daughters) was Mr. Bingley's intention when he agreed to rent Netherfield Park.

6. B: The passage discusses Helen Keller's life beginning with her birth and continuing on into her adulthood.

7. E: The passage does mention that Helen graduated from Radcliffe College (choice A), and the passage does tell about Anne's role as Helen's teacher (choice B), but the passage as a whole does not focus on Helen's time at college or Anne's life outside of her role as teacher. The passage does not mention services available for the deaf and blind (choice C). The passage does tell about Helen Keller's life.

8. C: The second paragraph explains why Anne Sullivan was crucial to Helen's life, and the third paragraph elaborates on how Anne helped Helen succeed.

9. C: The author's use of the phrase "Helen learned at an incredible rate" and the word "remarkable" to describe Helen's life are two examples of the author's admiration.

10. D: Although all of the answer choices represent major events in Helen's life, the passage specifies that the advent of Anne Sullivan was the turning point in Helen's life when she began to learn to communicate with other people. "All of that began to change in March 1887 when Anne Sullivan came to live with the Kellers and be Helen's teacher. Anne taught Helen to communicate by forming letters with her fingers held in another person's hand."

11. A: The passage does not indicate that Helen's parents were jealous of Anne (choice B), glad to give Anne responsibility for Helen (choice C), had any preference in their daughter's choice of a college (choice D), or wished that they had asked for Mrs. Sullivan's help at an earlier time (choice E). The passage does say that Helen's parents loved her and that they brought Anne to their home to be Helen's teacher. This implies that they were frustrated by their own inability to help Helen and were looking for someone who could help.

12. C: The passage describes several distinctive features of annelid anatomy and tells how some of them differ from other worms.

13. E: The text gives the example of feet specializing into grasping organs to illustrate this evolutionary advantage of segmental plasticity.

14. C: The text defines metemeres as segments, and discusses segmentation as the distinguishing feature of the phylum.

15. D: The paragraph tells us that annelids can live in salt or fresh water and on land, and then gives examples.

16. D: The author compares (A) annelids and nematodes as both having a fluid-filled internal *coelom* or cavity separating the body wall and gut, and both having this cavity involved in their locomotion. The author also contrasts (B) the two phyla in that annelids develop this cavity much later during both embryonic growth and ("presumably") evolutionary progress. Hence both comparison and contrast (D) relationships are established, meaning (C) and (E) are incorrect.

17. B: After the initial topic sentence, the first paragraph discusses metameric segmentation as a distinctive feature of annelids. The second paragraph discusses annelid body parts, i.e., the gut, body wall, and *coelom*, including their functions, development, and differences and similarities of the latter between annelids and nematodes. The third paragraph discusses annelid body systems, including excretory, circulatory, respiratory, and nervous. The fourth and final paragraph includes annelid habitat adaptations and names three well-known types.

18. D: Hughes uses (extended) metaphor by describing the concrete presence of an animal, a fox, to represent the abstract entity of an inspiration for the writer to produce poetry. From beyond the blank window, starless sky, and dark forest, the fox, as a totem for the writer's imagination, approaches from without to inspire, its pawprints in the snow symbolizing print appearing on the blank page. Foreshadowing (A) is the literary device of hinting earlier in a work at something that will become more apparent later. Irony (B) is the device of creating a discrepancy between what is expected and what really occurs (verbal, dramatic, or situational irony). Hughes's work is notable for NOT including any overused expressions known as clichés (C). Finally, there is no significant literary or historical reference for an allusion (E).

19. C: The poem describes how the poet is inspired to write, using the fox to embody the thought that enters the poet's mind (hence the title "The Thought-Fox"). The fox's natural actions (A) are thus symbolic rather than literal. The poet is not inspired by nature (B); in this poem, he uses an element of nature (the fox) to represent the thought that he receives and writes. The fox's entering "the head" is not a literal attack (D) but a symbolic representation of having or getting that thought. The poet does not work for a print shop (E), instead he is writing down his ideas of inspiration.

20. E: The poet's passivity and lack of control over the thought, or content, of his writing can be interpreted from Hughes's separation of the thought, which does not arise from within his head, but approaches symbolically in the form of a fox from outside of his head, his body, and even his house. This separation is emphasized by the description of the Thought-Fox as "Coming about its own business." The poet as passive recipient is further shown in the last stanza, where the fox "...enters the dark hole of the head." This passivity of the artist is further reflected in the last line, "The page is printed," wherein Hughes uses the passive voice to represent the thought/writing process, rather than saying that he himself prints the page.

21. B: Lincoln begins this speech by discussing the founding of the U.S. and what the original purpose of the U.S. was. Then, he goes on to talk about how the U.S. is currently engaged in a war intended to fracture the nation, and he states that the battle being discussed was one large tragedy that came out of the war. Next, Lincoln says that his speech and even the memorial itself can't truly honor those who died, and that it's up to those who survived to continue the fight to ensure the nation does not break apart. Answer B best communicates this message.

22. E: The sentence in which this phrase is found is: The world will little note, nor long remember, what we say here, but can never forget what they did here. In this context, the phrase "the world will little note" means that no one outside of those in attendance or possibly those outside the country will pay attention to the speech or the ceremony. This eliminates all of the answer choices except E.

23. A: The ideals of the revolution are addressed in the first paragraph: Four score and seven years ago our fathers brought forth, upon this continent, a new nation, conceived in Liberty, and dedicated to the proposition that all men are created equal. This introduces the point that Lincoln is trying to make about the battle at hand and the war as a whole: the Civil War is threatening the ideas upon which the nation was created.

24. C: There is a comparison between the ideas of the Revolution and the Civil War in this speech. To facilitate understanding of this comparison, Lincoln has to set the stage by telling his audience about the past event he is referencing. This establishes the context of his message.

25. A: This line directly references the idea in the previous paragraph, which is that the U.S. is a nation that was created to ensure liberty and equality. This sentence talks about how the Civil War is testing whether or not a nation that was created to ensure liberty and equality can really survive.

26. B: When President Lincoln argues that the people who died at Gettysburg did not die in vain, he asserts that their passing was not frivolous or unimportant or meaningless.

27. D: This information is all given in the second paragraph.

28. C: In the fourth paragraph, the author states that the transient nature of relationships based solely on shared interests is keeping us "socially busy without building the lasting relationships and communities that we want."

29. B: The author lists urban sprawl, long work hours, and devotion to television and the internet as causes of problems for American communities.

30. B: This is the only one of the answer choices that is not listed in the fourth paragraph as suggestions put forth by the Harvard University study.

31. E: The author states in the fourth paragraph that Harvard University School of Government put forth 150 suggestions for increasing social capital.

32. D: Foreshadowing is the best choice. Choice (A), first person point of view, does not answer the question and is incorrect because the story is told from the third person point of view. Choice (B) is incorrect because "hyperbole" generally refers to unrealistic exaggeration, but the imagery in this passage is realistic, even if it does describe extreme conditions. Choice (C), onomatopoeia, is incorrect because the passage contains no words like "cluck" or "quack" that sound like what they describe. Choice (E), symbolism, does not adequately answer the question posed.

33. D: Choice (E) is close to being the answer, but Choice (D) is the best answer because the narrator can enter the consciousness of both the man and the dog, making it third person omniscient. Choices (A) and (B) can be ruled out because the narrator does not use the pronouns "I" or "we." Choice (C) does not seem likely because the passage gives us no reason to believe that the narrator's account of this information cannot be trusted.

34. A: Choice A offers the best interpretation. The passage refers to immortality and man's place in the universe; the man does not have the imagination to contemplate such issues, and he does not seem to realize the frailty of humans on the planet. Choices (B), (C), and (E) contradict or misinterpret the meaning of the passage. Choice (D) is not really implied by the passage; in fact, the dog's instincts make it seem more intelligent than the man in a certain sense.

35. C: It can be supported by the following quotation: "[The dog's] instinct told it a truer tale than was told to the man by the man's judgment." Choice (A) may sound possible, but it does not really capture the narrator's main point of comparison. Choice (B) can be contradicted by the following quotation: "In its brain there was no sharp consciousness of a condition of very cold such as was in the man's brain." Choices (D) and (E) can also be contradicted by the preceding quotation.

36. B: The second sentence in the passage notes that comets are distinguishable from asteroids by the presence of comas or tails.

37. C: The third paragraph notes that there are over 3,500 known comets. It also notes that this represents only a small portion of those in existence.

38. C: The second paragraph notes that because they have low mass, they don't become spherical and have irregular shapes.

39. E: The second paragraph notes that some comets may be tens of kilometers across. The passage also notes that comas may be larger than the Sun.

40. D: The passage defines single apparition comets as those whose trajectories make them pass the sun once and then exit our solar system permanently. It also describes most comets as having oval orbits wherein they are nearer to the sun during part of their orbit and then move farther away from the sun, but still within the solar system. The passage defines short and long orbital periods, but does not include long orbital periods in the definition apparition comets.

Section 3: Verbal

1. D: To enthrall is to fascinate or mesmerize.

2. C: A coward is someone who is gutless or lacks courage when facing danger.

3. A: A novice is someone who is new to the circumstances, or the person is a beginner.

4. C: Temperate means to be moderate or restrained.

5. C: Something authentic is genuine or true.

6. B: To salvage something is to save or recover it from wreckage, destruction, or loss.

7. B: Vernacular is the speech or language of a place.

8. D: To attest is to vouch for or to certify.

9. A: Derelict means to be neglected or abandoned, e.g., "a derelict old home."

10. C: To ordain is to order or command.

11. A: To be haughty is to be proud or arrogant.

12. B: A lapse is an error or mistake, e.g., "a lapse of memory."

13. C: To nauseate is to disgust or repulse.

14. A: Something paltry is cheap, base, or common.

15. C: To be refined is to be cultured and well-bred.

16. C: Virtual means to be simulated, especially as related to computer software.

17. D: To loathe is to hate or abhor.

18. C: When you mimic, you imitate or copy someone or something.

178

19. B: Something brittle is fragile and easily damaged or destroyed.

20. C: Wretched means miserable or woeful.

21. E: A fallible person or object is one that is faulty or imperfect.

22. D: Somebody who is experiencing or feeling anguish is experiencing sorrow or sadness.

23. E: A volatile situation or person is one that is unstable or changeable.

24. B: A person who is said to be pallid is feeble or sickly.

25. C: An individual who is described as demure is someone who is modest or timid.

26. E: When someone is told that they need to adhere to the group, they are being asked to become attached or united with the others of their group.

27. A: Something that is soiled is stained or dirty. When somebody says their clothing is soiled, it is the same as saying that their clothing is dirty.

28. E: An object that is pliable is understood to be very flexible or spongy.

29. D: When you have disdain for something or someone, you despise or scorn that person or thing.

30. B: A stoic is an individual that is very tolerant, or one who can suffer a great deal without raising a complaint.

31. C: This analogy focuses on synonyms. *Reprimand* and *punishment* are close synonyms. *Impetuous* is a sudden or impulsive action with little or no thoughtful planning. So, the best choice is *hasty* which means rapid or very quick.

32. B: This analogy focuses on homonyms. *Cue* and *queue* have different spellings, but they sound very similar. The best answer choice of *joule* and *jewel* also has different spellings with similar pronunciations.

33. B: The category of amphibians contains frogs. The order of this analogy begins with something that is specific and moves to the general category. Since you are given the specific item of *hydrogen*, then you are looking for the general category which would be choice B: *element*.

34. E: A *hologram* is an image that is made up of beams of *light* from a laser. So, we could say that the order of this analogy is a piece of a whole. The start of the next comparison is *film* which would be a piece of a *video camera*.

35. E: *Superficial* means shallow or lacking detail. *Mature* means complete development or ripe. So, this combination points to antonyms. The best answer choice is choice E which has the antonyms of *submissive* and *defiant*. *Submissive* means compliant or prone to submitting. *Defiant* means resisting opposition or disobedient.

36. C: The rare individual with insight into his or her craft at a very young age and makes startling *innovations* can receive the title of *prodigy*. The connection between these two words can be understood as a product being put together by a producer. Then, the best choice is the product of a *manuscript* (i.e., a document that is written by hand or has not been published) being produced by a *composer* (i.e., person who writes music).

37. B: *Rubber* material has the characteristic of being very flexible or *pliable*. So, the comparison to be made is how something or someone has a certain characteristic or attribute. The best choice is choice B as a characteristic of a *legacy* is its durability or *immutability*.

38. C: Among the many uses of a *kayak* is to depart on *quests*. The best choice is how an *intercom* is used to spread *communication*.

39. A: This analogy focuses on synonyms. *Particle* and *remnant* are close synonyms. *Ameliorate* means to improve, and *alleviate* means to lessen pain or trouble in an attempt to improve the situation. The other choices are antonyms.

40. D: A *cardiologist* is a doctor who focuses on the functions and diseases of the heart. This doctor is different than a general practice doctor because *cardiologists* are considered *specialists*. A *specialist* is a category of several kinds of doctors that includes dermatologists (focus on skin), immunologists (focus on immune system), neurologists (focus on nervous system), and many others. The best choice is how a *parable* (e.g., short story with a moral or religious teaching) stands among the many pieces of the category of *fiction*.

41. B: A *politician* is someone who has experience in government and normally is an elected official. A *policy* is a plan with general goals for a government that will influence decisions or actions in matters that are foreign or domestic. So, a *politician* is someone who would use *policy*. The comparison to be made is how a *critic* who can review books, television shows, movies, and many other things will also need to be able to write a *synopsis* (e.g., a summary or overview) of the work.

42. E: This analogy is a matter of degree as starting with something basic and escalating to something more significant. The question begins with *error* which is basic and general, and this is matched with *iniquity* which is a wicked act. So, the best choice is choice E which starts with a basic wave and escalates to a tsunami which is an incredibly high and large wave that can be the cause of destruction when meeting land.

43. E: This analogy focuses on homonyms. *Gorilla* and *guerilla* have different spellings, but they sound very similar. The best answer choice of *sign* and *sine* also has different spellings with similar pronunciations.

44. D: This analogy focuses on antonyms. *Apathy* and *persistence* are opposites as *apathy* means an absence of interest or feeling emotion, and *persistence* is a dedication to continue with an action despite opposition. *Profuse* means produced in large quantities, and *sparse* is an antonym as it means thin or existing in small quantities.

45. D: As a reference at the end of a *book*, an *index* may be provided that contains key terms or phrases with page numbers where those terms or phrases can be found. So, we can say that an *index* is a part to the whole of a *book*. The comparison involves an *elegy* which can be a song or a poem that expresses terrible sadness for the death of a person. This *elegy* would then be a part to the whole of a *funeral* service.

46. C: In a classroom or in research, a *professor* will speak on a topic or share his or her opinions that come from experience or study. Some of these opinions will come from the professor's *tenets* which are doctrines or principles that are held as being true. So, the comparison is one of a principle being produced by a *professor*. When you consider the options, the best choice is how a *parody* (e.g., imitation with comic intent) is produced by a *comedian*.

47. B: When a strong opponent competes against an unlikely challenger, we sometimes call the unlikely challenger an *underdog* who will face the incredible odds of defeating the strong opponent. An attribute or characteristic of an underdog can be their *audacious* (i.e., confident or bold) attitude. Now, a *conspirator* is a person who is participating in a plan that has some illegal intent. So, a conspirator has the characteristic of being *elusive* (i.e., easily escaping capture).

48. B: This analogy focuses on homonyms. *Marshal* and *martial* have different spellings, but they sound very similar. The best answer choice of *earn* and *urn* also has different spellings with similar pronunciations.

49. D: This analogy is a matter of degree as starting with something basic and escalating to something more significant. The question starts with a basic and general dollar which is escalated to a salary (i.e., a fixed amount of money that a person makes over a regular schedule). A *tear* is connected to sadness and weeping. So, a *tear* would be the basic or general start that escalates to the significant of being *melancholy*.

50. C: An *intermission* is a pause between acts of a play. Two common types of plays are *dramas* and comedies. So, we can determine that an *intermission* is a piece to the whole of a *drama*. Now, the comparison begins with *plant* as in vegetation. So, the best answer choice is *habitat* (i.e., the place where animal and plant life are naturally living) which fills the role of being the whole to the piece of *plant*.

51. D: This analogy focuses on synonyms. *Copious* (i.e., large in amount or number) and *extensive* (i.e., large in amount or size) are close synonyms. *Resilient* means flexible or able to recover or change after going through strain, and *supple* means able to fold or bend without much difficulty.

52. C: In fiction, you can find that many stories have both a protagonist and an *antagonist*. The protagonist is the person who is the main character of a story, and the *antagonist* is the person who is the opposing character to the protagonist. Now, an antagonist is a small piece to the whole of fiction. So, the best answer in the same order of piece to whole is *journal* to *database*. An example would be a peer-reviewed scientific journal that is found in an online research database.

53. C: A *novella* is a story with a number of pages that is less than a novel but is more than a short story. So, a certain characteristic of a *novella* is that it is *brief*. Then, you need to know which answer choice has the correct comparison for a characteristic. Among the choices, an *infant* being *naïve* (i.e., innocent) is the best option.

54. A: This analogy is a matter of degree as starting with something basic and escalating to something more significant. The question begins with *jog* which is basic and general, and this is matched with *marathon* which is a 26.2 mile race that takes several hours to complete. So, the best choice is choice A which starts with a basic *hypothesis* (i.e., educated guess) and escalates to a *discovery*.

55. A: *Connoisseurs* are critics or experts about their field or area of study who often lend their *opinions* to the general public. One could understand this as a product of an *opinion* that is produced by a *connoisseur*. Then, the comparison to be made is that a *hybrid* (i.e., combination or mixture) is produced by an *innovator* (i.e., a person who works on new ideas or methods).

56. A: When a *decision* needs to be made, some prefer to go with their instincts and others prefer to have wisdom or *insight* provided before making a commitment. So, one could say that *insight* is used to make *decisions*. Now, the correct comparison comes with an *advocate* (e.g., a lawyer) who *defends* someone or something against opposition.

57. B: This analogy focuses on antonyms. *Antipathy* and *sympathy* are opposites as *antipathy* means a strong feeling of opposition, and *sympathy* is the act of understanding another person's feeling or situation. You are given *convivial* which means sociable or cheerful, and you know that you are looking for the antonym of sociable and cheerful. So, *gloomy* means depressed or miserable, and this is the clear opposite to *convivial*.

58. D: *Espionage* is the service of spying on opposition in order to gain intelligence. So, the nature (or characteristic) of this task is easily understood to be *discreet* (i.e., tactful and cautious). The analogy continues with *kindling* which are the pieces of material used to start a fire. In many situations, a fire is characteristic of something tragic that is about to happen to someone or something. A name for this foreboding sense of tragedy can be *ominous*. In short, a characteristic of *kindling* is *ominous*.

59. B: A *benediction* is a prayer of blessing or expression of hope that is the final part of some religious services or general *ceremonies*. Since a *benediction* is a piece to the whole of a *ceremony*, you need to look for the choice that has a similar comparison. A *landmark* is a building or place in a town or *city* that is marked by historical significance and is sometimes officially recognized and preserved. So, the piece would be a *landmark*, and the whole would be a *city*.

60. E: While an *interjection* is commonly understood as one of the eight parts of speech, the term is also applicable to a statement that interrupts a situation or dialogue. An example could be a prosecutor that interrupts the dialogue between the defense attorney and a witness on the stand because he or she wants to make a plea to the judge. So, in this example an *interjection* is being used by an *attorney*. The best comparison comes with choice E as a *voucher* (i.e., coupon) needs to be redeemed (i.e., claimed) in order for the *redeemer* to receive the benefit of the *voucher*.

Section 4: Quantitative

1. B: The ratio of correct to incorrect answers is 2:3, giving a whole of 5. It takes 12 sets of 5 questions to total 60 questions. To determine how many correct answers Sam gave, multiply 2 by 12, for a total of 24.

2. B: Use the FOIL method (First, Outer, Inner, Last) to expand this expression, then combine like terms:

$$(3x + 1)(7x + 10) = (3x)(7x) + (3x)(10) + (1)(7x) + (1)(10)$$
$$= 21x^2 + 30x + 7x + 10$$
$$= 21x^2 + 37x + 10$$

3. B: The listed angles are located in the alternate interior angles position. According to the Alternate Interior Angle Theorem, when a transversal cuts across parallel lines, the alternate interior angles are congruent. Since lines a and b are parallel, it means that $2x + 5 = 3x - 25$. After subtracting $2x$ from both sides and adding 25 to both sides, the equation simplifies to $30 = x$.

4. A: The answer is expanded to simplify the calculations. The total of Choice A is $8.00 + $1.60, which is the same as the total calculated in the problem.

5. E: In order to determine the number of questions Joshua must answer correctly, consider the number of points he must earn. Joshua will receive 4 points for each question he answers correctly, and x represents the number of questions. Therefore, Joshua will receive a total of $4x$ points for all the questions he answers correctly. Joshua must earn more than 92 points. Therefore, to determine the number of questions he must answer correctly, solve the inequality $4x > 92$.

6. D: To solve the equation, first get rid of the denominators by multiplying both sides of the equation by $x(x-3)$ and simplifying the result:

$$\frac{4}{x-3} - \frac{2}{x} = 1$$

$$x(x-3)\left[\frac{4}{x-3} - \frac{2}{x}\right] = x(x-3) \times 1$$

$$4x - 2(x-3) = x(x-3)$$

$$4x - 2x + 6 = x^2 - 3x$$

$$2x + 6 = x^2 - 3x$$

The result is a quadratic equation. Move everything to one side and then solve for x by factoring the left side and applying the zero-product rule:

$$x^2 - 5x - 6 = 0$$

$$(x+1)(x-6) = 0$$

$$x + 1 = 0 \qquad x - 6 = 0$$

$$x = -1 \qquad x = 6$$

Therefore, the possible solutions are $x = -1$ and $x = 6$. Since neither of these values will cause division by zero when substituted back into the original equation, they are both valid solutions.

7. C: The score that has approximately 50% above and 50% below is approximately 500 (517 to be exact). The scores can be manually written by choosing either the lower or upper end of each interval and using the frequency to determine the number of times to record each score, i.e., using the lower end of each interval shows an approximate value of 465 for the median; using the upper end of each interval shows an approximate value of 530 for the median. A score of 500 (and the exact median of 517) is found between 465 and 530.

8. C: To divide expressions that contain variables, divide pairs of like variables (or constants) that appear in both the numerator and denominator. For this problem, first divide the constants: $12 \div 3$, then divide the a's: $a^2 \div a$. Since $a^2 \div a$ is equivalent to $\frac{a^2}{a^1}$, use the quotient rule, $\frac{x^a}{x^b} = x^{a-b}$, to simplify it. There is no change to b since the divisor does not contain the variable b:

$$\frac{12a^2b}{3a} = \frac{4a^{2-1}b}{1}$$

$$= 4ab$$

9. C: "The square of twice the sum of x and three is equal to the product of twenty-four and x" is represented by the equation $[2(x+3)]^2 = 24x$. Solve for x.

$$[2x + 6]^2 = 24x$$

$$4x^2 + 24x + 36 = 24x$$

$$4x^2 = -36$$

$$x^2 = -9$$

$$x = \pm\sqrt{-9}$$

$$x = \pm 3i$$

So, $-3i$ is a possible value of x.

10. B: If a line-of-fit is drawn through the points, the slope will be -1/5 so the snow melts 5 centimeters every day.

11. D: The expected value is equal to the sum of the products of each card value and its probability. Thus, the expected value is $\left(1 \times \frac{1}{5}\right) + \left(2 \times \frac{1}{5}\right) + \left(3 \times \frac{1}{5}\right) + \left(4 \times \frac{1}{5}\right) + \left(5 \times \frac{1}{5}\right)$, which equals 3.

12. B: The number of tails he can expect after 6 coin tosses is equal to the product of the probability of getting tails on one coin toss and the number of coin tosses. Thus, the expected value is $\frac{1}{2} \times 6$, or 3.

13. C: In ΔABC, the midpoints are marked as D, E, and F. The medians of the triangle are then drawn in as $\overline{AF}$, $\overline{BD}$ and $\overline{CE}$. The medians intersect at a point called the centroid. Based on this intersection, it is the case that $\overline{AG} = 2\overline{GF}$, $\overline{BG} = 2\overline{GD}$, and $\overline{CG} = 2\overline{GE}$. Since we are given that $\overline{BG} = 6x - 4$ and $\overline{GD} = 2x + 8$, we can set up the equation as $6x - 4 = 2(2x + 8)$. Simplifying that equation, it becomes $6x - 4 = 4x + 16$. After subtracting $4x$ from both sides and adding 4 to both sides, the equation becomes $2x = 20$. Divide both sides by 2 to get $x = 10$. Then, the length of $\overline{GD}$ is calculated as $2(10) + 8 = 20 + 8 = 28$.

14. E: First solve for the number of questions Matthew must answer correctly. To determine the number of correct answers Matthew needs, solve the following inequality:

$$3x > 96$$
$$x > \frac{96}{3}$$
$$x > 32$$

Therefore, Matthew must correctly answer at more than 32 questions to qualify for varsity sports. Since the test has 40 questions, he must answer less than 8 questions incorrectly. Matthew could also answer 0 questions incorrectly. Hence, the best inequality to describe the number of questions Matthew can answer incorrectly is $0 \leq x < 8$.

15. C: Use the formula for volume of a rectangular solid:

$$Volume = length \times width \times height$$
$$200 = 5 \times 5 \times h$$
$$200 = 25h \rightarrow 25h = 200$$

16. B: First, determine how many miles can be driven on one tank of gas by multiplying the numbers of gallons in a tank by the miles per gallon:

$$\frac{12 \text{ gallons}}{\text{tank}} \times \frac{30 \text{ miles}}{\text{gallon}} = 360 \frac{\text{miles}}{\text{tank}}$$

Next, divide the total miles for the trip by the number of miles driven per tank of gas to determine how many total tanks of gas Robert will need:

$$1,800 \text{ miles} \times \frac{\text{tank}}{360 \text{ miles}} = 5 \text{ tanks}$$

17. B: The slope of a line is a number that represents its steepness. Lines with positive slope go from the bottom-left to the top-right, lines with negative slope go from the top-left to the bottom-right, and horizontal lines have zero slope. You can also think of slope as being $\frac{rise}{run}$. In particular, a slope of 2 (which is equivalent to a slope of 2/1) means that the line rises (goes up) 2 units every time it runs (goes to the right) 1 unit. Looking closely at line k, notice that for every 2 units it goes up, it goes to the right 1 unit.

18. C: The average time can be represented by the expression, $\frac{3}{4}(16) + \frac{1}{4}(12)$, which equals the sum of 12 and 3, or 15. Thus, the average time overall was 15 seconds.

19. B: The events are dependent, since the first marble was not replaced. The sample space of the second draw will decrease by 1 because there will be one less marble to choose. The number of possible red marbles for the second draw will also decrease by 1. Thus, the probability may be written as $P(A \text{ and } B) = \frac{8}{15} \times \frac{7}{14}$. The probability he draws a red marble, does not replace it, and draws another red marble is $\frac{4}{15}$.

20. B: Start by squaring both sides of the equation and simplifying the result:

$$\left(\sqrt{3x - 2}\right)^2 = (x - 2)^2$$
$$3x - 2 = x^2 - 4x + 4$$

Next, move everything to one side and factor to find solutions for x:

$$x^2 - 7x + 6 = 0$$
$$(x - 1)(x - 6) = 0$$
$$x - 1 = 0 \qquad x - 6 = 0$$
$$x = 1 \qquad x = 6$$

Therefore, the possible solutions are $x = 1$ and $x = 6$. Substitute these solutions into the original equation to see if they are valid solutions:

$$\sqrt{3(1) - 2} = (1) - 2 \qquad \sqrt{3(6) - 2} = (6) - 2$$
$$\sqrt{1} = 1 - 2 \qquad \sqrt{16} = 6 - 2$$
$$1 = 1 - 2 \text{ False} \qquad 4 = 6 - 2 \text{ True}$$

Since only $x = 6$ leads to a true equality, that is the only solution.

21. E: Get all of the variables on one side of the equation and solve.

$$7\sqrt{x} + 16 = 79 \quad \text{Subtract 16 from both sides of the equation}$$
$$7\sqrt{x} = 63 \quad \text{Divide both sides by 7}$$
$$\sqrt{x} = 9 \quad \text{Square both sides}$$
$$x = 81$$

22. B: The product given for Choice B can be written as $27x^3 - 9x^2y + 3xy^2 + 9x^2y - 3xy^2 + y^3$, which reduces to $27x^3 + y^3$.

23. D: If $\frac{1}{4}$ inch represents 8 miles, then 1 inch represents $4 \times 8 = 32$ miles. Two inches represents $2 \times 32 = 64$ miles. An $\frac{1}{8}$ of an inch represents $8 \div 2 = 4$ miles. Therefore, $2\frac{1}{8}$ inches represent $64 + 4 = 68$ miles.

24. D: To determine the scale factor of the dilation, compare the coordinates of $\Delta J'K'L'$ to the coordinates of ΔJKL. J is at $(-2\ -3)$ and J' is at $(-4, -6)$, which means that the coordinates of J were multiplied by a scale factor of 2 to get the coordinates of J'. K is at $(1, 3)$ and K' is at $(2, 6)$. L is at $(4, -1)$ and L' is at $(8, -2)$. As can be seen, the coordinates of K and L were also multiplied by a scale factor of 2 to get to the coordinates of K' and L'.

25. B: The length of an arc is proportional to the measure of the arc, relative to the circle. Here, the length of arc $\overparen{AB}$ is in a ratio of 4:48, or 1:12, with the total circle perimeter. Thus, the measure of arc $\overparen{AB}$ has a ratio of 1:12 with the total circle measure, which is always 360°. To find the unknown arc measure, set up a proportion with the known information as follows: $\dfrac{1}{12} = \dfrac{x}{360°}$. Solving for x gives $12x = 360°$, or $x = 30°$.

Practice Test #2

Writing Sample

25 Minutes

Instructions: Read the following prompt, taking a few moments to plan a response. Then, write your response in essay form.

Prompt: *Fast food restaurants should be held legally responsible for the current rise in obesity in children.*

Do you agree or disagree with this statement? Use examples from history, literature, or your own personal experience to support your point of view.

Quantitative (Math)

Read each question, perform the appropriate calculations, and determine the correct answer.

1. Mrs. Patterson's classroom has sixteen empty chairs. All the chairs are occupied when every student is present. If 2/5 of the students are absent, how many students make up her entire class?

 a. 16
 b. 32
 c. 24
 d. 40
 e. 36

2. Rachel spent $24.15 on vegetables. She bought 2 lbs of onions, 3 lbs of carrots, and 1 ½ lbs of mushrooms. If the onions cost $3.69 per lb, and the carrots cost $ 4.29 per lb, what is the price per lb of mushrooms?

 a. $2.60
 b. $2.25
 c. $2.80
 d. $3.10
 e. $2.75

3. In the figure, A, B, and C are points on the number line, where O is the origin. What is the ratio of the distance BC to distance AB?

 a. 3:5
 b. 8:5
 c. 8:11
 d. 3:11
 e. 8:6

4. In an election in Kimball County, Candidate A obtained 36,800 votes. His opponent, Candidate B, obtained 32,100 votes. 2,100 votes went to write-in candidates. What percentage of the vote went to Candidate A?

 a. 51.8%
 b. 53.4%
 c. 45.2%
 d. 46.8%
 e. 56.2%

5. Lauren had $80 in her savings account. When she received her paycheck, she made a deposit which brought the balance up to $120. By what percentage did the total amount in her account increase as a result of this deposit?

    a.   50%
    b.   40%
    c.   35%
    d.   80%
    e.   120%

6. Find the length of the side labeled x. The triangle represented in the figure is a right triangle, as shown.

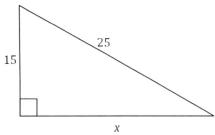

    a.   18
    b.   20
    c.   22
    d.   24
    e.   25

7. A motorcycle manufacturer offers 3 different models, each available in 6 different colors. How many different combinations of model and color are available?

    a.   9
    b.   6
    c.   12
    d.   18
    e.   24

8. Which of the following expressions is equivalent to $x^3 x^5$?

    a. $2x^8$
    b. x^{15}
    c. x^2
    d. x^8
    e. $2x^{15}$

9. If $\frac{12}{x} = \frac{30}{6}$, what is the value of x?

    a.   3.6
    b.   2.4
    c.   3.0
    d.   2.0
    e.   2.75

10. $\triangle ABC$ is a right triangle, and $\angle ACB = 30°$. What is the measure of $\angle BAC$?

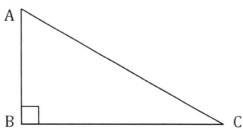

    a. 40°
    b. 50°
    c. 60°
    d. 45°
    e. 70°

11. Carrie wants to decorate her party with bundles of balloons containing three balloons each. Balloons are available in 4 different colors. There must be three different colors in each bundle. How many different kinds of bundles can she make?

    a. 18
    b. 12
    c. 4
    d. 6
    e. 10

12. In the figure below, $\overline{BC}$ is 4 units long, $\overline{CD}$ is 8 units long, and $\overline{DE}$ is 6 units long. What is the length of $\overline{AC}$?

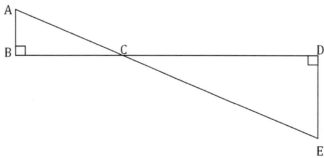

    a. 7 units
    b. 5 units
    c. 3 units
    d. 2.5 units
    e. 4 units

13. In a game of chance, 3 dice are cast simultaneously. What is the probability that all three will land with a 6 showing?

    a. 1 in 6
    b. 1 in 18
    c. 1 in 216
    d. 1 in 30
    e. 1 in 36

14. Arrange the following numbers in order from the least to greatest $2^3, 4^2, 6^0, 9, 10^1$.

a. $2^3, 4^2, 6^0, 9, 10^1$
b. $6^0, 9, 10^1, 2^3, 4^2$
c. $10^1, 2^3, 6^0, 9, 4^2$
d. $6^0, 2^3, 9, 10^1, 4^2$
e. $9, 6^0, 10^1, 4^2, 2^3$

15. A combination lock uses a 3-digit code. Each digit can be any one of the ten available integers 0-9. How many different combinations are possible?

a. 9
b. 1000
c. 30
d. 81
e. 100

16. Which of the following expressions represents the ratio of the area of a circle to its circumference?

a. πr^2
b. $\dfrac{\pi r^2}{2\pi}$
c. $\dfrac{2\pi r}{r^2}$
d. $2\pi r^{\frac{1}{2}}$
e. $\dfrac{r}{2}$

Questions 17 and 18 are based upon the following table:

Kyle bats third in the batting order for the Badgers baseball team. The table shows the number of hits that Kyle had in each of 7 consecutive games played during one week in July.

Day of Week	Number of Hits
Monday	1
Tuesday	2
Wednesday	3
Thursday	1
Friday	1
Saturday	4
Sunday	2

17. What is the mode of the numbers in the distribution shown in the table?

a. 1
b. 2
c. 3
d. 4
e. 7

18. What is the mean of the numbers in the distribution shown in the table?

a. 1
b. 2
c. 3
d. 4
e. 7

19. 32 is what percent of 80?

a. 25%
b. 32%
c. 40%
d. 44%
e. 48%

20. Jack and Kevin play in a basketball game. If the ratio of points scored by Jack to points scored by Kevin is 4 to 3, which of the following could NOT be the total number of points scored by the two boys?

a. 7
b. 14
c. 16
d. 28
e. 35

21. The average of six numbers is 4. If the average of two of those numbers is 2, what is the average of the other four numbers?

a. 5
b. 6
c. 7
d. 8
e. 9

22. Dean's Department Store reduces the price of a $30 shirt by 20%, but later raises it again by 20% of the sale price. What is the final price of the shirt?

a. $24.40
b. $32
c. $30
d. $28.80
e. $26.60

23. Sheila, Janice, and Karen, working together at the same rate, can complete a job in 3 1/3 days. Working at the same rate, how much of the job could Janice and Karen do in one day?

a. 1/5
b. 1/4
c. 1/3
d. 1/9
e. 1/8

24. $4^6 \div 2^8 =$

    a. 2
    b. 8
    c. 16
    d. 32
    e. 64

25. What is 20% of $\frac{12}{5}$, expressed as a percentage?

    a. 48%
    b. 65%
    c. 72%
    d. 76%
    e. 84%

Reading Comprehension

Read each passage closely and answer the associated questions. Be sure to choose the answer that BEST answers the question being asked.

Questions 1-4 refer to the following passage:

It is most likely that you have never had diphtheria. You probably don't even know anyone who has suffered from this disease. In fact, you may not even know what diphtheria is. Similarly, diseases like whooping cough, measles, mumps, and rubella may all be unfamiliar to you. In the nineteenth and early twentieth centuries, these illnesses struck hundreds of thousands of people in the United States each year, mostly children, and tens of thousands of people died. The names of these diseases were frightening household words. Today, they are all but forgotten. That change happened largely because of vaccines.

You probably have been vaccinated against diphtheria. You may even have been exposed to the bacterium that causes it, but the vaccine prepared your body to fight off the disease so quickly that you were unaware of the infection. Vaccines take advantage of your body's natural ability to learn how to combat many disease-causing germs, or microbes. What's more, your body remembers how to protect itself from the microbes it has encountered before. Collectively, the parts of your body that remember and repel microbes are called the immune system. Without the proper functioning of the immune system, the simplest illness—even the common cold—could quickly turn deadly.

On average, your immune system needs more than a week to learn how to fight off an unfamiliar microbe. Sometimes, that isn't enough time. Strong microbes can spread through your body faster than the immune system can fend them off. Your body often gains the upper hand after a few weeks, but in the meantime you are sick. Certain microbes are so virulent that they can overwhelm or escape your natural defenses. In those situations, vaccines can make all the difference.

Traditional vaccines contain either parts of microbes or whole microbes that have been altered so that they don't cause disease. When your immune system confronts these harmless versions of the germs, it quickly clears them from your body. In other words, vaccines trick your immune system in order to teach your body important lessons about how to defeat its opponents.

1. What is the main idea of the passage?
  a. The nineteenth and early twentieth centuries were a dark period for medicine.
  b. You have probably never had diphtheria.
  c. Traditional vaccines contain altered microbes.
  d. Vaccines help the immune system function properly.

2. Which statement is not a detail from the passage?

   a. Vaccines contain microbe parts or altered microbes.
   b. The immune system typically needs a week to learn how to fight a new disease.
   c. The symptoms of disease do not emerge until the body has learned how to fight the microbe.
   d. A hundred years ago, children were at the greatest risk of dying from now-treatable diseases.

3. What is the meaning of the word virulent as it is used in the third paragraph?

   a. tiny
   b. malicious
   c. contagious
   d. annoying

4. What is the author's primary purpose in writing the essay?

   a. to entertain
   b. to persuade
   c. to inform
   d. to analyze

Questions 5-8 refer to the following passage:

Foodborne illnesses are contracted by eating food or drinking beverages contaminated with bacteria, parasites, or viruses. Harmful chemicals can also cause foodborne illnesses if they have contaminated food during harvesting or processing. Foodborne illnesses can cause symptoms ranging from upset stomach to diarrhea, fever, vomiting, abdominal cramps, and dehydration. Most foodborne infections are undiagnosed and unreported, though the Centers for Disease Control and Prevention estimates that every year about 76 million people in the United States become ill from pathogens in food. About 5,000 of these people die.

Harmful bacteria are the most common cause of foodborne illness. Some bacteria may be present at the point of purchase. Raw foods are the most common source of foodborne illnesses because they are not sterile; examples include raw meat and poultry contaminated during slaughter. Seafood may become contaminated during harvest or processing. One in 10,000 eggs may be contaminated with Salmonella inside the shell. Produce, such as spinach, lettuce, tomatoes, sprouts, and melons, can become contaminated with Salmonella, Shigella, or Escherichia coli (E. coli). Contamination can occur during growing, harvesting, processing, storing, shipping, or final preparation. Sources of produce contamination vary, as these foods are grown in soil and can become contaminated during growth, processing, or distribution. Contamination may also occur during food preparation in a restaurant or a home kitchen. The most common form of contamination from handled foods is the calicivirus, also called the Norwalk-like virus.

When food is cooked and left out for more than two hours at room temperature, bacteria can multiply quickly. Most bacteria don't produce an odor or change in color or texture, so they can be impossible to detect. Freezing food slows or stops bacteria's growth but does not destroy the bacteria. The microbes can become reactivated when the food is thawed. Refrigeration also can slow the growth of some bacteria. Thorough cooking is required to destroy the bacteria.

5. What is the subject of the passage?
- a. foodborne illnesses
- b. the dangers of uncooked food
- c. bacteria
- d. proper food preparation

6. Which statement is not a detail from the passage?
- a. Every year, more than 70 million Americans contract some form of foodborne illness.
- b. Once food is cooked, it cannot cause illness.
- c. Refrigeration can slow the growth of some bacteria.
- d. The most common form of contamination in handled foods is calicivirus.

7. What is the meaning of the word pathogens as it is used in the first paragraph?
- a. diseases
- b. vaccines
- c. disease-causing substances
- d. foods

8. What is the meaning of the word sterile as it is used in the second paragraph?
- a. free of bacteria
- b. healthy
- c. delicious
- d. impotent

Questions 9-12 refer to the following passage:

There are a number of health problems related to bleeding in the esophagus and stomach. Stomach acid can cause inflammation and bleeding at the lower end of the esophagus. This condition, usually associated with the symptom of heartburn, is called esophagitis, or inflammation of the esophagus. Sometimes a muscle between the esophagus and stomach fails to close properly and allows the return of food and stomach juices into the esophagus, which can lead to esophagitis. In another unrelated condition, enlarged veins (varices) at the lower end of the esophagus rupture and bleed massively. Cirrhosis of the liver is the most common cause of esophageal varices. Esophageal bleeding can be caused by a tear in the lining of the esophagus (Mallory-Weiss syndrome). Mallory-Weiss syndrome usually results from vomiting but may also be caused by increased pressure in the abdomen from coughing, hiatal hernia, or childbirth. Esophageal cancer can cause bleeding.

The stomach is a frequent site of bleeding. Infections with Helicobacter pylori (H. pylori), alcohol, aspirin, aspirin-containing medicines, and various other medicines (such as nonsteroidal anti-inflammatory drugs [NSAIDs]—particularly those used for arthritis) can cause stomach ulcers or inflammation (gastritis). The stomach is often the site of ulcer disease. Acute or chronic ulcers may enlarge and erode through a blood vessel, causing bleeding. Also, patients suffering from burns, shock, head injuries, cancer, or those who have undergone extensive surgery may develop stress ulcers. Bleeding can also occur from benign tumors or cancer of the stomach, although these disorders usually do not cause massive bleeding.

9. What is the main idea of the passage?
- a.   The digestive system is complex.
- b.   Of all the digestive organs, the stomach is the most prone to bleeding.
- c.   Both the esophagus and the stomach are subject to bleeding problems.
- d.   Esophagitis afflicts the young and old alike.

10. Which statement is not a detail from the passage?
- a.   Alcohol can cause stomach bleeding.
- b.   Ulcer disease rarely occurs in the stomach.
- c.   Benign tumors rarely result in massive bleeding.
- d.   Childbirth is one cause of Mallory-Weiss syndrome.

11. What is the meaning of the word rupture as it is used in the first paragraph?
- a.   tear
- b.   collapse
- c.   implode
- d.   detach

12. What is the meaning of the word erode as it is used in the second paragraph?
- a.   avoid
- b.   divorce
- c.   contain
- d.   wear away

Questions 13-16 refer to the following passage:

We met Kathy Blake while she was taking a stroll in the park . . . by herself. What's so striking about this is that Kathy is completely blind, and she has been for more than 30 years.

The diagnosis from her doctor was retinitis pigmentosa, or RP. It's an incurable genetic disease that leads to progressive visual loss. Photoreceptive cells in the retina slowly start to die, leaving the patient visually impaired.

"Life was great the year before I was diagnosed," Kathy said. "I had just started a new job; I just bought my first new car. I had just started dating my now-husband. Life was good. The doctor had told me that there was some good news and some bad news. 'The bad news is you are going to lose your vision; the good news is we don't think you are going to go totally blind.' Unfortunately, I did lose all my vision within about 15 years."

Two years ago, Kathy got a glimmer of hope. She heard about an artificial retina being developed in Los Angeles. It was experimental, but Kathy was the perfect candidate.

Dr. Mark Humayun is a retinal surgeon and biomedical engineer. "A good candidate for the artificial retina device is a person who is blind because of retinal blindness," he said. "They've lost the rods and cones, the light-sensing cells of the eye, but the

197

rest of the circuitry is relatively intact. In the simplest rendition, this device basically takes a blind person and hooks them up to a camera."

It may sound like the stuff of science fiction . . . and just a few years ago it was. A camera is built into a pair of glasses, sending radio signals to a tiny chip in the back of the retina. The chip, small enough to fit on a fingertip, is implanted surgically and stimulates the nerves that lead to the vision center of the brain. Kathy is one of twenty patients who have undergone surgery and use the device.

It has been about two years since the surgery, and Kathy still comes in for weekly testing at the University of Southern California's medical campus. She scans back and forth with specially made, camera-equipped glasses until she senses objects on a screen and then touches the objects. The low-resolution image from the camera is still enough to make out the black stripes on the screen. Impulses are sent from the camera to the 60 receptors that are on the chip in her retina. So, what is Kathy seeing?

"I see flashes of light that indicate a contrast from light to dark—very similar to a camera flash, probably not quite as bright because it's not hurting my eye at all," she replied.

Humayun underscored what a breakthrough this is and how a patient adjusts. "If you've been blind for 30 or 50 years, (and) all of a sudden you get this device, there is a period of learning," he said. "Your brain needs to learn. And it's literally like seeing a baby crawl—to a child walk—to an adult run."

While hardly perfect, the device works best in bright light or where there is a lot of contrast. Kathy takes the device home. The software that runs the device can be upgraded. So, as the software is upgraded, her vision improves. Recently, she was outside with her husband on a moonlit night and saw something she hadn't seen for a long time.

"I scanned up in the sky (and) I got a big flash, right where the moon was, and pointed it out. I can't even remember how many years ago it's been that I would have ever been able to do that."

This technology has a bright future. The current chip has a resolution of 60 pixels. Humayun says that number could be increased to more than a thousand in the next version.

"I think it will be extremely exciting if they can recognize their loved ones' faces and be able to see what their wife or husband or their grandchildren look like, which they haven't seen," said Humayun.

Kathy dreams of a day when blindness like hers will be a distant memory. "My eye disease is hereditary," she said. "My three daughters happen to be fine, but I want to know that if my grandchildren ever have a problem, they will have something to give them some vision."

13. What is the primary subject of the passage?

a. a new artificial retina
b. Kathy Blake
c. hereditary disease
d. Dr. Mark Humayun

14. What is the meaning of the word progressive as it is used in the second paragraph?

a. selective
b. gradually increasing
c. diminishing
d. disabling

15. Which statement is not a detail from the passage?

a. The use of an artificial retina requires a special pair of glasses.
b. Retinal blindness is the inability to perceive light.
c. Retinitis pigmentosa is curable.
d. The artificial retina performs best in bright light.

16. What is the author's intention in writing the essay?

a. to persuade
b. to entertain
c. to analyze
d. to inform

Questions 17-21 refer to the following passage:

Usher syndrome is the most common condition that affects both hearing and vision. The major signs of Usher syndrome are hearing loss and an eye disorder called retinitis pigmentosa, or RP. Retinitis pigmentosa causes night blindness and a loss of peripheral vision (side vision) through the progressive degeneration of the retina. The retina, which is crucial for vision, is a light-sensitive tissue at the back of the eye. As RP progresses, the field of vision narrows, until only central vision (the ability to see straight ahead) remains. Many people with Usher syndrome also have severe balance problems.

There are three clinical types of Usher syndrome. In the United States, types 1 and 2 are the most common. Together, they account for approximately 90 to 95 percent of all cases of juvenile Usher syndrome. Approximately three to six percent of all deaf and hearing-disabled children have Usher syndrome. In developed countries, such as the United States, about four in every 100,000 newborns have Usher syndrome.

Usher syndrome is inherited as an autosomal recessive trait. The term autosomal means that the mutated gene is not located on either of the chromosomes that determine sex; in other words, both males and females can have the disorder and can pass it along to a child. The word recessive means that in order to have Usher syndrome, an individual must receive a mutated form of the Usher syndrome gene from each parent. If a child has a mutation in one Usher syndrome gene but the other gene is normal, he or she should have normal vision and hearing. Individuals with a mutation in a gene that can cause an autosomal recessive disorder are called carriers, because they carry the mutated gene but show no symptoms of the disorder. If both parents are carriers of a mutated gene for Usher syndrome, they will have a one-in-four chance of producing a child with Usher syndrome.

Usually, parents who have normal hearing and vision do not know if they are carriers of an Usher syndrome gene mutation. Currently, it is not possible to determine whether an individual without a family history of Usher syndrome is a carrier. Scientists at the National Institute on Deafness and Other Communication Disorders (NIDCD) are hoping to change this, however, as they learn more about the genes responsible for Usher syndrome.

17. What is the main idea of the passage?
   a. Usher syndrome is an inherited condition that affects hearing and vision.
   b. Some people are carriers of Usher syndrome.
   c. Usher syndrome typically skips a generation.
   d. Scientists hope to develop a test for detecting the carriers of Usher syndrome.

18. What is the meaning of the word *signs* as it is used in the first paragraph?
   a. qualifications
   b. conditions/diseases
   c. subjective markers
   d. measurable indicators

19. Which statement is not a detail from the passage?
   a. Types 1 and 2 Usher syndrome are the most common in the United States.
   b. Usher syndrome affects both hearing and smell.
   c. Right now, there is no way to identify a carrier of Usher syndrome.
   d. Central vision is the ability to see straight ahead.

20. What is the meaning of the word juvenile as it is used in the second paragraph?
   a. bratty
   b. serious
   c. occurring in children
   d. improper

21. What is the meaning of the word mutated as it is used in the third paragraph?
   a. selected
   b. altered
   c. composed
   d. destroyed

Questions 22-27 refer to the following passage:

The immune system is a network of cells, tissues, and organs that defends the body against attacks by foreign invaders. These invaders are primarily microbes—tiny organisms such as bacteria, parasites, and fungi—that can cause infections. Viruses also cause infections but are too primitive to be classified as living organisms. The human body provides an ideal environment for many microbes. It is the immune system's job to keep the microbes out or destroy them.

The immune system is amazingly complex. It can recognize and remember millions of different enemies, and it can secrete fluids and cells to wipe out nearly all of them.

The secret to its success is an elaborate and dynamic communications network. Millions of cells, organized into sets and subsets, gather and transfer information in response to an infection. Once immune cells receive the alarm, they produce powerful chemicals that help to regulate their own growth and behavior, enlist other immune cells, and direct the new recruits to trouble spots.

Although scientists have learned much about the immune system, they continue to puzzle over how the body destroys invading microbes, infected cells, and tumors without harming healthy tissues. New technologies for identifying individual immune cells are now allowing scientists to determine quickly which targets are triggering an immune response. Improvements in microscopy are permitting the first-ever observations of living B cells, T cells, and other cells as they interact within lymph nodes and other body tissues.

In addition, scientists are rapidly unraveling the genetic blueprints that direct the human immune response, as well as those that dictate the biology of bacteria, viruses, and parasites. The combination of new technology with expanded genetic information will no doubt reveal even more about how the body protects itself from disease.

22. What is the main idea of the passage?

a. Scientists fully understand the immune system.
b. The immune system triggers the production of fluids.
c. The body is under constant invasion by malicious microbes.
d. The immune system protects the body from infection.

23. Which statement is not a detail from the passage?

a. Most invaders of the body are microbes.
b. The immune system relies on excellent communication.
c. Viruses are extremely sophisticated.
d. The cells of the immune system are organized.

24. What is the meaning of the word ideal as it is used in the first paragraph?

a. thoughtful
b. confined
c. hostile
d. perfect

25. Which statement is not a detail from the passage?

a. Scientists can now see T cells.
b. The immune system ignores tumors.
c. The ability of the immune system to fight disease without harming the body remains mysterious.
d. The immune system remembers millions of different invaders.

26. What is the meaning of the word enlist as it is used in the second paragraph?

a. call into service
b. write down
c. send away
d. put across

27. What is the author's primary purpose in writing the essay?

a. to persuade
b. to analyze
c. to inform
d. to entertain

Questions 28-31 refer to the following passage:

The federal government regulates dietary supplements through the United States Food and Drug Administration (FDA). The regulations for dietary supplements are not the same as those for prescription or over-the-counter drugs. In general, the regulations for dietary supplements are less strict.

To begin with, a manufacturer does not have to prove the safety and effectiveness of a dietary supplement before it is marketed. A manufacturer is permitted to say that a dietary supplement addresses a nutrient deficiency, supports health, or is linked to a particular body function (such as immunity), if there is research to support the claim. Such a claim must be followed by the words "This statement has not been evaluated by the Food and Drug Administration. This product is not intended to diagnose, treat, cure, or prevent any disease."

Also, manufacturers are expected to follow certain good manufacturing practices (GMPs) to ensure that dietary supplements are processed consistently and meet quality standards. Requirements for GMPs went into effect in 2008 for large manufacturers and are being phased in for small manufacturers through 2010.

Once a dietary supplement is on the market, the FDA monitors safety and product information, such as label claims and package inserts. If it finds a product to be unsafe, it can take action against the manufacturer and/or distributor and may issue a warning or require that the product be removed from the marketplace. The Federal Trade Commission (FTC) is responsible for regulating product advertising; it requires that all information be truthful and not misleading.

The federal government has taken legal action against a number of dietary supplement promoters or Web sites that promote or sell dietary supplements because they have made false or deceptive statements about their products or because marketed products have proven to be unsafe.

28. What is the main idea of the passage?

a. Manufacturers of dietary supplements have to follow good manufacturing practices.
b. The FDA has a special program for regulating dietary supplements.
c. The federal government prosecutes those who mislead the general public.
d. The FDA is part of the federal government.

29. Which statement is not a detail from the passage?

a. Promoters of dietary supplements can make any claims that are supported by research.
b. GMP requirements for large manufacturers went into effect in 2008.
c. Product advertising is regulated by the FTC.
d. The FDA does not monitor products after they enter the market.

30. What is the meaning of the phrase *phased in* as it is used in the third paragraph?
   a. stunned into silence
   b. confused
   c. implemented in stages
   d. legalized

31. What is the meaning of the word deceptive as it is used in the fifth paragraph?
   a. misleading
   b. malicious
   c. illegal
   d. irritating

Questions 32-35 refer to the following passage:

Anemia is a condition in which there is an abnormally low number of red blood cells (RBCs). This condition also can occur if the RBCs don't contain enough hemoglobin, the iron-rich protein that makes the blood red. Hemoglobin helps RBCs carry oxygen from the lungs to the rest of the body.

Anemia can be accompanied by low numbers of RBCs, white blood cells (WBCs), and platelets. Red blood cells are disc-shaped and look like doughnuts without holes in the center. They carry oxygen and remove carbon dioxide (a waste product) from your body. These cells are made in the bone marrow and live for about 120 days in the bloodstream. Platelets and WBCs also are made in the bone marrow. White blood cells help fight infection. Platelets stick together to seal small cuts or breaks on the blood vessel walls and to stop bleeding.

If you are anemic, your body doesn't get enough oxygenated blood. As a result, you may feel tired or have other symptoms. Severe or long-lasting anemia can damage the heart, brain, and other organs of the body. Very severe anemia may even cause death.

Anemia has three main causes: blood loss, lack of RBC production, or high rates of RBC destruction. Many types of anemia are mild, brief, and easily treated. Some types can be prevented with a healthy diet or treated with dietary supplements. However, certain types of anemia may be severe, long lasting, and life threatening if not diagnosed and treated.

If you have the signs or symptoms of anemia, you should see your doctor to find out whether you have the condition. Treatment will depend on the cause and severity of the anemia.

32. What is the main idea of the passage?
   a. Anemia presents in a number of forms.
   b. Anemia is a potentially dangerous condition characterized by low numbers of RBCs.
   c. Anemia is a deficiency of WBCs and platelets.
   d. Anemia is a treatable condition.

33. Which statement is not a detail from the passage?

a. There are different methods for treating anemia.
b. Red blood cells remove carbon dioxide from the body.
c. Platelets are made in the bone marrow.
d. Anemia is rarely caused by blood loss.

34. What is the meaning of the word oxygenated as it is used in the third paragraph?

a. containing low amounts of oxygen
b. containing no oxygen
c. consisting entirely of oxygen
d. containing high amounts of oxygen

35. What is the meaning of the word severity as it is used in the fifth paragraph?

a. seriousness
b. disconnectedness
c. truth
d. swiftness

Questions 36-39 refer to the following passage:

Contrary to previous reports, drinking four or more cups of coffee a day does not put women at risk of rheumatoid arthritis (RA), according to a new study partially funded by the National Institute of Arthritis and Musculoskeletal and Skin Diseases (NIAMS). The study concluded that there is little evidence to support a connection between consuming coffee or tea and the risk of RA among women.

Rheumatoid arthritis is an inflammatory autoimmune disease that affects the joints. It results in pain, stiffness, swelling, joint damage, and loss of function. Inflammation most often affects the hands and feet and tends to be symmetrical. About one percent of the U.S. population has rheumatoid arthritis.

Elizabeth W. Karlson, M.D., and her colleagues at Harvard Medical School and Brigham and Women's Hospital in Boston, Massachusetts, used the Nurses' Health Study, a long-term investigation of nurses' diseases, lifestyles, and health practices, to examine possible links between caffeinated beverages and RA risk. The researchers were able to follow up more than 90 percent of the original pool of 83,124 participants who answered a 1980 food frequency questionnaire, and no links were found. They also considered changes in diet and habits over a prolonged period of time, and when the results were adjusted for other factors, such as cigarette smoking, alcohol consumption, and oral contraceptive use, the outcome still showed no relationship between caffeine consumption and risk of RA.

Previous research had suggested an association between consuming coffee or tea and RA risk. According to Dr. Karlson, the data supporting that conclusion were inconsistent. Because the information in the older studies was collected at only one time, she says, consideration was not given to the other factors associated with RA, such as cigarette smoking and changes in diet and lifestyle over a follow-up period. The new study presents a more accurate picture of caffeine and RA risk.

36. What is the main idea of the passage?

    a. In the past, doctors have cautioned older women to avoid caffeinated beverages.
    b. Rheumatoid arthritis affects the joints of older women.
    c. A recent study found no link between caffeine consumption and RA among women.
    d. Cigarette smoking increases the incidence of RA.

37. Which statement is not a detail from the passage?

    a. Alcohol consumption is linked with RA.
    b. The original data for the study came from a 1980 questionnaire.
    c. Rheumatoid arthritis most often affects the hands and feet.
    d. This study included tens of thousands of participants.

38. What is the meaning of the word symmetrical as it is used in the second paragraph?

    a. affecting both sides of the body in corresponding fashion
    b. impossible to treat
    c. sensitive to the touch
    d. asymptomatic

39. What is the author's primary purpose in writing the essay?

    a. to entertain
    b. to inform
    c. to analyze
    d. to persuade

40. This passage describes Toni Morrison's writing as all of the following EXCEPT:

Toni Morrison, who name was originally Chloe Anthony Wofford, is a writer of great distinction who has won many awards, one of which was the Pulitzer Prize in 1988. From her very first novel, *The Bluest Eye*, the writer has portrayed the struggles of black people, and especially black women, in America. Her writing is multifaceted and profound with the distinctive African-American culture as the backbone. Morrison's novels are literary epics with strong, descriptive dialogue and black characters with powerful depth.

    a. multifaceted
    b. award-winning
    c. profound
    d. struggling

Verbal

30 minutes, 60 questions

For questions 1-30: Select the synonym. Each question has a word in all capital letters followed by five answer choices in all lower-case letters. Select the answer choice with a definition closest to the capitalized word.

1. OBSCURE:

a. opinionated
b. unclear
c. offensive
d. benign

2. REMISS:

a. timely
b. diligent
c. negligent
d. meticulous

3. GRIEVOUS:

a. casual
b. frightening
c. delighted
d. serious

4. EXHILARATION:

a. exhalation
b. aimlessness
c. curiosity
d. elation

5. SIEGE:

a. slip
b. blockade
c. severity
d. odor

6. COURTEOUS:

a. conscientious
b. polite
c. interested
d. aware

7. RECEDE:

a. excel
b. increase
c. abut
d. wane

8. BRANDISHED:
   a. threw
   b. waved menacingly
   c. smacked
   d. peered

9. BESOTTED:
   a. infatuated
   b. infuriated
   c. perplexed
   d. engrossed

10. VICINITY:
   a. neighborhood
   b. parish
   c. mindset
   d. idea

11. PROGNOSIS:
   a. forecast
   b. description
   c. outline
   d. schedule

12. ABSTAIN:
   a. offend
   b. retrain
   c. to refrain from
   d. defenestrate

13. OMINOUS:
   a. threatening
   b. emboldening
   c. destructive
   d. insightful

14. INCIDENCE:
   a. random events
   b. sterility
   c. autonomy
   d. rate of occurrence

15. OCCLUDED:
   a. closed
   b. deformed
   c. enlarged
   d. engorged

16. POTENT:

a. frantic
b. determined
c. feverish
d. powerful

17. PRECIPITOUS:

a. detached
b. sordid
c. encompassed
d. steep

18. INSIDIOUS:

a. stealthy
b. deadly
c. collapsed
d. new

19. PROSCRIBE:

a. anticipate
b. prevent
c. defeat
d. forbid

20. DISTENDED:

a. concave
b. sore
c. swollen
d. empty

21. OVERT:

a. concealed
b. apparent
c. expert
d. delectable

22. CARNIVORE:

a. hungry
b. meat-eating
c. infected
d. demented

23. BELLIGERENT:

a. retired
b. sardonic
c. pugnacious
d. acclimated

24. FLACCID:

a. defended
b. limp
c. slender
d. outdated

25. TERRESTRIAL:

a. alien
b. earthly
c. foreign
d. domestic

26. ENDOGENOUS:

a. contagious
b. painful to the touch
c. continuous
d. growing from within

27. DISCRETE:

a. calm
b. subtle
c. hidden
d. separate

28. EXACERBATE:

a. implicate
b. aggravate
c. heal
d. decondition

29. HOLISTIC:

a. insensitive
b. ignorant
c. specialized
d. concerned with the whole rather than the parts

30. REPUGNANT:

a. destructive
b. selective
c. collective
d. offensive

For questions 31-60: These questions ask you to identify and compare relationships between pairs of words. Select the answer that best completes the comparison.

31. shovel is to dig as spoon is to

a. stir
b. knife
c. silverware
d. eat

32. shoot is to gun as drive is to

    a. road
    b. way
    c. automobile
    d. golf

33. simmer is to boil as tremor is to

    a. earth
    b. earthquake
    c. shake
    d. nervous

34. intelligent is to stupid as enthusiastic is to

    a. happy
    b. passionate
    c. action
    d. indifferent

35. bouquet is to flowers as recipe is to

    a. success
    b. cookbook
    c. ingredients
    d. chef

36. cool is to freezing as warm is to

    a. boiling
    b. summer
    c. heat
    d. cozy

37. France is to Europe as China is to

    a. Japan
    b. Asia
    c. country
    d. continent

38. fable is to story as sandal is to

    a. strap
    b. summer
    c. foot
    d. shoe

39. shell is to beach as rock is to

    a. roll
    b. stone
    c. mountain
    d. dune

40. kitchen is to cook as library is to

   a. peace
   b. read
   c. play
   d. pray

41. rug is to floor as sheet is to

   a. pillowcase
   b. bedspread
   c. sail
   d. bed

42. smokestack is to factory as steeple is to

   a. church
   b. chase
   c. dome
   d. high

43. rain is to wet as fire is to

   a. ash
   b. ember
   c. hot
   d. spark

44. sentence is to paragraph as brick is to

   a. mortar
   b. cement
   c. slate
   d. wall

45. try is to attempt as dare is to

   a. challenge
   b. devil
   c. fear
   d. defy

46. laugh is to joy as sneer is to

   a. snicker
   b. snob
   c. contempt
   d. face

47. hospital is to surgeon as store is to

   a. clerk
   b. inventory
   c. warehouse
   d. customer

48. weave is to basket as knit is to

    a. brow
    b. scarf
    c. sew
    d. needle

49. hungry is to eat as tired is to

    a. bed
    b. awake
    c. sick
    d. sleep

50. desert is to dune as ocean is to

    a. deep
    b. continent
    c. sea
    d. wave

51. oil is to squeak as salve is to

    a. burn
    b. medicine
    c. soothe
    d. ointment

52. nudge is to shove as nibble is to

    a. morsel
    b. devour
    c. tiny
    d. swallow

53. cavity is to tooth as wart is to

    a. hog
    b. blemish
    c. skin
    d. virus

54. had is to have as saw is to

    a. tool
    b. sawed
    c. see
    d. wood

55. racket is to tennis as paddle is to

    a. hit
    b. punishment
    c. wheel
    d. ping pong

56. etch is to glass as paint is to

 a. canvas
 b. draw
 c. color
 d. brush

57. debt is to pay as law is to

 a. obey
 b. break
 c. order
 d. legal

58. president is to government as principal is to

 a. belief
 b. teacher
 c. school
 d. student

59. pearl is to oyster as seed is to

 a. plant
 b. grape
 c. sow
 d. grow

60. rake is to hoe as hammer is to

 a. head
 b. build
 c. pound
 d. screwdriver

Quantitative (Math)

Read each question, perform the appropriate calculations, and determine the correct answer.

1. Archie's gas tank is 1/3 full. If Archie adds 3 gallons of gas to the tank, it will be ½ full. What is the capacity in gallons of Archie's tank?

    a. 28
    b. 12
    c. 20
    d. 16
    e. 18

2. If 30 kids on one team average 8 points each, and 20 kids on another team average 7 points each, what is the average of all kids?

    a. 7
    b. 7.2
    c. 7.4
    d. 7.6
    e. 7.8

3. Juice that is normally $3.49 a gallon is on sale at two gallons for $5.99. How much money can be saved by buying 4 gallons at the sale price?

    a. $3.00
    b. $2.98
    c. $1.98
    d. $1.50
    e. $0.98

4. Which of the following is equal to three fourths of 0.01 percent?

    a. 0.75
    b. 0.075
    c. 0.0075
    d. 0.00075
    e. 0.000075

5. $(10 - 9 - 8 - 7) - (11 - 10 - 9 - 8) =$

    a. -30
    b. 2
    c. -2
    d. 0
    e. -1

6. If $4x - 7 = 9,$ then $7x =$

    a. 4
    b. 16
    c. 28
    d. 2
    e. 3

7. If four friends had an average score of 92 on a test, what was Annie's score if Bill got an 86, Clive got a 98 and Demetrius got a 90?

    a. 88
    b. 90
    c. 92
    d. 94
    e. 96

8. What percent of 8 is 9?

    a. 89%
    b. 99%
    c. 102.5%
    d. 112.5%
    e. 122.5%

9. If $3x - 2 = 1$, then $x =$

    a. 4
    b. 3
    c. 2
    d. 1
    e. -1

10. If $2^4 = 4^x$, then $x =$

    a. 2
    b. 3
    c. 4
    d. 8
    e. 16

11. If $2x + 3y = 13$ and $4x - y = 5$, then $3x + 2y =$

    a. 2
    b. 3
    c. 6
    d. 12
    e. 24

12. What is the value of $(-5) + (-3)$?

    a. -2
    b. 2
    c. -1
    d. -8
    e. 8

13. A rectangle is divided into two squares, each with a perimeter of 20. What is the perimeter of the rectangle?

   a. 20
   b. 30
   c. 40
   d. 50
   e. 60

Use the following graph to answer questions 14-16:

Top Three Majors at Greenly Community College

Class	History	Engineering	Spanish
Freshmen	30	25	17
Sophomore	33	21	18
Junior	36	22	14
Senior	29	28	19

14. What percentage of freshmen are studying a major other than history, engineering or Spanish?

   a. 8%
   b. 18%
   c. 28%
   d. 38%
   e. 48%

15. If class sizes are the same for all 4 years, what percentage of the overall student body is studying history?

   a. 29
   b. 30
   c. 31
   d. 32
   e. 33

16. Which of the following are the lowest terms for expressing the ratio of the percentage of juniors majoring in Spanish to the percentage of juniors majoring in history?

   a. 14:36
   b. 14:22
   c. 7:11
   d. 7:18
   e. 14:18

17. The ski team has 16 boys and 24 girls. What fraction of the ski team are girls?

   a. 2/3
   b. 2/5
   c. 3/4
   d. 3/5
   e. 4/5

18. For what real number x is it true that $3(2x - 10) = x$?

    a. -6
    b. -5
    c. 5
    d. 6
    e. 30

19. A two-digit number is chosen at random. What is the probability that the chosen number is a multiple of 7?

    a. 1/10
    b. 1/9
    c. 11/90
    d. 12/90
    e. 13/90

20. If the ratio of the measures of the three angles in a triangle are $2 : 6 : 10$, what is the actual measure of the smallest angle?

    a. 20 degrees
    b. 40 degrees
    c. 60 degrees
    d. 80 degrees
    e. 100 degrees

21. If $a = 3, b = 4, c = 5$, then $(a + b + c)^2 + (a - b - c) =$

    a. 124
    b. 136
    c. 138
    d. 150
    e. 118

22. If $x = 2$ then $x^4(x + 3) =$

    a. 72
    b. 80
    c. 96
    d. 114
    e. 85

23. $160\% =$

    a. 5/6
    b. 6/5
    c. 8/5
    d. 9/6
    e. 7/4

24. Which of the following is equivalent to 5.30×10^{-4}?

    a.   0.000053

    b.   0.00053

    c.   53,000

    d.   5,300,000

    e.   0.0053

25. $45^x/5^x =$

    a. 9^x

    b.   9

    c. 11^x

    d.   11

    e. $9x^2$

Answer Key and Explanations for Test #2

Quantitative (Math)

1. D: Since 16 chairs are empty, and this represents 2/5 of the total enrollment, then the full class must consist of $\frac{5}{2} \times 16 = 40$ students.

Using proportions:

$$\frac{2}{5} = \frac{16}{x} \qquad \text{Cross multiply}$$
$$2x = 80 \qquad \text{Divide each side by 2}$$
$$x = 40$$

2. A: Begin by determining the total cost of the onions and carrots, since these prices are given. This will equal $(2 \times \$3.69) + (3 \times \$4.29) = \$20.25$. Next, this sum is subtracted from the total cost of the vegetables to determine the cost of the mushrooms: $\$24.15 - \$20.25 = \$3.90$. Finally, the cost of the mushrooms is divided by the quantity (lbs) to determine the cost per pound:

$$\text{Cost per lb} = \frac{\$3.90}{1.5} = \$2.60$$

3. D: Since the figure represents the number line, the distance from point A to point B will be the difference, $B - A$, which is $5 - (-6) = 11$. The distance from point B to point C will also be the difference, $C - B$, otherwise $8 - 5 = 3$. So, the ratio $BC{:}AB$ will be 3:11.

4. A: Candidate A's vote ratio is the number of votes that he obtained divided by the total number of votes cast. Then, multiply that decimal by 100 to convert the decimal into a percentage. Therefore, Candidate A's Vote is: $\frac{36,800}{36,800+32,100+2,100} \times 100 = 51.8\%$

5. A: The rate of increase equals the change in the account balance divided by the original amount, $\$80$. Multiply that decimal by 100 to yield the percentage of increase. To determine the change in the balance, subtract the original amount from the new balance: Change $= \$120 - \$80 = \$40$. Now, determine the percentage of increase as described above: Percent $= \frac{\$40}{\$80} \times 100 = 50\%$.

6. B: Since the figure is a right triangle, the Pythagorean Theorem may be applied. The side which is 25 units long is the hypotenuse, and its square will equal the sum of the squares of the other two sides. That is, $25^2 = 15^2 + x^2$. Solve for x^2 by subtracting 15^2 from each side of this equation, and then take the square root to determine x.

$$x = \sqrt{25^2 - 15^2} = \sqrt{625 - 225} = \sqrt{400} = 20$$

7. D: Since each of the 3 models is available in each of the 6 different colors, there are $6 \times 3 = 18$ different combinations available.

8. D: In order to multiply two powers that have the same base, add their exponents. Therefore, $x^3 x^5 = x^{3+5} = x^8$. Also, note that $x^3 = x \times x \times x$. Therefore, the expression is equivalent to $(x \times x \times x) \times (x \times x \times x \times x \times x)$.

9. B: A proportion such as this can be solved by taking the cross product of the numerators and denominators from either side.

$$\frac{12}{x} = \frac{30}{6}$$ Cross multiply
$$72 = 30x$$ Divide each side by 30
$$2.4 = x$$

10. C: The internal angles of a triangle always add up to 180°. Since ΔABC is a right triangle, then $\angle ABC = 90°$, and $\angle ACB$ is given as 30°. The middle letter represents the vertex. By using triangle addition theorem, the answer must be: $\angle BAC = 180 - (90 + 30)$ which equals 60°.

11. C: Since there are four different colors, one color must be excluded from each balloon bundle. Therefore, there is one color set for each excluded color, or four in all.

This problem can also be solved mathematically as follows. An arrangement such as this, in which the order of the individual components is not important, is called a combination. The number of combinations of n objects taken k at a time is given by $C = \frac{n!}{(n-k)!k!}$. The ! notation indicates a *factorial* product, where $n! = 1 \times 2 \times 3 \times ... \times (n-1) \times n$. In this case, $n = 4$ colors, and $k = 3$ balloons per bundle. Substituting into the equation above, and simplifying:

$$C = \frac{4!}{(4-3)! \times 3!} = \frac{1 \times 2 \times 3 \times 4}{(1)(1 \times 2 \times 3)} = 4$$

12. B: The two right triangles are similar because they share a pair of vertical angles. Vertical angles are always congruent ($\angle ACB$ and $\angle DCE$). Obviously both right angles ($\angle B$ and $\angle D$) are congruent. Thus, $\angle A$ and $\angle E$ are congruent because of the triangular sum theorem.

With similar triangles, corresponding sides will be proportional. Segment $\overline{BC}$ is half the length of $\overline{CD}$, therefore $\overline{AC}$ will be half the length of $\overline{CE}$. The length of $\overline{CE}$ can be computed from the Pythagorean theorem, since it is the hypotenuse of a right triangle for which the lengths of the other two sides are known: $\overline{CE} = \sqrt{6^2 + 8^2} = \sqrt{100} = 10$.

The length of $\overline{AC}$ will be ½ of this value, or 5 units.

13. C: For each die there is 1 chance in 6 that a 6 will emerge on top, since the die has 6 sides. The probability that a 6 will show for each die is not affected by the results obtained for any other. Since these probabilities are independent, the overall probability of throwing 3 sixes is the product of the individual probabilities, or

$$P = \frac{1}{6} \times \frac{1}{6} \times \frac{1}{6}$$
$$= \frac{1}{6^3}$$
$$= \frac{1}{216}$$

14. D: When a number is raised to a power, it is multiplied by itself as many times as the power indicates. For example, $2^3 = 2 \times 2 \times 2 = 8$. A number raised to the power of 0 is always equal to 1, so 6^0 is the smallest number shown. Similarly, for the other numbers: $9 = 9^1 = 9$; $10^1 = 10$; $4^2 = 4 \times 4 = 16$.

15. B: In this probability problem, there are three independent events (the codes for each digit), each with ten possible outcomes (the numerals 0-9). Since the events are independent, the total possible outcomes equals the product of the possible outcomes for each of the three events, that is $P = P_1 \times P_2 \times P_3 = 10 \times 10 \times 10 = 1,000$.

This makes sense when you also relate the problem to a sequence, beginning with the combinations 0-0-0, 0-0-1, 0-0-2......In ascending order, the last 3 digit combination would be 9-9-9. Although it may seem that there would be 999 possible combinations, you must include the initial combination, 0-0-0.

16. E: The area of the circle is πr^2 while the circumference is $2\pi r$. Taking the ratio of these two expressions and reducing gives: Ratio $= \frac{\pi r^2}{2\pi r} = \frac{r}{2}$

17. A: The mode is the number that appears most often in a set of data. If no item appears most often, then the data set has no mode. In this case, Kyle achieved one hit a total of three times, two hits twice, three hits once, and four hits once. One hit occurred the most times, therefore the mode of the data set is 1.

18. B: The mean, or average, is the sum of the numbers in a data set divided by the total number of items. This data set contains seven items, one for each day of the week. The total number of hits that Kyle had during the week is the sum of the numbers in the right-hand column, or 14. This gives: Mean $= \frac{14}{7} = 2$.

19. C: This problem is solved by finding x in this equation: $\frac{32}{80} = \frac{x}{100}$. Cross-multiply to get $80x = 3,200$, then divide 3,200 by 80 to get $x = 40$.

20. C: Every possible combination of scores is a multiple of 7, since the two terms of the ratio have a sum of seven.

21. A: A set of six numbers with an average of 4 must have a collective sum of 24. The two numbers that average 2 will add up to 4, so the remaining numbers must add up to 20. The average of these four numbers can be calculated: $20/4 = 5$.

22. D: Multiply 30 by 0.2 and subtract this from the original price of the shirt to find the sale price: $24. Then multiply 24 by 0.2 and add the product to the sale price to find the final price.

23. A: If it takes 3 people 3 1/3 days to do the job, then it would take one person 10 days: $3 \times \left(3\frac{1}{3}\right) = 10$.Thus, it would take 2 people 5 days, and one day of work for two people would complete 1/5 of the job.

24. C: Since 4 is the same as 2^2, $4^6 = 2^{12}$. When dividing exponents with the same base, simply subtract the exponent in the denominator from the exponent in the numerator.

$$2^{12} \div 2^8 = 2^{12-8} = 2^4 = 16$$

25. A: Convert 20% to the fraction 1/5, then multiply by 12/5. The resulting fraction, 12/25, must have both numerator and denominator multiplied by 4 to become a percentage.

Reading Comprehension

1. D: The main idea of this passage is that vaccines help the immune system function properly. Identifying main ideas is one of the key skills tested by the exam. One of the common traps that many test-takers fall into is assuming that the first sentence of the passage will express the main idea. Although this will be true for some passages, often the author will use the first sentence to attract interest or to make an introductory, but not central, point. On this question, if you assume that the first sentence contains the main idea, you will incorrectly choose answer B. Finding the main idea of a passage requires patience and thoroughness; you cannot expect to know the main idea until you have read the entire passage. In this case, a diligent reading will show you that answer choices A, B, and C express details from the passage, but only answer choice D is a comprehensive summary of the author's message.

2. C: This passage does not state that the symptoms of disease will not emerge until the body has learned to fight the disease. The reading comprehension section of the exam will include several questions that require you to identify details from a passage. The typical structure of these questions is to ask you to identify the answer choice that contains a detail not included in the passage. This question structure makes your work a little more difficult, because it requires you to confirm that the other three details are in the passage. In this question, the details expressed in answer choices A, B, and D are all explicit in the passage. The passage never states, however, that the symptoms of disease do not emerge until the body has learned how to fight the disease-causing microbe. On the contrary, the passage implies that a person may become quite sick and even die before the body learns to effectively fight the disease.

3. B: In the third paragraph, the word *virulent* means "malicious." The reading comprehension section of the exam will include several questions that require you to define a word as it is used in the passage. Sometimes the word will be one of those used in the vocabulary section of the exam; other times, the word in question will be a slightly difficult word used regularly in academic and professional circles. In some cases, you may already know the basic definition of the word. Nevertheless, you should always go back and look at the way the word is used in the passage. The exam will often include answer choices that are legitimate definitions for the given word, but which do not express how the word is used in the passage. For instance, the word *virulent* could in some circumstances mean contagious. However, since the passage is not talking about transfer of the disease, but the effects of the disease once a person has caught it, malicious is the more appropriate answer.

4. C: The author's primary purpose in writing this essay is to inform. The reading comprehension section of the exam will include a few questions that ask you to determine the purpose of the author. The answer choices are always the same: The author's purpose is to entertain, to persuade, to inform, or to analyze. When an author is *writing to entertain*, he or she is not including a great deal of factual information; instead, the focus is on vivid language and interesting stories. *Writing to persuade* means "trying to convince the reader of something." When a writer is just trying to provide the reader with information, without any particular bias, he or she is *writing to inform*. Finally, *writing to analyze* means to consider a subject already well known to the reader. For instance, if the above passage took an objective look at the pros and cons of various approaches to fighting disease, we would say that the passage was a piece of analysis. Because the purpose of this passage is to present new information to the reader in an objective manner, it is clear that the author's intention is to inform.

5. A: The subject of this passage is foodborne illnesses. Identifying the subject of a passage is similar to identifying the main idea. Do not assume that the first sentence of the passage will declare the subject. Oftentimes, an author will approach his or her subject by first describing some related, familiar subject. In this passage, the author does introduce the subject of the passage in the first sentence. However, it is only by reading the rest of the passage that you can determine the subject. One way to figure out the subject of a passage is to identify the main idea of each paragraph, and then identify the common thread in each.

6. B: This passage never states that cooked food cannot cause illness. Indeed, the first sentence of the third paragraph states that harmful bacteria can be present on cooked food that is left out for two or more hours. This is a direct contradiction of answer choice B. If you can identify an answer choice that is clearly contradicted by the text, you can be sure that it is not one of the ideas advanced by the passage. Sometimes the correct answer to this type of question will be something that is contradicted in the text; on other occasions, the correct answer will be a detail that is not included in the passage at all.

7. C: In the first paragraph, the word *pathogens* means "disease-causing substances." The vocabulary you are asked to identify in the reading comprehension section of the exam will tend to be health related. The exam administrators are especially interested in your knowledge of the terminology used by doctors and nurses. Some of these words, however, are rarely used in normal conversation, so they may be unfamiliar to you. The best way to determine the meaning of an unfamiliar word is to examine how it is used in context. In the last sentence of the first paragraph, it is clear that pathogens are some substances that cause disease. Note that the pathogens are not diseases themselves; we would not say that an uncooked piece of meat "has a disease," but rather that consuming it "can cause a disease." For this reason, answer choice C is better than answer choice A.

8. A: In the second paragraph, the word *sterile* means "free of bacteria." This question provides a good example of why you should always refer to the word as it is used in the text. The word *sterile* is often used to describe "a person who cannot reproduce." If this definition immediately came to mind when you read the question, you might have mistakenly chosen answer D. However, in this passage the author describes raw foods as *not sterile*, meaning that they contain bacteria. For this reason, answer choice A is the correct response.

9. C: The main idea of the passage is that both the esophagus and the stomach are subject to bleeding problems. The structure of this passage is simple: The first paragraph discusses bleeding disorders of the esophagus, and the second paragraph discusses bleeding disorders of the stomach. Remember that statements can be true, and can even be explicitly stated in the passage, and can yet not be the main idea of the passage. The main idea given in answer choice A is perhaps true but is too general to be classified as the main idea of the passage.

10. B: The passage never states that ulcer disease rarely occurs in the stomach. On the contrary, in the second paragraph the author states that ulcer disease *can* affect the blood vessels in the stomach. The three other answer choices can be found within the passage. The surest way to answer a question like this is to comb through the passage, looking for each detail in turn. This is a time-consuming process, however, so you may want to follow any initial intuition you have. In other words, if you are suspicious of one of the answer choices, see if you can find it in the passage. Often you will find that the detail is expressly contradicted by the author, in which case you can be sure that this is the right answer.

11. A: In the first paragraph, the word *rupture* means "tear." All of the answer choices are action verbs that suggest destruction. In order to determine the precise meaning of rupture, then, you must examine its usage in the passage. The author is describing a condition in which damage to a vein causes internal bleeding. Therefore, it does not make sense to say that the vein has *collapsed* or *imploded*, as neither of these verbs suggests a ripping or opening in the side of the vein. Similarly, the word *detach* suggests an action that seems inappropriate for a vein. It seems quite possible, however, for a vein to *tear*: Answer choice A is correct.

12. D: In the second paragraph, the word *erode* means "wear away." Your approach to this question should be the same as for question 11. Take a look at how the word is used in the passage. The author is describing a condition in which ulcers degrade a vein to the point of bleeding. Obviously, it is not appropriate to say that the ulcer has *avoided*, *divorced*, or *contained* the vein. It *is* sensible, however, to say that the ulcer has *worn away* the vein.

13. A: The primary subject of the passage is a new artificial retina. This question is a little tricky, because the author spends so much time talking about the experience of Kathy Blake. As a reader, however, you have to ask yourself whether Mrs. Blake or the new artificial retina is more essential to the story. Would the author still be interested in the story if a different person had the artificial retina? Probably. Would the author have written about Mrs. Blake if she hadn't gotten the artificial retina? Almost certainly not. Really, the story of Kathy Blake is just a way for the author to make the artificial retina more interesting to the reader. Therefore, the artificial retina is the primary subject of the passage.

14. B: In the second paragraph, the word *progressive* means "gradually increasing." The root of the word is *progress*, which you may know means "advancement toward a goal." With this in mind, you may be reasonably certain that answer choice B is correct. It is never a bad idea to examine the context, however. The author is describing *progressive visual loss*, so you might be tempted to select answer choice C or D, since they both suggest loss or diminution. Remember, however, that the adjective *progressive* is modifying the noun *loss*. Since the *loss* is increasing, the correct answer is B.

15. C: The passage never states that retinitis pigmentosa (RP) is curable. This question may be somewhat confusing, since the passage discusses a new treatment for RP. However, the passage never declares that researchers have come up with a cure for the condition; rather, they have developed a new technology that allows people who suffer from RP to regain some of their vision. This is not the same thing as curing RP. Kathy Blake and others like her still have RP, though they have been assisted by this exciting new technology.

16. D: The author's intention in writing this essay is to inform. You may be tempted to answer that the author's intention is to entertain. Indeed, the author expresses his message through the story of Kathy Blake. This story, however, is not important by itself. It is clearly included as a way of explaining the new camera glasses. If the only thing the reader learned from the passage was the story of Kathy Blake, the author would probably be disappointed. At the same time, the author is not really trying to persuade the reader of anything. There is nothing controversial about these new glasses: Everyone is in favor of them. The mission of the author, then, is simply to inform the reader.

17. A: The main idea of the passage is that Usher syndrome is an inherited condition that affects hearing and vision. Always be aware that some answers may be included in the passage but not the main idea. In this question, answer choices B and D are both true details from the passage, but neither of them would be a good summary of the article. One way to approach this kind of question is to consider what you would be likely to say if someone asked you to describe the article in a single sentence. Often, the sentence you come up with will closely mimic one of the answer choices. If so, you can be sure that answer choice is correct.

18. D: In the first paragraph, the word signs means "measurable indicators." The word sign is used frequently in medical contexts, though many people do not entirely understand its meaning. Signs are those objective (measurable) indicators of illness that can be observed by someone besides the person with the illness. A stomachache, for instance, is not technically considered a sign, since it cannot be observed by anyone other than the person who has it, and therefore must be expressed by the individual experiencing it. This would be known as a symptom. Change in vital signs, a failed hearing test, or a low Snellen (vision) chart score, however, would all be considered signs because practitioners can measure or observe them. The best definition for signs, then, is "measurable indicators," that is, objective markers of a disease or condition.

19. B: The passage does not state that Usher syndrome affects both hearing and smell. On the contrary, the passage only states that Usher syndrome affects hearing and vision. You should not be content merely to note that sentence in the passage and select answer choice B. In order to be sure, you need to quickly scan the passage to determine whether there is any mention of problems with the sense of smell. This is because the mention of impaired hearing and vision does not make it impossible for smell to be damaged as well. It is a good idea to practice scanning short articles for specific words. In this case, you would want to scan the article looking for words like *smell* and *nose*.

20. C: In the second paragraph, the word *juvenile* means "occurring in children." Examine the context in which the word is used. Remember that the context extends beyond just the immediate sentence in which the word is found. It can also include adjacent sentences and paragraphs. In this case, the word juvenile is immediately followed by a further explanation of Usher syndrome as it appears in children. You can be reasonably certain, then, that juvenile Usher syndrome is the condition as it presents in children. Although the word *juvenile* is occasionally used in English to describe immature or annoying behavior, it is clear that the author is not here referring to a *bratty* form of Usher syndrome.

21. B: In the third paragraph, the word *mutated* means "altered." This word comes from the same root as mutant; a *mutant* is an organism in which the chromosomes have been changed somehow. The context in which the word is used makes it clear that the author is referring to a scenario in which one of the parent's chromosomes has been altered. One way to approach this kind of problem is to substitute the answer choice into the passage to see if it still makes sense. Clearly, it would not make sense for a chromosome to be *selected*, since chromosomes are passed on and inherited without conscious choice. Neither does it make sense for a chromosome to be destroyed, because a basic fact of biology is that all living organisms have chromosomes.

22. D: The main idea of the passage is that the immune system protects the body from infection. The author repeatedly alludes to the complexity and mystery of the immune system, so it cannot be true that scientists fully understand this part of the body. It is true that the immune system triggers the production of fluids, but this description misses the point. Similarly, it is true that the body is under constant invasion by malicious microbes; however, the author is much more interested in the body's response to these microbes. For this reason, the best answer choice is D.

23. C: The passage never states that viruses are extremely sophisticated. In fact, the passage explicitly states the opposite. However, in order to know this, you need to understand the word *primitive*. The passage says that viruses are too primitive, or early in their development, to be classified as living organisms. A primitive organism is simple and undeveloped—exactly the opposite of sophisticated. If you do not know the word *primitive*, you can still answer the question by finding all three of the answer choices in the passage.

24. D: In the first paragraph, the word *ideal* means "perfect." Do not be confused by the similarity of the word *ideal* to *idea* and mistakenly select answer choice A. Take a look at the context in which the word is used. The author is describing how many millions of microbes can live inside the human body. It would not make sense, then, for the author to be describing the body as a *hostile* environment for microbes. Moreover, whether or not the body is a confined environment would not seem to have much bearing on whether it is good for microbes. Rather, the paragraph suggests that the human body is a perfect environment for microbes.

25. B: The passage never states that the immune system ignores tumors. Indeed, at the beginning of the third paragraph, the author states that scientists remain puzzled by the body's ability to fight tumors. This question is a little tricky, because it is common knowledge that many tumors prove fatal to the human body. However, you should not take this to mean that the body does not at least try to fight tumors. In general, it is best to seek out direct evidence in the text rather than to rely on what you already know. You will have enough time on the exam to fully examine and research each question.

26. A: In the second paragraph, the word *enlist* means "call into service." The use of this word is an example of figurative language, the use of a known image or idea to elucidate an idea that is perhaps unfamiliar to the reader. In this case, the author is describing the efforts of the immune system as if they were a military campaign. The immune system *enlists* other cells, and then directs these *recruits* to areas where they are needed. You are probably familiar with *enlistment* and *recruitment* as they relate to describe military service. The author is trying to draw a parallel between the enlistment of young men and women and the enlistment of immune cells. For this reason, "call into service" is the best definition for *enlist*.

27. C: The author's primary purpose in writing this essay is to inform. As you may have noticed, the essays included in the reading comprehension section of the exam were most often written to inform. This should not be too surprising; after all, the most common intention of any writing on general medical subjects is to provide information rather than to persuade, entertain, or analyze. This does not mean that you can automatically assume that "to inform" will be the answer for every question of this type. However, if you are in doubt, it is probably best to select this answer. In this case, the passage is written in a clear, declarative style with no obvious prejudice on the part of the author. The primary intention of the passage seems to be providing information about the immune system to a general audience.

28. B: The main idea of the passage is that the Food and Drug Administration (FDA) has a special program for regulating dietary supplements. This passage has a straightforward structure: The author introduces his subject in the first paragraph and uses the four succeeding paragraphs to elaborate. All of the other possible answers are true statements from the passage but cannot be considered the main idea. One way to approach questions about the main idea is to take sentences at random from the passage and see which answer choice they could potentially support. The main idea should be strengthened or supported by most of the details from the passage.

29. D: The passage never states that the Food and Drug Administration (FDA) ignores products after they enter the market. In fact, the entire fourth paragraph describes the steps taken by the FDA to regulate products once they are available for purchase. In some cases, questions of this type will contain answer choices that are directly contradictory. Here, for instance, answer choices A and B cannot be true if answer choice D is true. If there are at least two answer choices that contradict another answer choice, it is a safe bet that the contradicted answer choice cannot be correct. If you are at all uncertain about your logic, however, you should refer to the passage.

30. C: In the third paragraph, the phrase *phased in* means "implemented in stages." Do not be tempted by the similarity of this phrase to the word *fazed*, which can mean "confused or stunned." The author is referring to manufacturing standards that have already been implemented for large manufacturers and are in the process of being implemented for small manufacturers. It would make sense, then, for these standards to be implemented in *phases*: that is, to be *phased in*.

31. A: In the fifth paragraph, the word *deceptive* means "misleading." The root of the word *deceptive* is the same as for the words *deceive* and *deception*. Take a look at the context in which the word is used. The author states that the FDA prevents certain kinds of advertising. It would be somewhat redundant for the author to mean that the FDA prevents *illegal* advertising; this goes without saying. At the same time, it is unlikely that the FDA spends its time trying to prevent merely *irritating* advertising; the persistent presence of such advertising makes this answer choice inappropriate. Left with a choice between *malicious* and *misleading* advertising, it makes better sense to choose the latter, since being mean and nasty would be a bad technique for selling a product. It is common, however, for an advertiser to deliberately mislead the consumer.

32. B: The main idea of the passage is that anemia is a potentially dangerous condition characterized by low numbers of RBCs (red blood cells). All of the other answer choices are true (although answer C leaves out RBCs), but only answer choice C expresses an idea that is supported by the others. When you are considering a question of this type, try to imagine the answer choices as they would appear on an outline. If the passage above were placed into outline form, which answer choice would be the most appropriate title? Which answer choices would be more appropriate as supporting details? Try to get in the habit of imagining a loose outline as you are reading the passages on the exam.

33. D: The passage never states that anemia is rarely caused by blood loss. On the contrary, in the first sentence of the fourth paragraph the author lists three causes of anemia, and blood loss is listed first. Sometimes, answer choices for this type of question will refer to details not explicitly mentioned in the passage. For instance, answer choice A is true without ever being stated in precisely those terms. Since the passage mentions several different treatments for anemia, however, you should consider the detail in answer choice A to be in the passage. In other words, it is not enough to scan the passage looking for an exact version of the detail. Sometimes, you will have to use your best judgment.

34. D: In the third paragraph, the word *oxygenated* means "containing high amounts of oxygen." This word is not in common usage, so it is absolutely essential for you to refer to its context in the passage. The author states in the second paragraph that anemia is in part a deficiency of the red blood cells that carry oxygen throughout the body. Then in the first sentence of the third paragraph, the author states that anemic individuals do not get enough oxygenated blood. Given this information, it is clear that *oxygenated* must mean carrying high amounts of oxygen, because it has already been stated that anemia consists of a lack of oxygen-rich blood.

35. A: In the fifth paragraph, the word *severity* means "seriousness." This word shares a root with the word *severe*, but not with the word *sever*. As always, take a look at the word as it is used in the passage. In the final sentence of the passage, the author states that the treatment for anemia will depend on the *cause and severity* of the condition. In the previous paragraph, the author outlined a treatment for anemia and indicated that the proper response to the condition varies. The author even refers to the worst cases of anemia as being *severe*. With this in mind, it makes the most sense to define *severity* as seriousness.

36. C: The main idea of the passage is that a recent study found no link between caffeine consumption and rheumatoid arthritis (RA) among women. As is often the case, the first sentence of the passage contains the main idea. However, do not assume that this will always be the case. Furthermore, do not assume that the first sentence of the passage will only contain the main idea. In this passage, for instance, the author makes an immediate reference to the previous belief in the correlation between caffeine and RA. It would be incorrect, however, to think that this means answer choice A is correct. Regardless of whether or not the main idea is contained in the first sentence of the passage, you will need to read the entire text before you can be sure.

37. A: The passage never states that alcohol consumption is linked with RA. The passage does state that the new study took into account alcohol consumption when evaluating the long-term data. This is a good example of a question that requires you to spend a little bit of time rereading the passage. A quick glance might lead you to believe that the new study had found a link between alcohol and RA. Tricky questions like this make it even more crucial for you to go back and verify each answer choice in the text. Working through this question by using the process of elimination is the best way to ensure the correct response.

38. A: In the second paragraph, the word *symmetrical* means "affecting both sides of the body in corresponding fashion." This is an example of a question that is hard to answer even after reviewing its context in the passage. If you have no idea what *symmetrical* means, it will be hard for you to select an answer: All of them sound plausible. In such a case, the best thing you can do is make an educated guess. One clue is that the author has been describing a condition that affects the hands and the feet. Since people have both right and left hands and feet, it makes sense that inflammation would be described as *symmetrical* if it affects both the right and left hand or foot.

39. B: The author's primary purpose in writing this essay is to inform. You may be tempted to select answer choice D on the grounds that the author is presenting a particular point of view. However, there is no indication that the author is trying to persuade the reader of anything. One clear sign that an essay is written to persuade is a reference to what the reader already thinks. A persuasive essay assumes a particular viewpoint held by the reader and then argues against that viewpoint. In this passage, the author has no allegiance to any idea; he or she is only reporting the results of the newest research.

40. D: Although the passage does use the word "struggles" in the second sentence, the word does not describe the writing. The struggles are ones that Morrison's characters are dealing with rather than a description of Morrison's writing.

Verbal

1. B: The word "obscure" means "unclear" and "difficult to understand."

2. C: The word "remiss" means "negligent or forgetful."

3. D: Serious most closely means the same thing as grievous.

4. D: Elation most closely means the same thing as exhilaration.

5. B: Blockade most closely means the same thing as siege.

6. B: Polite most closely means the same things as courteous.

7. D: Wane most closely means the same thing as recede.

8. B: Brandish means to wave menacingly.

9. A: Besotted means infatuated.

10. A: Vicinity means neighborhood.

11. A: The best definition for the word *prognosis* is "forecast."

12. C: The best definition for the word *abstain* is "to refrain from."

13. A: The best synonym for *ominous* is "threatening."

14. D: The word *incidence* means "rate of occurrence."

15. A: The closest meaning for the word *occluded* is "closed."

16. D: The best definition for the word *potent* is "powerful."

17. D: The word *precipitous* means "steep."

18. A: The best definition of the word *insidious* is "stealthy."

19. D: The word *proscribe* means "forbid."

20. C: The word *distended* means "swollen."

21. B: The word *overt* means "apparent."

22. B: The word *carnivore* means "meat-eating."

23. C: The word *belligerent* means "pugnacious." *Pugnacious* means "ready to fight."

24. B: The best description for the word *flaccid* is "limp.

25. B: The word *terrestrial* means "earthly."

26. D: The word *endogenous* means "growing from within."

27. D: The best description for the word *discrete* is "separate."

28. B: The word *exacerbate* means "aggravate."

29. D: The word *holistic* means "concerned with the whole rather than the parts."

30. D: The word *repugnant* means "offensive, especially to the senses or the morals."

31. A: A shovel is used to dig and a spoon is used to stir. While a spoon can also be used to eat, it isn't the direct instrument of eating in the way that a shovel is the direct instrument of digging.

32. C: Shoot is an action done with a gun and drive is an action done with an automobile.

33. B: Simmer is a milder form of boil and tremor is a milder form of earthquake.

34. D: Intelligent is the opposite of stupid and enthusiastic is the opposite of indifferent.

35. C: A bouquet is made up of flowers and a recipe is made up of ingredients.

36. A: Cool is a mild temperature and freezing is extreme; warm is a mild temperature and boiling is extreme.

37. B: France is a country on the continent of Europe and China is a country on the continent of Asia.

38. D: A fable is a type of story and a sandal is a type of shoe.

39. C: A shell can be found on the beach and a rock can be found on a mountain.

40. B: You cook in a kitchen and you read in a library.

41. D: A rug covers the floor and a sheet covers a bed.

42. A: A smokestack extends from the roof of a factory and a steeple extends from the roof of a church.

43. C: Rain feels wet and fire feels hot.

44. D: Sentences make up a paragraph and bricks make up a wall.

45. A: Try is another word for attempt and challenge is another word for dare.

46. C: To laugh is to show joy and to sneer is to show contempt.

47. A: A surgeon works in a hospital and a clerk works in a store.

48. B: A basket can be made by weaving and a scarf can be made by knitting.

49. D: To eat is a solution to being hungry and to sleep is a solution to being tired.

50. D: A dune is a feature of the desert and a wave is a feature of the ocean.

51. A: Oil is applied to relieve a squeak and salve is applied to relieve a burn.

52. B: A nudge is less extreme as compared to a shove and nibble is less extreme as compared to devour.

53. C: A cavity is a flaw in a tooth and a wart is a flaw on the skin.

54. C: Had is the past tense of have and saw is the past tense of see.

55. D: A racket is used to play tennis and a paddle is used to play ping pong.

56. A: To etch is to embellish glass and to paint is to embellish a canvas.

57. A: A debt must be paid and a law must be obeyed.

58. C: A president heads the government and a principal heads the school.

59. B: A pearl can be found inside an oyster and a seed can be found inside a grape.

60. D: A rake and a hoe are both tools for gardening and a hammer and a screwdriver are both tools for building.

Quantitative (Math)

1. E: This problem can be solved with the following equation, in which x is the total capacity of the tank: $\frac{1}{2}x = \frac{1}{3}x + 3$.

2. D: To find the average, we divide the total points for both teams by the total number of players on both teams. The total score for the first team is $8 \times 30 = 240$. The total score for the second team is $7 \times 20 = 140$. This gives a total for both teams of $240 + 140 = 380$. The total number of kids on both teams is 50, so the average score for both teams is $380 \div 50 = 7.6$.

3. C: The savings per gallon can be found by dividing the sale price by 2 and then subtracting that from the regular price: $3.49 - (5.99 \div 2) = 3.49 - 2.995 = 0.495$ per gallon. Buying 4 gallons would therefore generate a savings of $4 \times 0.495 = 1.98$.

4. E: One percent is equivalent to 0.01. Therefore, 0.01 percent is $0.01 \times 0.01 = 0.0001$. Taking $\frac{3}{4}$, or 0.75, of that gives us $0.75 \times 0.0001 = 0.000075$. Note that the number of decimal places in the product is the sum of the number decimal places in each of the factors being multiplied.

5. B: The order of operations requires that we perform all operations inside the parentheses before performing the subtraction in the middle. $10 - 9 - 8 - 7 = -14$ and $11 - 10 - 9 - 8 = -16$. So, we are left with $(-14) - (-16) = -14 + 16 = 2$.

6. C: Solving for x, we add 7 to both sides to get $4x = 16$, then divide both sides by 4 to see that $x = 4$. Therefore $7x = 7 \times 4 = 28$.

7. D: This is a simple average problem. If x denotes Annie's score, $86 + 98 + 90 + x$, divided by 4 equals 92. To solve, multiply each side by 4 and add the known scores together to get $274 + x = 368$. Subtract 274 from 368 to solve. $x = 94$.

8. D: To determine what percent of 8 9 is, set up the following equality: $9/8 = x/100$. Then, solve for x:

$$8x = 90$$
$$x = 900/8$$
$$x = 112.5\%$$

9. D: If $3x - 2 = 1$, then $3x = 3$. Therefore, $x = 1$.

10. A: Recall and apply the rules for multiplying exponents:

$$2^4 = 4^x$$
$$2^{2\times2} = 4^x$$
$$(2^2)^2 = 4^x$$
$$4^2 = 4^x$$

Therefore, $x = 2$.

11. D: This system can be solved by substitution. Begin by solving for y in the second equation and then substituted into the first equation:

$$4x - y = 5$$
$$4x - 5 = y$$

Copyright © Mometrix Media. You have been licensed one copy of this document for personal use only. Any other reproduction or redistribution is strictly prohibited. All rights reserved. This content is provided for test preparation purposes only and does not imply an endorsement by Mometrix of any particular political, scientific, or religious point of view.

Next, substitute this expression for y into the first equation:

$$2x + 3(4x - 5) = 13$$
$$2x + 12x - 15 = 13$$
$$14x = 28$$
$$x = 2$$

Then, plug the value of x into the expression found for y.

$$4x - 5 = y$$
$$y = 3$$

Finally, find the value of $3x + 2y$:

$$3x + 2y = 3(2) + 2(3)$$
$$= 6 + 6$$
$$= 12$$

12. D: Recall the sum of two negative numbers is a negative number: $(-5) + (-3) = -8$.

13. B: The perimeter of a square is four times the length of any one of its sides. If a square's perimeter is 20, the length of any side is 5. The perimeter of this rectangle is six times the length of a side, which is 30.

14. C: The percentage of freshmen studying history, engineering, or Spanish is $30 + 25 + 17 = 72$. Therefore, the percentage of freshmen studying something else is $100 - 72$. The percentage is 28%.

15. D: Since class size is the same for all four years, we can average to get the percentage of the overall student body studying history.

$$\frac{30\% + 33\% + 36\% + 29\%}{4} = \frac{128\%}{4} = 32\%$$

16. D: The percentage of juniors majoring in Spanish is 14. The percentage of juniors majoring in history is 36. $\frac{14}{36}$ in lowest terms is $\frac{7}{18}$.

17. D: The ski team has 24 girls out of 40 total students. $\frac{24}{40} = \frac{3}{5}$ or 60%.

18. D: To solve, follow the order of operations and isolate the variable:

$$3(2x - 10) = x$$
$$6x - 30 = x$$
$$5x = 30$$
$$x = 6$$

19. E: There are 90 two-digit numbers (all integers from, and including, 10 to, and including, 99). Of those, there are 13 multiples of 7: $14, 21, 28, 35, 42, 49, 56, 63, 70, 77, 84, 91, 98$.

20. A: The sum of the measures of the three angles of any triangle is 180 degrees. The equation for the sum of the angles of this triangle can be written as $2x + 6x + 10x = 180$, or $18x = 180$. Therefore, $x = 10$. We multiply 2 by 10 to find that the measure of the smallest angle is 20 degrees.

21. C: Substitute the given values for a, b, and c into the expression and simplify:

$$(a + b + c)^2 + (a - b - c) = (3 + 4 + 5)^2 + (3 - 4 - 5)$$
$$= 12^2 + (-6)$$
$$= 144 - 6$$
$$= 138$$

22. B: Substitute the given value for x into the expression and simplify:

$$x^4(x + 3) = (2^4) \times (2 + 3)$$
$$= 16 \times 5$$
$$= 80$$

23. C: To convert a percentage to a fraction, recall that "percent" means per one hundred:

$$160\% = \frac{160}{100}$$
$$= \frac{8 \times 20}{5 \times 20}$$
$$= \frac{8}{5}$$

24. B: In scientific notation, the exponent on the 10 is the key to determining the decimal equivalent. A negative exponent means the value is decimal less than 1 in other words, move the decimal point to the left. In this case, it will move 4 places:

$$5.30 \times 10^{-4} = 5.3 \times 0.0001$$
$$= 0.00053$$

25. A: Begin by factoring 45^x into 9^x and 5^x, since $45^x = (9 \times 5)^x = 9^x \times 5^x$. The 5^x cancels out and the remainder is 9^x.

Practice Test #3

Writing Sample

25 Minutes

Instructions: Read the following prompt, taking a few moments to plan a response. Then, write your response in essay form.

Prompt: *A professional athlete should be held to a higher standard in his or her personal life than the average citizen.*

Do you agree or disagree with this statement? Use examples from history, literature, or your own personal experience to support your point of view.

Quantitative (Math)

Read each question, perform the appropriate calculations, and determine the correct answer.

1. A boy has a spinner labeled with the numbers from 1 to 10. He spins it 100 times and records his results in a table, shown below. Give the experimental probability that the boy will spin the number 6.

Number on Spinner	Frequency
1	12
2	13
3	11
4	6
5	12
6	14
7	8
8	9
9	12
10	3

a. $\dfrac{6}{100}$

b. $\dfrac{100}{100}$

c. $\dfrac{10}{100}$

d. $\dfrac{14}{100}$

e. $\dfrac{4}{100}$

2. Which of the following are complementary angles?

    a. 71° and 19°
    b. 18° and 18°
    c. 90° and 90°
    d. 90° and 45°
    e. 15° and 30°

3. A man decided to buy new furniture from Futuristic Furniture for $2,600. Futuristic Furniture gave the man two choices: pay the entire amount in one payment with cash, or pay $1,000 as a down payment and $120 per month for two full years in the financial plan. If the man chooses the financial plan, how much more would he pay?

    a. $1,480 more
    b. $1,280 more
    c. $1,600 more
    d. $2,480 more
    e. $3,720 more

4. What is the value of r in the following equation?

$$29 + r = 420$$

    a. $r = 29/420$
    b. $r = 420/29$
    c. $r = 391$
    d. $r = 449$
    e. $r = 478$

5. Find the area of the rectangle.

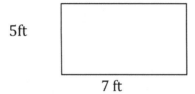

5ft   7 ft

    a. 5 ft^2
    b. 12 ft^2
    c. 24 ft^2
    d. 35 ft^2
    e. 70 ft^2

6. If 35% of a paycheck was deducted for taxes and 4% for insurance, what is the total percentage taken out of the paycheck?

    a. 20%
    b. 31%
    c. 39%
    d. 42%
    e. 48%

7. In the year 2000, 35% of the company sales were in electronics. The table below shows how electronic sales have changed for the company over the years. Find the percentage of electronics sold in 2005.

Years	Change
2000 − 2001	−2%
2001 − 2002	−1%
2002 − 2003	+6%
2003 − 2004	−1%
2004 − 2005	+2%

    a. 2%
    b. 11%
    c. 39%
    d. 42%
    e. 47%

8. Which of the following choices expresses 5/8 as a percentage?

    a. 40%
    b. 58%
    c. 62.5%
    d. 65%
    e. 72%

9. In the following figure, angle b = 120°. What is the measurement of angle a?

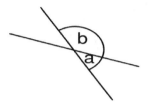

    a. 40°
    b. 60°
    c. 90°
    d. 100°
    e. 180°

10. Determine the following difference to 3 significant figures:

$$(3.667 \times 10^6) - 51,011$$

    a. 3.62×10^6
    b. 3.616×10^6
    c. 3.67×10^6
    d. -4.734×10^4
    e. -5.10×10^4

11. A woman wants to stack two small bookcases beneath a window that is 26½ inches from the floor. The larger bookcase is 14½ inches tall. The other bookcase is 8¾ inches tall. How tall will the two bookcases be when they are stacked together?

    a. 12 inches tall
    b. 23¼ inches tall
    c. 35¼ inches tall
    d. 41 inches tall
    e. 49¾ inches tall

12. A plane is flying 345 miles per hour at an altitude of 35,000 feet. If the speed stays the same, how many miles will the plane travel in 3 hours?

    a. 690 miles
    b. 1,035 miles
    c. 2,596 miles
    d. 33,965 miles
    e. 35,000 miles

13. A man has $1,000. He adds 10% to the total amount of money. Then he takes away 10% of the total amount. How much money does he have now?

 a. $800
 b. $900
 c. $990
 d. $1,000
 e. $1,100

14. An analog wall clock runs on a battery. If the clock runs out of power, what is the probability of the second hand stopping on an even number?

 a. 20%
 b. 30%
 c. 40%
 d. 50%
 e. 100%

15. What is the perimeter of the following figure?

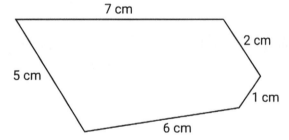

 a. 15 cm
 b. 18 cm
 c. 21 cm
 d. 36 cm
 e. 45 cm

16. Angle AEC is a straight line. Angle BEC is 45°. What is the measure for angle AEB?

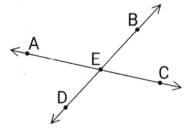

a. Angle AEB is 90°
b. Angle AEB is 115°
c. Angle AEB is 135°
d. Angle AEB is 180°
e. Angle AEB is 360°

17. To begin making her soup, Jennifer added four containers of chicken broth with 1 liter of water into the pot. Each container of chicken broth contains 410 milliliters. How much liquid is in the pot?

a. 1.64 liters
b. 2.64 liters
c. 5.44 liters
d. 6.12 liters
e. 17.4 liters

18. Which of the following demonstrates 25,125,652 in scientific notation?

a. $2,512,565.2 \times 10$
b. $251,256.52 \times 10^2$
c. $25,125.652 \times 10^3$
d. 25.125652×10^6
e. 2.5125652×10^7

19. What is 44/99 in the simplest form?

a. 4/9
b. 4/5
c. 11/99
d. 14/19
e. 44/99

20. Which of the following fractions is halfway between 2/5 and 4/9?

a. 2/3
b. 2/20
c. 17/40
d. 19/45
e. 20/45

21. Fifteen ring boxes can fit into each case. If you have 100 ring boxes, how many cases do you need?

a. 4 cases
b. 5 cases
c. 6 cases
d. 7 cases
e. 8 cases

22. Which of the following is the largest number?

a. 1/2
b. 3/8
c. 7/16
d. 13/54
e. 89/216

240

23. Which number has no remainder when divided into 250?

    a. 5

    b. 15

    c. 20

    d. 30

    e. 75

24. Of the following expressions, which is equal to $6\sqrt{10}$?

    a. 36

    b. $\sqrt{600}$

    c. $\sqrt{360}$

    d. $\sqrt{6}$

    e. $10\sqrt{6}$

25. A box of laundry detergent contains 16.5 oz of product. What is the maximum number of loads that can be washed if each load requires a minimum of $\frac{3}{4}$ oz of detergent?

    a. 10 loads

    b. 18 loads

    c. 16.5 loads

    d. 22 loads

    e. 50 loads

Mometrix

Reading Comprehension

Read each passage closely and answer the associated questions. Be sure to choose the answer that BEST answers the question being asked.

Questions 1-4 refer to the following passage:

Protozoa are microscopic, one-celled organisms that can be free-living or parasitic in nature. They are able to multiply in humans, a factor which contributes to their survival and also permits serious infections to develop from just a single organism. Transmission of protozoa that live in the human intestine to another human typically occurs by a fecal-oral route (for example, contaminated food or water, or person-to-person contact). Protozoa that thrive in the blood or tissue of humans are transmitted to their human hosts by an arthropod vector (for example, through the bite of a mosquito or sand fly).

Helminths are large, multicellular organisms that are generally visible to the naked eye in their adult stages. Like protozoa, helminths can be either free-living or parasitic in nature. In their adult form, helminths cannot multiply in humans. There are three main groups of helminths (derived from the Greek word for worms) that are human parasites:

1. Flatworms (platyhelminths) – these include the trematodes (flukes) and cestodes (tapeworms).
2. Thorny-headed worms (acanthocephalins) – the adult forms of these worms reside in the gastrointestinal tract. The acanthocephala are thought to be intermediate between the cestodes and nematodes.
3. Roundworms (nematodes) – the adult forms of these worms can reside in the gastrointestinal tract, blood, lymphatic system or subcutaneous tissues. Alternatively, the immature (larval) states can cause disease through their infection of various body tissues.

1. As used in this passage, the word "parasite" means
   a.   a person who lives in Paris
   b.   an organism that live on or in another organism
   c.   microscopic insects
   d.   a person who takes advantage of the generosity of others

2. According to the passage, adult Roundworms can live in
   a.   the arthropod vector
   b.   fecal matter
   c.   the subcutaneous tissue of humans
   d.   contaminated water

3. You can infer from this passage that
   a.   larval stages of parasites are more dangerous than the adult forms
   b.   mosquitoes do not transmit parasites
   c.   worms cannot infect humans
   d.   clean sanitary conditions will keep you free of protozoa

4. According to the passage, which of the following is true?

> I. Protozoa live in the blood or tissue of humans.
> II. Adult helminthes cannot reproduce in humans.
> III. Adult thorny-headed worms live in the intestinal tract.

a. I only
b. II only
c. I and II only
d. I, II, and III

Questions 5-9 refer to the following passage:

What do you think is the biggest American holiday? The most significant and uniquely American holiday would have to be the Fourth of July, the day when the United States celebrates its independence from Britain. You might think that the Fourth of July became a holiday immediately after the signing of the Declaration of Independence on July 4, 1776, but actually it didn't become a tradition until after the War of 1812.

By the 1870s, the Fourth of July was the most important nonreligious holiday on the calendar. All across the country, on that day, towns and cities held celebrations with parades, barbecues, and fireworks displays.

Back in the 1870s, the Fourth of July was "the big event of the year," according to Nettie Spencer, a pioneer from Portland, Oregon. The holiday included a parade with floats, a band, and a speaker. "First, the speaker would challenge England to a fight and berate the King and say that he was a skunk. In the afternoon, we had what we called the 'plug uglies'--funny floats and clowns who took off on the political subjects of the day," said Spencer. At that time, the Fourth of July made people think about what it meant to be independent from Britain.

More than 200 years have passed since the signing of the Declaration of Independence, and our independence from Britain is sometimes taken for granted.

Today, the Fourth of July holiday is still a popular day for celebrations with family and friends. The holiday's importance has inspired the creation of everything from the lyrics to "Yankee Doodle Dandy" ("I'm a Yankee Doodle Dandy ...born on the Fourth of July...") to movies like *Independence Day*. America's independence has always been an important concept of our country, and Americans will protect it from I any and all challenges facing it.

5. The author wrote this passage to

a. tell about the Declaration of Independence
b. encourage the reader to watch movies about America's independence
c. give the reader the history of an American holiday
d. explain why America's independence from Britain is taken for granted

6. This passage is primarily about

a. the most important nonreligious holiday in America
b. how the Fourth of July did not become a tradition until after the War of 1812
c. how Americans will always protect their independence
d. how the Fourth of July no longer makes people think about independence from Britain

7. According to the passage, when did Americans first begin celebrating the Fourth of July?

 a. Immediately after signing the Declaration of Independence
 b. After the War of 1812
 c. In the 1870s
 d. Two hundred years after the Declaration of Independence was signed

8. The word "berate" in the third passage can best be replaced with

 a. compliment
 b. praise
 c. inform
 d. scold

9. The tone of this passage can best be described as

 a. confused
 b. neutral
 c. admiring
 d. condescending

Questions 10-13 refer to the following passage:

Nutria (Myocastor coypu) are large rodents that look like beavers with long, thin tails. Nutria may weigh up to 20 lbs. but on average weigh between 12-15 lbs. with males slightly larger than females. They have dense, grayish under-fur overlaid by long, glossy guard hairs that vary in color from dark brown to yellowish brown. Their large front teeth are yellow-orange to orange-red on the outer surface. The forepaws have four well-developed clawed toes and one non-functional toe. The hind feet have five clawed toes: four webbed and one that hangs free. Nutria have several other adaptations to help them in the water. Their eyes, ears and nostrils are set high on their heads. The nostrils and mouth have valves that seal out water while swimming, diving or feeding underwater. The female's teats are located high on her sides to allow the young to suckle while in the water. Nutria are primarily nocturnal (active at night), with peak activity occurring near midnight. When food is abundant, nutria rest and groom during the day and feed at night. When food is limited, daytime feeding increases, especially in wetlands free from disturbance.

Nutria inhabit fresh and brackish marshes, rivers, bayous, farm ponds, freshwater impoundments, drainage canals, swamps and various other types of wetlands. Although found in sixteen U.S. states, nutria are native to South America. Their original range includes Argentina, Chile, Bolivia, Uruguay, Paraguay and southern Brazil. After escaping from captivity in the U.S. and elsewhere, they now inhabit a much greater area. Nutria were first imported into the United States between 1899 and 1930 in an attempt to establish a fur farm industry. Many of the fur farms failed in the late 1940s because fur prices fell and nutria did not reproduce well in captivity. Many nutria were released into the wild. Nutria are now reported in every Maryland Eastern Shore county and are found from Bombay Hook National Wildlife Refuge in Delaware through the Delmarva Peninsula to Virginia's Eastern Shore. They have also been reported on the western shore of Maryland in the Potomac and Patuxent Rivers and in Virginia as far south as the Northern Neck near the Rappahanock River.

Nutria are highly prolific and breed all year. Reproductive peaks occur in late winter, early summer, and mid-autumn. Reproduction and survival may be influenced by extreme weather conditions. Nutria reach sexual maturity at four to six months. Sexually mature male nutria can breed throughout the year. Females are pregnant from 128 to 130 days and are ready to breed within forty-eight hours after giving birth. Litters average four to five young; however, nutria can have up to thirteen young per litter and may have three litters per year. Young are born fully furred and active, weighing 8 oz. at birth. They can swim and eat vegetation shortly thereafter, still feeding on mother's milk for up to eight weeks. Within five days of life, nutria can survive away from the mother.

10. Where would you most likely find this passage?
   a. In a tourist guidebook
   b. In a history textbook
   c. In an online encyclopedia
   d. In a comic book

11. It can be inferred from the passage that nutrias' eyes, ears, and nostrils are set high on their heads
   a. so they can see their young while they are in the water
   b. to prevent water from getting in them while they are swimming
   c. so that they can eat at night
   d. so that they are balanced with the rest of their body

12. According to the passage, how long does it take for nutria to reach sexual maturity?
   a. 4 to 6 months
   b. 128 to 130 days
   c. 48 hours
   d. 8 weeks

13. The author states that fur farms failed in the 1940s because
   a. nutria were released into the wild
   b. of limited amounts of food for the nutria
   c. nutria are highly prolific
   d. nutria did not reproduce well in captivity

Questions 14-18 refer to the following passage:

Born Ehrich Weiss, Harry Houdini was a master of illusion. Houdini earned an international reputation as an escape artist who dramatically freed himself from ropes, shackles, and handcuffs. He was married to Wilhelmina Rahner, who, as Beatrice Houdini, was his stage assistant. He performed on vaudeville and was also in many motion pictures.

In 1899, when Houdini decided to stop doing traditional magic and instead concentrate on escapes, his career took off. He created several dramatic escape tricks. In 1908, in St. Louis, Houdini introduced his escape from a giant milk can filled with water. It became a very popular trick and he took it on tour throughout the U.S., England, and Germany. What kind of escape could top this?

For his next escape, Houdini had to come up with something even more dramatic than the Giant Milk Can Escape, and he did. His new trick, which he began to perform in 1913, was known as the Upside Down Water Torture Cell. In this trick, Houdini's ankles were secured in a brace and he was put under water, upside down, and locked in place in full view of the audience. From this position, he freed himself and escaped from the water cell. Another escape was called the underwater burial. Houdini called this "the greatest feat I have ever attempted."

Some magicians might make a rabbit jump out of a hat or a bird disappear into thin air, but that was too easy for Houdini. He had to work with an elephant! In 1918, in the middle of the brightly lit stage of the Hippodrome Theater in New York City, Houdini made a 10,000-pound elephant named Jennie disappear. The act was called "The Vanishing Elephant," and when Houdini fired a pistol, Jennie vanished from view. Houdini had created a sensation. This incredible trick helped make Houdini a world-famous master of illusion.

14. The best title for this passage is
- a. Hippodrome Theater
- b. The Giant Milk Can Escape
- c. The Master of Illusion
- d. Rabbit in the Hat

15. The author wrote this passage to
- a. inform the reader
- b. entertain the reader
- c. persuade the reader
- d. humor the reader

16. Who was Beatrice Houdini?
- a. A 10,000 pound elephant
- b. Houdini's mother
- c. The owner of Houdini's vaudeville show
- d. Wilhelmina Rahner, Houdini's wife

17. According to the passage, what was Houdini's most sensational act?
- a. The Giant Milk Can Escape
- b. The Upside Down Water Torture Cell
- c. The Vanishing Elephant
- d. Escape from Handcuffs

18. Which word best replaces the word "feat" in the fourth paragraph without changing the meaning?
- a. exploit
- b. failure
- c. discovery
- d. surrender

Questions 19-22 refer to the following passage:

Volcanoes destroy and volcanoes create. The catastrophic eruption of Mount St. Helens on May 18, 1980, made clear the awesome destructive power of a volcano. Yet, over a time span longer than human memory and record, volcanoes have played a key role in forming and modifying the planet upon which we live. More than 80 percent of the earth's surface--above and below sea level--is of volcanic origin. Gaseous emissions from volcanic vents, scoring and shaping the earth over hundreds of millions of years, formed the earth's earliest oceans and atmosphere, and supplied the ingredients vital to generate and sustain life. Over geologic eons, countless volcanic eruptions have produced mountains, plateaus, and plains, which subsequent erosion and weathering have sculpted into majestic landscapes and fertile soils.

Ironically, these volcanic soils and inviting terrains have attracted people, and continue to attract people, to an existence on the flanks of volcanoes. Thus, as population density increases in regions of active or potentially active volcanoes, mankind must become increasingly aware of the hazards and learn not to "crowd" the volcanoes. People living in the shadow of volcanoes must live in harmony with them, expecting and planning for periodic violent unleashings of their pent-up energy.

19. According to the passage, how were the earth's early oceans and atmosphere formed?
   a.   By gaseous emissions from volcanic vents
   b.   Through erosion and weathering
   c.   By volcanic eruptions
   d.   By hurricanes

20. According to the context of the passage, "crowd" means
   a.   a group of people gathered in one spot
   b.   to press or throng into a space
   c.   a group of people with something in common
   d.   the common people

21. This passage would most likely be found in
   a.   an almanac
   b.   a science textbook
   c.   a social studies textbook
   d.   a novel

22. How does erosion and weathering affect the earth's surface?
   a.   They create mountains and plateaus
   b.   They create volcanic emissions
   c.   They destroy the landscape
   d.   They help to form fertile soils

Questions 23-27 refer to the following passage:

Jazz singer Billie Holiday, later nicknamed "Lady Day," was born on April 7, 1915, in Baltimore, Maryland. In her autobiography, "Lady Sings the Blues," Holiday says, "Mom and Pop were just a couple of kids when they got married; he was 18, she was

16, and I was three." Despite a challenging childhood and no formal musical training, Billie Holiday made her professional singing debut in Harlem nightclubs in 1931. By 1933, she had made her first recordings. Do you think her parents really named her "Billie?"

Born Eleanora Fagan, she gave herself the stage name Billie after Billie Dove, an early movie star. While becoming a star, Holiday faced racism. Laws at that time created separate facilities, public spaces, and seats on public buses for black people and, in the private sector, there were restaurants that would serve only white people. As a result, Holiday sometimes found herself singing in clubs that refused service to black people. Her 1939 version of "Strange Fruit," a song about lynching, was described in the album's liner notes as the most haunting and sad "expression of protest against man's inhumanity to man that has ever been made in the form of vocal jazz."

Billie Holiday worked with many jazz greats including Count Basie and Benny Goodman. She sang in small clubs, large concert halls, and in the film *New Orleans*. She even arranged and composed her own songs such as "I Love My Man" and "God Bless the Child." Many people mourned the loss of "Lady Day" when she died in New York at the age of 44.

23. The best title for this passage is

a. Mom and Pop
b. Harlem
c. Lady Day Sings the Blues
d. Jazz in the 1930s

24. According to the passage, which of the following is true?

I. Billie Holiday had no formal musical training.
II. Billie Holiday's parents were very young when they got married.
III. Billie Holiday sang in clubs that refused service to white people.

a. I only
b. II only
c. I and II only
d. I, II, and III

25. It can be inferred from the passage that Holiday

a. felt strongly about racism
b. despised her given name, Eleanora Fagan
c. preferred singing in large concert halls
d. died of a heart attack

26. The author wrote this passage to

a. tell a story
b. make the reader laugh
c. describe the life of a famous singer
d. convince the reader to buy a Billie Holiday CD

27.When did Billie Holiday make her professional singing debut in Harlem?

  a. 1915
  b. 1931
  c. 1933
  d. 1939

Questions 28-31 refer to the following passage:

When you think of a web, you probably don't think of earthworms, do you? What comes to mind? A spider web? The World Wide Web? How about a duck's webbed feet? Well, there's another kind of web you might not know about. It's the soil food web.

The soil food web is the set of organisms that work underground to help plants grow. There are billions of organisms that make up the soil food web. These include bacteria, fungi, protozoa, nematodes, arthropods and earthworms. Each type of organism plays an important role in keeping the soil healthy for all living things.

Earthworms eat just about every other organism in the soil. They're miniature topsoil factories—all the soil you have ever seen has passed through the stomachs of lots of earthworms. When they eat, they leave behind "castings," which are high in organic matter and plant nutrients and are a valuable fertilizer.

Earthworms move through the soil creating tunnels—areas that can be filled by air and water. Fields that are "tilled" by earthworm tunneling can absorb water at a rate 4 to 10 times that of fields without worm tunnels. This reduces water runoff, restores groundwater, and helps store more water for dry spells.

This burrowing also helps nutrients enter the subsoil at a faster rate and opens up pathways for roots to grow into. During droughts, the tunnels allow plant roots to penetrate more deeply, enabling them to reach the water they need to thrive.

Earthworms help keep soil healthy by moving organic matter from the surface into the soil. Normally, a tree leaf may take three to five years to decompose and be incorporated into the soil. In forests infested with night crawlers, this process can take as little as four weeks! By speeding up the breakdown of plant material, earthworms also speed up the rate at which nutrients are recycled back to the plants.

Earthworms and other soil organisms are a necessary part of the soil food web. Without them, all the organic matter would build up on the soil surface and never get down into the soil. To grow healthy, productive plants, you need healthy, productive soil. Organisms in the soil provide the food for plants—when they need it and in a form they can use!

28. The tone of this passage can be described as

  a. confused
  b. neutral
  c. mournful
  d. positive

29. Which of the following are part of the soil food web?

> I. bacteria
> II. protozoa
> III. nematodes

   a. I only
   b. II only
   c. I and II only
   d. I, II, and III

30. According to the context of the passage, "tilled" means

   a. plowed
   b. hardened
   c. moistened
   d. destroyed

31. What benefits do earthworms provide by burrowing in the soil?

   a. They provide valuable fertilizer
   b. They open pathways for roots to grow in
   c. They slow the decomposition rate
   d. They allow bacteria into the soil

Questions 32-36 refer to the following passage:

The Missouri territory came to the United States as part of the 1803 Louisiana Purchase, one of the best real estate deals the United States ever made. Before Missouri became the 24th state on August 10, 1821, certain compromises had to be made to keep a balance in the Union between the slave and non-slave states. Those compromises would later turn neighbor against neighbor.

Under the Missouri Compromise of 1820, designed by statesman Henry Clay, Missouri entered the Union as a slave state, and Maine entered as a free state, thus keeping the number of slave and non-slave states equal at 12 each.

John F. Smith recalled in an interview an incident when Jayhawkers, a group opposed to slavery, came to his house in 1861. One of the Jayhawkers threatened to shoot his father, a Missouri slave owner. "... (then) we heard a shout and looked up the road... The man dropped his gun to his side, when Judge Myers rode up, he was shaking his head and his eyes were blazing fire...All the Jayhawkers turned around and sulked off like whipped dogs."

The Civil War continued to divide Missourians. Although the state remained with the Union, some of its citizens chose to fight for the Confederacy. Smith's father and his rescuer, Judge Myers, remained best friends despite their conflicting views on slavery, but the two ended up fighting on opposite sides of the war.

32. This passage would most likely be found in a(n)

   a. World history textbook
   b. American history textbook
   c. Ancient history textbook
   d. Art history textbook

33. According to the passage, how did the Missouri Territory become part of the United States?

a. Through the Missouri Compromise
b. Through the defeat of the Confederacy
c. Through the Louisiana Purchase
d. As a result of a Jayhawkers revolt

34. What can you infer from the statement "Those compromises would later turn neighbor against neighbor" at the end of the first paragraph?

a. All Missourians wanted a free state
b. All Missourians wanted a slave state
c. Missourians disagreed on the issue of slave ownership
d. Neighbors were arguing over property lines

35. According to the passage, Jayhawkers were

a. part of the Ku Klux Klan
b. a slavery opposition group
c. Confederate soldiers
d. judges

36. What is the author most likely to discuss next?

a. Missouri's role in the Civil War
b. Different judges' rulings on slavery
c. The biography of Henry Clay
d. The history of the Jayhawkers

Questions 37-40 refer to the following passage:

Corals in the deep sea? When asked to describe corals, most people think of those that make up tropical, shallow-water reefs like the Great Barrier Reef. However, there are corals that live in much deeper, colder waters where there is no sunlight. Over the past 8 years, my colleagues and I have been studying these deep-sea corals in North Atlantic waters deeper than 1,000 meters.

Between 2003-2005, we visited a previously unexplored group of extinct underwater volcanoes in the western North Atlantic—the New England Seamounts and Corner Rise Seamounts—looking for deep-sea coral communities living between 1,000 and 2,500 meters. Our explorations revealed some spectacular assemblages of bamboo corals, bubblegum corals, black corals, and a variety of other sea fan and sea whip species.

Living amidst the corals were a myriad of animals, including shrimp, crabs, snake stars, sea stars, feather stars, scale worms and many species of deep-sea fish. Most of the species we found were new to science, while others (or their close relatives) were known only from the eastern North Atlantic and were being observed in the western Atlantic for the first time.

As a follow-up to those discoveries, we planned this expedition to explore the deep slopes of the northern Bahamas. In the western North Atlantic, a major deep-sea current flows from north to south along the slope of the continental USA, but as it approaches the tropics, it encounters deep, cold water flowing northward from

Antarctica. Our goal is to determine if the coral species, and their associated fauna, living in the subtropical Bahamas are the same as those on the seamounts to the north, or will we begin to see a different group of species reflecting a southern influence?

37. The best title for this passage is

    a. Underwater Volcanoes
    b. The Western North Atlantic
    c. Bubblegum Coral
    d. Coral Reefs in the Deep Sea

38. Deep sea coral reefs are unique because

    a. they are less than 1,000 meters deep
    b. they survive where there is no sunlight
    c. they are found in tropical waters
    d. they are composed of shallow water reefs

39. This passage was written in

    a. first person
    b. second person
    c. third person
    d. fourth person

40. What is the goal of the next expedition?

    a. To reach deep-sea communities at 2,500 meters
    b. To visit an unexplored group of extinct underwater volcanoes
    c. To determine if the corals living in the Bahamas are the same as those on the seamounts to the north
    d. To discover crabs, snake stars, sea stars, feather stars, and scale worms

Verbal

30 minutes, 60 questions

For questions 1-30: Select the synonym. Each question has a word in all capital letters followed by five answer choices in all lower-case letters. Select the answer choice with a definition closest to the capitalized word.

1. ENTHRALL:

    a. extreme
    b. fascinate
    c. devote
    d. bizarre

2. COWARD:

    a. gutless
    b. boor
    c. judge
    d. brave

3. NOVICE:

    a. expert
    b. nurse
    c. beginner
    d. naught

4. TEMPERATE:

    a. extreme
    b. lenient
    c. taut
    d. moderate

5. AUTHENTIC:

    a. genuine
    b. colorful
    c. flimsy
    d. laughable

6. SALVAGE:

    a. bless
    b. slobber
    c. swagger
    d. recover

7. VERNACULAR:

    a. poison
    b. language
    c. veracity
    d. ballad

8. ATTEST:
  a. bewitch
  b. accommodate
  c. vouch
  d. heed

9. DERELICT:
  a. abandoned
  b. corrupted
  c. dispirited
  d. depressed

10. ORDAIN:
  a. arrange
  b. create
  c. command
  d. adorn

11. HAUGHTY:
  a. obscure
  b. arrogant
  c. perilous
  d. bitter

12. LAPSE:
  a. prank
  b. margin
  c. error
  d. award

13. NAUSEATE:
  a. rival
  b. crave
  c. annoy
  d. repulse

14. PALTRY:
  a. cheap
  b. peaceful
  c. severely
  d. lurid

15. REFINED:
  a. aromatic
  b. blatant
  c. cultured
  d. frightened

16. VIRTUAL:
- a. real
- b. visible
- c. potent
- d. simulated

17. LOATHE:
- a. fear
- b. hate
- c. exist
- d. charge

18. MIMIC:
- a. recall
- b. delve
- c. imitate
- d. curtail

19. BRITTLE:
- a. fragile
- b. radical
- c. broad
- d. smooth

20. WRETCHED:
- a. wicked
- b. awry
- c. absorbed
- d. miserable

21. VEHEMENT:
- a. troubled
- b. intense
- c. changeable
- d. obstinate

22. DIATRIBE:
- a. criticism
- b. apology
- c. commend
- d. merit

23. COGITATE:
- a. surprise
- b. endanger
- c. confuse
- d. deliberate

24. INVIDIOUS:
    a. offensive
    b. pleasant
    c. ornate
    d. infectious

25. HYPERBOLE:
    a. reference
    b. amendment
    c. exaggeration
    d. demarcation

26. INNOCUOUS:
    a. harmful
    b. innocent
    c. scandalous
    d. hidden

27. CAPRICIOUS:
    a. steady
    b. unpredictable
    c. pleasant
    d. violent

28. INTERMITTENT:
    a. occasional
    b. intense
    c. frequent
    d. bursts

29. SOLITARY:
    a. single
    b. solid
    c. sturdy
    d. stoic

30. PRECIPITOUS:
    a. rugged
    b. dangerous
    c. steep
    d. wet

For questions 31-60: These questions ask you to identify and compare relationships between pairs of words. Select the answer that best completes the comparison.

31. surgeon is to operating room as
    a. chiropractor is to doctor
    b. novelist is to panel
    c. conductor is to symphony hall
    d. truck driver is to rest stop

32. opinionated is to indecisive as

a. diffident is to shy
b. frugal is to spendthrift
c. conspicuous is to obvious
d. thoughtful is to thought-provoking

33. pleased is to overjoyed as

a. dirty is to squalid
b. thrilled is to happy
c. determined is to decided
d. perceptive is to unaware

34. punitive is to punishment as

a. spatial is to measurement
b. exhausted is to sleep
c. perplexed is to answer
d. complimentary is to praise

35. considerable is to extensive as

a. enormous is to vacant
b. diminutive is to microscopic
c. outlandish is to undistinguished
d. descriptive is to straightforward

36. insipid is to boredom as

a. tasty is to craving
b. gratuitous is to freedom
c. morose is to rebellion
d. jovial is to optimistic

37. sedentary is to sit as

a. descry is to lampoon
b. espoused is to belief
c. perseverance is to endurance
d. peripatetic is to wander

38. querulous is to amiable as

a. sequential is to serial
b. ponderous is to insubstantial
c. illicit is to forbidden
d. pugnacious is to truculent

39. abstemious is to restraint as

a. discerning is to awareness
b. servile is to aggression
c. avowal is to affirm
d. exhilarate is to enlivened

257

40. Motorcycle is to bicycle as speedboat is to:

    a. Motor
    b. Paddleboat
    c. Float
    d. Transportation

41. Apple is to seed as person is to

    a. Parent
    b. Embryo
    c. Nourishment
    d. Cell

42. Fraction is to whole as slice is to

    a. Pie
    b. Cut
    c. Part
    d. Element

43. Temperature is to heat as pound is to

    a. Weight
    b. Height
    c. Measurement
    d. Heavy

44. Bank is to savings as safe is to

    a. Valuables
    b. Combination
    c. Crack
    d. Vault

45. Island is to sea as star is to

    a. Light
    b. Night
    c. Celestial
    d. Space

46. Inattention is to accidents as practice is to

    a. Improvement
    b. Performance
    c. Discipline
    d. Repetition

47. Sight is to sense as gravity is to

    a. Weight
    b. Pounds
    c. Distance
    d. Force

48. Dexterity is to skill as English is to

    a. Language

    b. Literature

    c. Japanese

    d. Linguistics

49. Coach is to team as teacher is to

    a. Knowledge

    b. School

    c. Students

    d. Principal

50. Article is to magazine as chapter is to

    a. Verse

    b. Book

    c. Number

    d. Paragraph

51. House is to neighborhood as tree is to

    a. leaf

    b. timber

    c. forest

    d. limb

52. Wallet is to money as envelope is to

    a. mail

    b. letter

    c. address

    d. post office

53. German shepherd is to dog as strawberry is to

    a. red

    b. vine

    c. seeds

    d. fruit

54. Joyful is to sad as empty is to

    a. bare

    b. crowded

    c. productive

    d. vacant

55. Automobile is to garage as dish is to

    a. plate

    b. food

    c. cupboard

    d. spoon

56. Doctor is to medicine as teacher is to

a. student
b. teaching
c. education
d. school

57. Chirp is to tweet as jump is to

a. leap
b. rope
c. high
d. street

58. Sleeping is to tired as drinking is to

a. glass
b. thirsty
c. swallow
d. water

59. Four-leaf clover is to luck as arrow is to

a. bow
b. Cupid
c. shoot
d. direction

60. Question is to answer as problem is to

a. mathematics
b. solution
c. worry
d. trouble

Quantitative (Math)

Read each question, perform the appropriate calculations, and determine the correct answer.

1. A bullet travels at 5×10^6 feet per hour. If it strikes its target in 2×10^{-4} hours, how far has it traveled?

   a. 50 feet
   b. 25 feet
   c. 100 feet
   d. 1000 feet
   e. 200 feet

2. A blouse normally sells for \$138, but is on sale for 25% off. What is the cost of the blouse?

   a. \$34.50
   b. \$67
   c. \$103.50
   d. \$113
   e. \$125

3. Which number equals 2^{-3}?

   a. $1/2$
   b. $1/4$
   c. $1/8$
   d. $1/12$
   e. $1/16$

4. A straight line with slope +4 is plotted on a standard Cartesian (x, y) coordinate system so that it intersects the y-axis at a value of $y = 1$. Which of the following points will the line pass through?

   a. (2,9)
   b. (0,-1)
   c. (0,0)
   d. (4,1)
   e. (1,4)

5. What is the average of $\frac{7}{5}$ and 1.4?

   a. 5.4
   b. 1.4
   c. 2.4
   d. 7.4
   e. None of these

6. What is the surface area, in square inches, of a cube if the length of one side is 3 inches?

   a. 9
   b. 27
   c. 54
   d. 18
   e. 21

7. Which of the following values is closest to the diameter of a circle with an area of 314 square inches?

    a. 20 inches
    b. 10 inches
    c. 100 inches
    d. 31.4 inches
    e. 2π inches

8. A circle has a circumference of 35 feet. Approximately what is its diameter.

    a. 3.5 feet
    b. 5.57 feet
    c. 6.28 feet
    d. 11.14 feet
    e. 14 feet.

9. Two angles of a triangle measure 15° and 70°, respectively. What is the size of the third angle?

    a. 90°
    b. 80°
    c. 75°
    d. 125°
    e. 95°

10. The triangle shown in the figure has angles A, B, and C, and sides a, b, and c. If $a = 14$ cm, $b = 12$ cm, and $\angle B = 35$ degrees, what is the approximate value of $\angle A$?

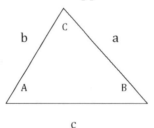

    a. 18°
    b. 28°
    c. 35°
    d. 42°
    e. 64°

11. A taxi service charges \$5.50 for the first $\frac{1}{5}$ of a mile, \$1.50 for each additional $\frac{1}{5}$ of a mile, and 20¢ per minute of waiting time. Joan took a cab from her place to a flower shop 8 miles away, where she bought a bouquet, then another 3.6 miles to her mother's place. The driver had to wait 9 minutes while she bought the bouquet. What was the fare?

    a. \$20
    b. \$90
    c. \$91
    d. \$92.80
    e. \$120.20

Use the following information to answer questions 12-13:

> An MP3 player is set to play songs at random from the fifteen songs it contains in memory. Any song can be played at any time, even if it is repeated. There are 5 songs by Band A, 3 songs by Band B, 2 by Band C, and 5 by Band D.

12. If the player has just played two songs in a row by Band D, what is the probability that the next song will also be by Band D?

a. 1 in 5
b. 1 in 3
c. 1 in 9
d. 1 in 27
e. Not enough data to determine.

13. What is the probability that the next two songs will both be by Band B?

a. 1 in 25
b. 1 in 3
c. 1 in 5
d. 1 in 9
e. Not enough data to determine.

14. Which of the following numbers is a prime number?

a. 15
b. 11
c. 33
d. 4
e. 88

15. Which of the following expressions is equivalent to $(3x^{-2})^3$?

a. $9x^{-6}$
b. $9x^{-8}$
c. $27x^{-8}$
d. $27x^{-4}$
e. $27x^{-6}$

16. Sally wants to buy a used truck for her delivery business. Truck A is priced at \$450 and gets 25 miles per gallon. Truck B costs \$650 and gets 35 miles per gallon. If gasoline costs \$4 per gallon, how many miles must Sally drive to make truck B the better buy?

a. 600
b. 7500
c. 340
d. 740
e. 1600

17. To determine a student's grade, a teacher throws out the lowest grade obtained on 5 tests, averages the remaining grades, and rounds up to the nearest integer. If Betty scored 68, 75, 88, 86, and 90 on her tests, what grade will she receive?

    a. 68
    b. 85
    c. 88
    d. 84.8
    e. 84

18. A rock group with 5 musicians gets 25% of the gross sales of their new album, but they have to give their agent 15% of their share. If the album grosses $20,000,000, what is each band member's share?

    a. $650,000
    b. $800,000
    c. $850,000
    d. $1,150,000
    e. $4,000,000

19. Given the equation $\frac{3}{y-5} = \frac{15}{y+4}$, what is the value of y?

    a. 45
    b. 54
    c. $\frac{29}{4}$
    d. $\frac{4}{29}$
    e. $\frac{4}{45}$

20. The weight in pounds of five students is 112, 112, 116, 133, 145. What is the median weight of the group?

    a. 123.6
    b. 116
    c. 112
    d. 118.5
    e. 140

21. Which of the following expressions is equivalent to $(a)(a)(a)(a)(a)$ for all values of a, positive or negative?

    a. $5a$
    b. a^{-5}
    c. $a^{-\frac{1}{5}}$
    d. a^5
    e. $5a^{\frac{1}{5}}$

22. Which value is equivalent to 7.5×10^{-4}?

    a. 0.075
    b. 0.00075
    c. 0.0075
    d. 0.75
    e. 0.0030

23. How many real-number solutions exist for the equation $x^2 + 1 = 0$?

   a. 0
   b. 1
   c. 2
   d. 3
   e. 4

24. Jamie had $6.50 in his wallet when he left home. He spent $4.25 on drinks and $2.00 on a magazine. Later, his friend repaid him $2.50 that he had borrowed the previous day. How much money does Jamie have in his wallet?

   a. $12.25
   b. $14.25
   c. $3.25
   d. $2.75
   e. $1.75

25. A sailboat is 19 meters long. What is its length in inches?

English-Metric Equivalents	
1 meter	1.094 yard
2.54 centimeter	1 inch
1 kilogram	2.205 pound
1 liter	1.06 quart

   a. 254
   b. 1094
   c. 4826
   d. 748
   e. 21

Answer Key and Explanations for Test #3

Quantitative (Math)

1. D: Experimental probability is a ratio of how many times the spinner will land on the specific number to the total number of times the spinner is spun. In this case, the boy landed on the number 6 a total of 14 times. He tried the spinner 100 times. The resulting ratio is 14/100.

2. A: Complementary angles are two angles that add to 90°.

3. B: Multiply $120 by 24 months (a full two years) to get $2880. Add the thousand dollars for the down payment to get $3880. Find the difference between the entire amount all at once ($2600) and the amount paid in the plan ($3880). To find the difference, you subtract. The difference shows that $1280 more is paid with the installment plan.

4. C: Remember to apply the same operation to both sides of the equation:

$$29 + r = 420$$
$$29 + r - 29 = 420 - 29$$
$$r = 391$$

5. D: Recall that the area of a rectangle is length times width:

$$A = 7 \text{ ft} \times 5 \text{ ft}$$
$$A = 35 \text{ ft}^2$$

6. C: To solve, find the sum. $35\% + 4\% = 39\%$

7. C: To find the percentage for 2005, add the change each year to the original amount:

$$\begin{aligned} \textit{Electronics sales} &= 35 + (-2) + (-1) + (+6) + (-1) + (+2) \\ &= (35 + 6 + 2) + \big((-2) + (-1) + (-1)\big) \\ &= (43) + (-4) \\ &= 39 \end{aligned}$$

8. C: Recall that percentage means per one hundred:

$$\frac{5}{8} = \frac{x}{100}$$
$$0.625 \times 100 = x$$
$$62.5 = x$$

9. B: These are supplementary angles. That means that the two angles will add up to a total of 180°, which is the angle of a straight line. $b = 180° - 120° = 60°$

266

10. A: To solve, put the values in terms of the same power of 10 and then evaluate:

$$\begin{aligned}(3.667 \times 10^6) - 51{,}011 &= (3.667 \times 10^6) - (5.1011 \times 10^4) \\ &= (366.7 \times 10^4) - (5.1011 \times 10^4) \\ &= (366.7 - 5.1011) \times 10^4 \\ &= 361.5989 \times 10^4 \\ &= 3.615989 \times 10^6 \\ &= 3.62 \times 10^6\end{aligned}$$

11. B: Add to solve. The height of the window from the floor is not needed in this equation. It is extra information. You only need to add the heights of the two bookcases. Change the fractions so that they have a common denominator. After you add, simplify the fraction.

$$\begin{aligned}14\frac{1}{2} + 8\frac{3}{4} &= 14\frac{2}{4} + 8\frac{3}{4} \\ &= (14 + 8) + \left(\frac{2+3}{4}\right) \\ &= 22\frac{5}{4} \\ &= 23\frac{1}{4}\end{aligned}$$

12. B: Multiply the speed by the number of hours traveled: $345 \frac{\text{miles}}{\text{hr}} \times 3 \text{ hr} = 1035$ miles

13. C: Apply each of the adjustments in sequence. Note that increasing by 10% is the same as multiplying by 1.1 and decreasing by 10% is the same as multiplying by 0.9:

$$\begin{aligned}\big((\$1{,}000 \times 1.1) \times 0.9\big) &= \$1{,}100 \times 0.9 \\ &= \$990\end{aligned}$$

14. D: Out of the twelve numbers, half are even. That means there is a 50% chance that the second hand will stop on an even number.

15. C: To find perimeter, add the sides: 1 cm + 2 cm + 7 cm + 5 cm + 6 cm = 21 cm.

16. C: A straight line is 180°. Subtract to solve: 180° − 45° = 135°

17. B: Since there are 4 containers of broth: 410 ml × 4 = 1640 ml

Change to liters: $1{,}640 \text{ mL} \times \frac{1 \text{ L}}{1{,}000 \text{ mL}} = 1.64 \text{ L}$

Add the liter of water that was already in the pot: 1.64 L + 1 L = 2.64 L

18. E: Scientific notation uses powers of ten to represent values in simplified form. There will be a non-zero digit in the ones place and possibly some digits to the right of the decimal multiplied by a power of ten. If you carry out the multiplication, you would be left with the original number.

19. A: Simplify the fraction by dividing both the numerator and the denominator by their greatest common factor. In this case, the greatest common factor is 11. When you do that, 44/99 becomes 4/9.

20. D: Find the common denominator for the two fractions so that you can compare them. You can use the common denominator of 45, as follows:

$$\frac{2}{5} = \frac{18}{45}, \quad \frac{4}{9} = \frac{20}{45}$$

Look at the numerators: 18 and 20. The number halfway between them is 19, so the answer is $\frac{19}{45}$.

21. D: You would need 7 cases because $15 \times 7 = 105$. You would have some extra room in the last case, but 6 cases would only give you room for 90 and you need to be able to fit 100 ring boxes into cases.

22. A: Convert each to the lowest common denominator and then compare the numerators. Since 2 and 8 are factors of 16, we only need to use 16, 54, and 216 to find the common denominator.

$$16 = 2 \times 2 \times 2 \times 2$$
$$54 = 2 \times 3 \times 3 \times 3$$
$$216 = 2 \times 2 \times 2 \times 3 \times 3 \times 3$$
$$LCD = 2 \times 2 \times 2 \times 2 \times 3 \times 3 \times 3 = 432$$

$$\frac{1}{2} = \frac{216}{432}$$
$$\frac{3}{8} = \frac{162}{432}$$
$$\frac{7}{16} = \frac{189}{432}$$
$$\frac{13}{54} = \frac{104}{432}$$
$$\frac{89}{216} = \frac{178}{432}$$

$216 > 189 > 178 > 162 > 104$. Therefore, 1/2 is the largest fraction.

23. A: Of the options, only dividing by 5 will have no remainder: $250 \div 5 = 50$. All of the other divisors leave a remainder, as follows:

$$250 \div 15 = 16 \text{ R}10$$
$$250 \div 20 = 12 \text{ R}10$$
$$250 \div 30 = 8 \text{ R}10$$
$$250 \div 75 = 3 \text{ R}25$$

24. C: $6\sqrt{10}$ is equal to $\sqrt{36} \times \sqrt{10}$ or $\sqrt{360}$. None of the other choices listed are equivalent.

25. D: To calculate how many loads can be washed, divide the amount of detergent in the box by the amount of detergent required for each load. Recall that dividing by a fraction is the same as multiplying by its reciprocal: $16.5 \div \frac{3}{4} = 16.5 \times \frac{4}{3} = 22$. Therefore, a maximum of 22 loads can be washed.

Reading Comprehension

1. B: As used in this passage, the word "parasite" means an organism that lives on or in another organism, Choice B. Choice A and C are obviously wrong, since the passage mentions nothing of Paris or insects. Choice D is another definition for "parasite," but does not fit the context of the word used in this passage.

2. C: According to the description of Roundworms, they can live in the subcutaneous tissue of humans, Choice C. Choices A, B, and D describe where protozoa live and how they are transmitted.

3. D: According to the first paragraph, protozoa are transmitted through food and water contaminated by fecal matter. It can then be inferred that clean sanitary conditions will prevent the spread of protozoa, Choice D. Choice A is an incorrect inference because the passage discusses both larval and adult forms of parasites that infect humans. Choice B is an incorrect inference, since the first paragraph states that protozoa are transmitted by mosquitoes. Choice C is an incorrect inference because the second paragraph is about worms that infect humans.

4. D: To answer this question, you will need to verify all three statements in the passage. All three of these statements are true and are supported by the passage.

5. C: This passage was written to give the reader the history of the American holiday, the Fourth of July, Choice C. With regard to Choice A, the Declaration of Independence is mentioned in the passage, but the main purpose of the passage does not focus on it. The same is true for Choice B. The passage does talk about movies associated with the Fourth of July, but the main purpose of the passage is not to encourage the reader to watch those movies. In Choice D, the passage does mention that independence from Britain is taken for granted, but the passage does not explain why.

6. A: This passage is primarily about the most popular American holiday, the Fourth of July, Choice A. The passage does relate to some extent to the other choices, but these do not reflect the main idea of the passage.

7. B: This detailed question offers four time periods mentioned in the passage as possible answer choices. Use caution when choosing the answer. Look back at the passage. The end of paragraph one offers the correct choice, Choice B.

8. D: As used in this passage, "berate" means to scold or rebuke, Choice D. Choices A and B are antonyms. Choice C does not fit the meaning.

9. C: The last sentence of the passage gives the best clue to the tone of the passage: "American independence has always been an important concept in our country, and Americans will protect it from any and all challenges facing it." Of the four options given, *admiring* would best describe the tone.

10. C: You could possibly find this passage in a tourist guidebook, Choice A, but you would most likely find the passage in an online encyclopedia, Choice C. Choices B and D can be eliminated, since a history text book and a comic book are the least likely choices.

11. B: The passage explains that nutria have several adaptations to help them in the water. The logical inference is that their eyes, ears, and nostrils are high on their heads to prevent water from entering them while they are swimming, Choice B.

12. A: Use caution when answering this detailed question, since all the choices given are quantitative possibilities used in the passage. According to the third paragraph, nutria reach sexual maturity in four to six months, Choice A.

13. D: Look back to the passage to answer this detailed question. According to the second paragraph, fur farms failed due to the drop in prices of fur and nutrias' failure to reproduce well in captivity, Choice D.

14. C: This passage is about Harry Houdini. In both the first paragraph and the last paragraph, the author refers to Houdini as a master of illusion. The best choice is Choice C. Choices A and D are both mentioned in the passage, but are not the main idea of the passage. Although Choice B seems like a possibility because a whole paragraph focuses on the escape, several other escapes are also described, making this a poor choice.

15. A: This passage gives facts and details about the life of Harry Houdini and was written in order to inform the reader, Choice A. Although the passage could be considered entertaining, its main purpose is to inform. There are no persuasive techniques used in the passage, nor is it humorous, making Choices C and D incorrect.

16. D: According to the first paragraph, Beatrice Houdini was Harry Houdini's stage assistant and wife, Choice D.

17. C: To answer this detail question, look back at the passage. The last paragraph states that "Houdini had created a sensation" with The Vanishing Elephant act, Choice C. Choices A and B are acts discussed in the passage, but they are not described as his most sensational. Choice D is not an actual act discussed in the passage, and therefore, an incorrect choice.

18. A: Choice A, "exploit" is a synonym for "feat." Choice B, "failure," is an antonym. Choices C and D do not fit the context of the sentence. The correct answer is Choice A.

19. A: The first paragraph describes how gaseous emissions from volcanic vents formed the early oceans and atmosphere, Choice A.

20. B: Although all of the answer choices point to the word "crowd," Choice B is the only logical choice based how the word is used in the context of the passage.

21. B: Of the choices given, this passage would most likely be found in a science textbook, Choice B.

22. D: The second paragraph states that erosion and weathering have sculpted "majestic landscapes and formed fertile soils", Choice D.

23. C: The best title for this passage is Choice C. The first paragraph tells the reader that Billie Holiday's nickname was Lady Day. The entire passage focuses on her career as a Jazz singer.

24. C: To answer this question, you will need to find supporting statements in the passage. Only the first two statements are supported by the passage, Choice C.

25. A: The second paragraph describes the racism that blacks were facing in the 1930s. It supports this inference, stating that one of Holiday's songs was a sad "expression of protest against man's inhumanity to man that has ever been made in the form of vocal jazz." There is no support in the passage for the other three answer choices. Choice A is the correct answer.

26. C: The purpose of this passage is to inform the reader. Choice C is the correct answer.

27. B: The answer choices are all dates from the passage. Refer back to the passage to check each date. The first paragraph gives the correct answer, Choice B.

28. D: Scan the passage for words that reveal how the author feels about the subject. The author states that Earthworms have an "important role" and play a "necessary part" in the soil food web. These words have a positive connotation. The last paragraph also exudes a positive feeling towards earthworms. Choice D is the correct answer.

29. D: To answer this question, you will need to verify all three options in the passage. The second paragraph lists all three organisms as members of the soil food web, Choice D.

30. A: To till means to plow or cultivate, Choice A. The other answer choices do not fit the context of the sentence.

31. B: According to the fifth paragraph, burrowing helps nutrients enter the subsoil at a faster rate and opens up pathways for roots to grow into, Choice B.

32. B: Because this passage is about how the Missouri Territory became a part of the United States, the most likely place to find this passage is in an American history textbook, Choice B.

33. C: According to the first paragraph, the Missouri Territory became part of the United States through the 1803 Louisiana Purchase, Choice C.

34. C: First, determine what the compromise was. According to the passage, compromises had to be made to keep a balance in the Union between the slave and non-slave states. An accurate inference would be that Missourians disagreed on the issue of slavery, Choice C.

35. B: According to the third paragraph, Jayhawkers were members of a group opposed to slavery.

36. A: All the answer choices are related to the passage in some way. However, the last paragraph of the passage begins discussing Missourians and the Civil War. The most logical choice, then, would be Choice A, a continued discussion of Missouri's role in the Civil War.

37. D: Although the first three answer choices are mentioned in the passage, the last answer choice is best in summarizing the passage as a whole. The correct answer is choice D.

38. B: All choices, except Choice B, describe shallow water coral reefs. According to the passage, deep sea coral reefs are found where sunlight does not reach, making them unique. The correct answer is Choice B.

39. A: This passage was written in the first-person format. The author refers to himself or herself with the pronouns "we" and "I." A passage written in second person would include the pronouns "you." A passage written in the third person would have a narrator telling the story, but not part of the events. There is no fourth person narrative. The correct answer is Choice A.

40. C: Answer Choices A, B, and D all refer back to the first expedition. The end of the passage clearly states that the next goal is to "determine if the coral species, and their associate fauna, living in the subtropical Bahamas are the same as those on the seamounts to the north." The correct answer is Choice C.

Verbal

1. B: To enthrall is to fascinate or mesmerize.

2. A: A coward is someone who is gutless, or lacks courage when facing danger.

3. C: A novice is someone who is new to the circumstances, or a beginner.

4. D: Temperate means to be moderate or restrained.

5. A: Something authentic is genuine or true.

6. D: To salvage something is to save or recover it from wreckage, destruction or - loss.

7. B: Vernacular is the speech or language of a place.

8. C: To attest is to vouch for or to certify.

9. A: Derelict means to be neglected or abandoned, e.g., "a derelict old home."

10. C: To ordain is to order or command.

11. B: To be haughty is to be proud or arrogant.

12. C: A lapse is an error or mistake, e.g., "a lapse of memory."

13. D: To nauseate is to disgust or repulse.

14. A: Something paltry is cheap, base, or common.

15. C: To be refined is to be cultured and well-bred.

16. D: Virtual means to be simulated, especially as related to computer software.

17. B: To loathe is to hate or abhor.

18. C: When you mimic, you imitate or copy someone or something.

19. A: Something brittle is fragile and easily damaged or destroyed.

20. D: Wretched means miserable or woeful.

21. B: Vehement most closely means the same thing as intense.

22. A: Diatribe most closely means the same thing as criticism.

23. D: Cogitate most closely means the same thing as deliberate.

24. A: Invidious most closely means the same thing as offensive.

25. C: Hyperbole most closely means the same thing as exaggeration.

26. B: Innocuous most closely means the same thing as innocent.

27. B: The word "capricious" means "unpredictable" or "changeable."

28. A: The word "intermittent" also means "occasional" or "discontinuous."

29. A: Solitary can mean a number of different things, but one meaning is single. For example, if you said there was a solitary tree in a yard, you would mean that there was a single tree.

30. C: The word "precipitous" means "steep."

31. C: The relationship sought is one of a professional to the place in which he/she performs his/her professional work. The only answer that has that relationship is that of conductor to symphony hall.

32. B: The relationship sought is that of antonyms. The only answer that has that relationship is that of frugal to spendthrift.

33. A: The relationship sought is one of an adjective to another adjective that is a stronger form of the first word. The only answer that has that relationship is that of dirty to squalid.

34. D: The relationship sought is one of an emotional state to the action taken as a result of being in that state. The only answer that has that relationship is that of complimentary to praise.

35. B: The relationship sought is that of synonyms. The only answer that has that relationship is that of diminutive to microscopic.

36. A: The relationship sought is one of an adjective to the state of mind something modified by that adjective creates. The only answer that has that relationship is that of tasty to craving.

37. D: The relationship sought is one of an adjective to the action which the state of being described by the adjective necessitates. The only answer that has that relationship is that of peripatetic to wander.

38. B: The relationship sought is that of antonyms. The only answer that has that relationship is that of ponderous to insubstantial.

39. A: The relationship sought is that of an adjective and an action or state of being exhibited by one accurately described by that adjective. The only answer that has that relationship is that of discerning to awareness.

40. B: A motorcycle is a motorized bicycle; a speedboat is a motorized paddleboat.

41. B: An apple develops from a seed; a person develops from an embryo.

42. A: A fraction is a part of a whole; a slice is a part of a pie.

43. A: Temperature is used to measure heat; pounds are used to measure weight.

44. A: A bank is a place to keep one's savings; a safe is a place to keep one's valuables.

45. D: An island is surrounded by the sea; a star is surrounded by space.

46. A: Inattention can lead to accidents; practice can lead to improvement.

47. D: Sight is an example of a sense; gravity is an example of a force.

48. A: Dexterity is a kind of skill; English is a kind of language.

49. C: A coach is in charge of a team; a teacher is in charge of students.

50. B: An article is a section of a magazine; a chapter is a section of a book.

51. C: A house is a part of the neighborhood and a tree is a part of the forest.

52. B: A wallet holds money and an envelope holds a letter.

53. D: A German shepherd is a type of dog and a strawberry is a type of fruit.

54. B: Joyful is an opposite of sad and empty is an opposite of crowded.

55. C: An automobile is stored in the garage and a dish is stored in a cupboard.

56. C: A doctor works in the field of medicine and a teacher works in the field of education.

57. A: Chirp is a similar action to tweet and jump is a similar action to leap.

58. B: Sleeping is a solution for being tired and drinking is a solution for being thirsty.

59. D: A four-leaf clover is a symbol of luck and an arrow is a symbol of direction.

60. B: A question requires an answer and a problem requires a solution.

Quantitative (Math)

1. D: Distance is the product of velocity and time, and

$$(5 \times 10^6) \times (2 \times 10^{-4}) = 10^1 \times 10^6 \times 10^{-4}$$
$$= 10^{1+6-4}$$
$$= 10^3$$
$$= 1000$$

2. C: 25% off is equivalent to $\frac{25}{100} \times \$138 = \$34.50$, so the sale price becomes $\$138 - \$34.50 = \$103.50$.

3. C: Recall the properties of exponents:

$$2^{-3} = \frac{1}{2^3} = \frac{1}{8}$$

4. A: As defined, the line will be described by the equation $y = 4x + 1$. Only point (2,9) is a valid solution to this equation:

$$9 = 4 \times 2 + 1$$
$$9 = 8 + 1$$
$$9 = 9$$

5. B: The value of the fraction $\frac{7}{5}$ can be evaluated by dividing 7 by 5, which yields 1.4. The average of 1.4 and 1.4 is $\frac{1.4+1.4}{2} = 1.4$.

6. C: The surface of a cube is obtained by multiplying the area of each face by 6, since there are 6 faces. The area of each face is the square of the length of one edge. Therefore $A = 6 \times 3^2 = 6 \times 9 = 54$.

7. A: The area A of a circle is given by $A = \pi \times r^2$, where r is the radius. Since π is approximately 3.14:

$$r = \sqrt{\frac{A}{\pi}} = \sqrt{\frac{314}{3.14}} = \sqrt{100} = 10 \text{ inches}$$

The diameter is twice the radius or 20 inches.

8. D: The circumference of a circle can be found using the formula $C = \pi d$, where d is the diameter of the circle.

$$35 = \pi d$$

$$d = \frac{35}{\pi} \approx 11.14$$

Therefore, the diameter of the circle is approximately 11.14 feet.

9. E: The sum of angles in a triangle is 180°. Solve for the remaining angle:

$$180° - (15° + 70°) = 95°$$

10. D: This answer may be determined using the law of sines, which relates the sides of a triangle and their opposing angles as follows.

$$\frac{a}{\sin A} = \frac{b}{\sin B} = \frac{c}{\sin C}$$

Substitute the known values, ignoring the angle C and side c since there is no information given or asked about these values.

$$\frac{14\ \text{cm}}{\sin A} = \frac{12\ \text{cm}}{\sin 35°}$$

From here, solve for A.

$$14 \sin 35° = 12 \sin A$$
$$\frac{14 \sin 35°}{12} = \sin A$$
$$\sin^{-1}\left(\frac{14 \sin 35°}{12}\right) = A$$
$$42° \approx A$$

Therefore, $\angle A \approx 42°$.

Alternatively, one can note that 14 is a little bit larger than 12, and consequently, angle A must be a little bit larger than angle B.

11. D: The total distance traveled was 8 miles + 3.6 miles = 11.6 miles. The first $\frac{1}{5}$ of a mile is charged at the higher rate. Since $\frac{1}{5} = 0.2$, the remainder of the trip is 11.4 miles. Thus, the fare for the distance traveled is computed as $5.50 + 5 \times 11.4 \times \$1.50 = \$91$. The charge for waiting time is added next, which is simply $9 \times 20¢ = 180¢ = \$1.80$. Finally, add the two charges, $\$91 + \$1.80 = \$92.80$.

12. B: The probability of playing a song by any band is proportional to the number of songs by that band over the total number of songs, or $\frac{5}{15} = \frac{1}{3}$ for Band D. The probability of playing any particular song is not affected by what has been played previously, since the choice is random.

13. A: Since 3 of the 15 songs are by Band B, the probability that any one song will be by that band is $\frac{3}{15} = \frac{1}{5}$. The probability that two successive events will occur is the product of the probabilities for any one event or, in this case $\frac{1}{5} \times \frac{1}{5} = \frac{1}{25}$.

14. B: A prime number is a natural, positive, non-zero number which can be factored only by itself and by 1. This is the case for 11.

15. E: Evaluate as follows: $(3x^{-2})^3 = 3^3 \times (x^{-2})^3 = 27x^{(-2 \times 3)} = 27x^{-6}$

16. D: Let P_A = the price of truck A and P_B that of truck B. Similarly let M_A and M_B represent the gas mileage obtained by each truck. The total cost of driving a truck n miles is

$$C = P + n \times \frac{\$4}{M}$$

To determine the break-even mileage, set the two cost equations equal to one another and solve for n:

$$P_A + n \times \frac{\$4}{M_A} = P_B + n \times \frac{\$4}{M_B}$$
$$n \times \left(\frac{\$4}{M_A} - \frac{\$4}{M_B}\right) = P_B - P_A$$
$$n = \frac{P_B - P_A}{(\frac{\$4}{M_A} - \frac{\$4}{M_B})}$$

Plugging in the given values:

$$n = \frac{650 - 450}{\left(\frac{4}{25} - \frac{4}{35}\right)} = \frac{200}{(0.16 - 0.11)} = 740 \text{ miles}$$

17. B: The lowest score, 68, is eliminated. The average of the remaining four grades is

$$\text{Avg} = \frac{75 + 88 + 86 + 90}{4} = 84.75$$

Rounding up to the nearest integer gives a final grade of 85.

18. C: The band's share, 25% of $20,000,000, is $5,000,000. After the agent's share is subtracted, the band gets $(1 - 0.15) \times \$5,000,000 = 0.85 \times \$5,000,000 = \$4,250,000$, and each band member gets one-fifth of that, or $850,000.

19. C: To find the value of y, cross multiply, isolate the variable, and simplify:

$$3(y + 4) = 15(y - 5)$$
$$15y - 3y = 12 + 75$$
$$12y = 87$$
$$y = \frac{87}{12} = \frac{29}{4}$$

20. B: The median is the value in a group of numbers that separates the upper half from the lower half, so that there are an equal number of values above and below it. In this distribution, there are two values greater than 116, and two values below it. 123.6 is the mean, or average of the distribution, not the median. 112 is the most common value, or mode of the distribution, not the median.

21. D: The product $(a)(a)(a)(a)(a)$ is defined as a to the fifth power, a^5.

22. B: $7.5 \times 10^{-4} = \frac{7.5}{10{,}000} = 0.00075$

23. A: Rearranging the equation gives $x^2 = -1$. However, the square of a real number cannot yield a negative result, so no real number solutions exist for the equation.

24. D: Jamet had $2.75 after all the transactions described. To solve this problem, first subtract $4.25 and $2.00 from the initial sum of $6.50, leaving $0.25. Then add $2.50, arriving at the final answer of $2.75.

25. D: Convert meters to centimeters and then use the conversion factor in the table to convert centimeters to inches. Recall that there are 100 centimeters in a meter (centi means "hundredth"). Therefore, $19 \text{ m} = 1900 \text{ cm} = \frac{1900}{2.54} = 748$ inches.

How to Overcome Test Anxiety

Just the thought of taking a test is enough to make most people a little nervous. A test is an important event that can have a long-term impact on your future, so it's important to take it seriously and it's natural to feel anxious about performing well. But just because anxiety is normal, that doesn't mean that it's helpful in test taking, or that you should simply accept it as part of your life. Anxiety can have a variety of effects. These effects can be mild, like making you feel slightly nervous, or severe, like blocking your ability to focus or remember even a simple detail.

If you experience test anxiety—whether severe or mild—it's important to know how to beat it. To discover this, first you need to understand what causes test anxiety.

Causes of Test Anxiety

While we often think of anxiety as an uncontrollable emotional state, it can actually be caused by simple, practical things. One of the most common causes of test anxiety is that a person does not feel adequately prepared for their test. This feeling can be the result of many different issues such as poor study habits or lack of organization, but the most common culprit is time management. Starting to study too late, failing to organize your study time to cover all of the material, or being distracted while you study will mean that you're not well prepared for the test. This may lead to cramming the night before, which will cause you to be physically and mentally exhausted for the test. Poor time management also contributes to feelings of stress, fear, and hopelessness as you realize you are not well prepared but don't know what to do about it.

Other times, test anxiety is not related to your preparation for the test but comes from unresolved fear. This may be a past failure on a test, or poor performance on tests in general. It may come from comparing yourself to others who seem to be performing better or from the stress of living up to expectations. Anxiety may be driven by fears of the future—how failure on this test would affect your educational and career goals. These fears are often completely irrational, but they can still negatively impact your test performance.

> **Review Video: 3 Reasons You Have Test Anxiety**
> Visit mometrix.com/academy and enter code: 428468

Elements of Test Anxiety

As mentioned earlier, test anxiety is considered to be an emotional state, but it has physical and mental components as well. Sometimes you may not even realize that you are suffering from test anxiety until you notice the physical symptoms. These can include trembling hands, rapid heartbeat, sweating, nausea, and tense muscles. Extreme anxiety may lead to fainting or vomiting. Obviously, any of these symptoms can have a negative impact on testing. It is important to recognize them as soon as they begin to occur so that you can address the problem before it damages your performance.

Review Video: 3 Ways to Tell You Have Test Anxiety
Visit mometrix.com/academy and enter code: 927847

The mental components of test anxiety include trouble focusing and inability to remember learned information. During a test, your mind is on high alert, which can help you recall information and stay focused for an extended period of time. However, anxiety interferes with your mind's natural processes, causing you to blank out, even on the questions you know well. The strain of testing during anxiety makes it difficult to stay focused, especially on a test that may take several hours. Extreme anxiety can take a huge mental toll, making it difficult not only to recall test information but even to understand the test questions or pull your thoughts together.

Review Video: How Test Anxiety Affects Memory
Visit mometrix.com/academy and enter code: 609003

Effects of Test Anxiety

Test anxiety is like a disease—if left untreated, it will get progressively worse. Anxiety leads to poor performance, and this reinforces the feelings of fear and failure, which in turn lead to poor performances on subsequent tests. It can grow from a mild nervousness to a crippling condition. If allowed to progress, test anxiety can have a big impact on your schooling, and consequently on your future.

Test anxiety can spread to other parts of your life. Anxiety on tests can become anxiety in any stressful situation, and blanking on a test can turn into panicking in a job situation. But fortunately, you don't have to let anxiety rule your testing and determine your grades. There are a number of relatively simple steps you can take to move past anxiety and function normally on a test and in the rest of life.

Review Video: How Test Anxiety Impacts Your Grades
Visit mometrix.com/academy and enter code: 939819

Physical Steps for Beating Test Anxiety

While test anxiety is a serious problem, the good news is that it can be overcome. It doesn't have to control your ability to think and remember information. While it may take time, you can begin taking steps today to beat anxiety.

Just as your first hint that you may be struggling with anxiety comes from the physical symptoms, the first step to treating it is also physical. Rest is crucial for having a clear, strong mind. If you are tired, it is much easier to give in to anxiety. But if you establish good sleep habits, your body and mind will be ready to perform optimally, without the strain of exhaustion. Additionally, sleeping well helps you to retain information better, so you're more likely to recall the answers when you see the test questions.

Getting good sleep means more than going to bed on time. It's important to allow your brain time to relax. Take study breaks from time to time so it doesn't get overworked, and don't study right before bed. Take time to rest your mind before trying to rest your body, or you may find it difficult to fall asleep.

Review Video: The Importance of Sleep for Your Brain
Visit mometrix.com/academy and enter code: 319338

Along with sleep, other aspects of physical health are important in preparing for a test. Good nutrition is vital for good brain function. Sugary foods and drinks may give a burst of energy but this burst is followed by a crash, both physically and emotionally. Instead, fuel your body with protein and vitamin-rich foods.

Also, drink plenty of water. Dehydration can lead to headaches and exhaustion, especially if your brain is already under stress from the rigors of the test. Particularly if your test is a long one, drink water during the breaks. And if possible, take an energy-boosting snack to eat between sections.

Review Video: How Diet Can Affect your Mood
Visit mometrix.com/academy and enter code: 624317

Along with sleep and diet, a third important part of physical health is exercise. Maintaining a steady workout schedule is helpful, but even taking 5-minute study breaks to walk can help get your blood pumping faster and clear your head. Exercise also releases endorphins, which contribute to a positive feeling and can help combat test anxiety.

When you nurture your physical health, you are also contributing to your mental health. If your body is healthy, your mind is much more likely to be healthy as well. So take time to rest, nourish your body with healthy food and water, and get moving as much as possible. Taking these physical steps will make you stronger and more able to take the mental steps necessary to overcome test anxiety.

281

Copyright © Mometrix Media. You have been licensed one copy of this document for personal use only. Any other reproduction or redistribution is strictly prohibited. All rights reserved. This content is provided for test preparation purposes only and does not imply an endorsement by Mometrix of any particular political, scientific, or religious point of view.

Mental Steps for Beating Test Anxiety

Working on the mental side of test anxiety can be more challenging, but as with the physical side, there are clear steps you can take to overcome it. As mentioned earlier, test anxiety often stems from lack of preparation, so the obvious solution is to prepare for the test. Effective studying may be the most important weapon you have for beating test anxiety, but you can and should employ several other mental tools to combat fear.

First, boost your confidence by reminding yourself of past success—tests or projects that you aced. If you're putting as much effort into preparing for this test as you did for those, there's no reason you should expect to fail here. Work hard to prepare; then trust your preparation.

Second, surround yourself with encouraging people. It can be helpful to find a study group, but be sure that the people you're around will encourage a positive attitude. If you spend time with others who are anxious or cynical, this will only contribute to your own anxiety. Look for others who are motivated to study hard from a desire to succeed, not from a fear of failure.

Third, reward yourself. A test is physically and mentally tiring, even without anxiety, and it can be helpful to have something to look forward to. Plan an activity following the test, regardless of the outcome, such as going to a movie or getting ice cream.

When you are taking the test, if you find yourself beginning to feel anxious, remind yourself that you know the material. Visualize successfully completing the test. Then take a few deep, relaxing breaths and return to it. Work through the questions carefully but with confidence, knowing that you are capable of succeeding.

Developing a healthy mental approach to test taking will also aid in other areas of life. Test anxiety affects more than just the actual test—it can be damaging to your mental health and even contribute to depression. It's important to beat test anxiety before it becomes a problem for more than testing.

> **Review Video: Test Anxiety and Depression**
> Visit mometrix.com/academy and enter code: 904704

Study Strategy

Being prepared for the test is necessary to combat anxiety, but what does being prepared look like? You may study for hours on end and still not feel prepared. What you need is a strategy for test prep. The next few pages outline our recommended steps to help you plan out and conquer the challenge of preparation.

STEP 1: SCOPE OUT THE TEST

Learn everything you can about the format (multiple choice, essay, etc.) and what will be on the test. Gather any study materials, course outlines, or sample exams that may be available. Not only will this help you to prepare, but knowing what to expect can help to alleviate test anxiety.

STEP 2: MAP OUT THE MATERIAL

Look through the textbook or study guide and make note of how many chapters or sections it has. Then divide these over the time you have. For example, if a book has 15 chapters and you have five days to study, you need to cover three chapters each day. Even better, if you have the time, leave an extra day at the end for overall review after you have gone through the material in depth.

If time is limited, you may need to prioritize the material. Look through it and make note of which sections you think you already have a good grasp on, and which need review. While you are studying, skim quickly through the familiar sections and take more time on the challenging parts. Write out your plan so you don't get lost as you go. Having a written plan also helps you feel more in control of the study, so anxiety is less likely to arise from feeling overwhelmed at the amount to cover.

STEP 3: GATHER YOUR TOOLS

Decide what study method works best for you. Do you prefer to highlight in the book as you study and then go back over the highlighted portions? Or do you type out notes of the important information? Or is it helpful to make flashcards that you can carry with you? Assemble the pens, index cards, highlighters, post-it notes, and any other materials you may need so you won't be distracted by getting up to find things while you study.

If you're having a hard time retaining the information or organizing your notes, experiment with different methods. For example, try color-coding by subject with colored pens, highlighters, or post-it notes. If you learn better by hearing, try recording yourself reading your notes so you can listen while in the car, working out, or simply sitting at your desk. Ask a friend to quiz you from your flashcards, or try teaching someone the material to solidify it in your mind.

STEP 4: CREATE YOUR ENVIRONMENT

It's important to avoid distractions while you study. This includes both the obvious distractions like visitors and the subtle distractions like an uncomfortable chair (or a too-comfortable couch that makes you want to fall asleep). Set up the best study environment possible: good lighting and a comfortable work area. If background music helps you focus, you may want to turn it on, but otherwise keep the room quiet. If you are using a computer to take notes, be sure you don't have any other windows open, especially applications like social media, games, or anything else that could distract you. Silence your phone and turn off notifications. Be sure to keep water close by so you stay hydrated while you study (but avoid unhealthy drinks and snacks).

Also, take into account the best time of day to study. Are you freshest first thing in the morning? Try to set aside some time then to work through the material. Is your mind clearer in the afternoon or evening? Schedule your study session then. Another method is to study at the same time of day that you will take the test, so that your brain gets used to working on the material at that time and will be ready to focus at test time.

STEP 5: STUDY!

Once you have done all the study preparation, it's time to settle into the actual studying. Sit down, take a few moments to settle your mind so you can focus, and begin to follow your study plan. Don't give in to distractions or let yourself procrastinate. This is your time to prepare so you'll be ready to fearlessly approach the test. Make the most of the time and stay focused.

Of course, you don't want to burn out. If you study too long you may find that you're not retaining the information very well. Take regular study breaks. For example, taking five minutes out of every hour to walk briskly, breathing deeply and swinging your arms, can help your mind stay fresh.

As you get to the end of each chapter or section, it's a good idea to do a quick review. Remind yourself of what you learned and work on any difficult parts. When you feel that you've mastered the material, move on to the next part. At the end of your study session, briefly skim through your notes again.

But while review is helpful, cramming last minute is NOT. If at all possible, work ahead so that you won't need to fit all your study into the last day. Cramming overloads your brain with more information than it can process and retain, and your tired mind may struggle to recall even previously learned information when it is overwhelmed with last-minute study. Also, the urgent nature of cramming and the stress placed on your brain contribute to anxiety. You'll be more likely to go to the test feeling unprepared and having trouble thinking clearly.

So don't cram, and don't stay up late before the test, even just to review your notes at a leisurely pace. Your brain needs rest more than it needs to go over the information again. In fact, plan to finish your studies by noon or early afternoon the day before the test. Give your brain the rest of the day to relax or focus on other things, and get a good night's sleep. Then you will be fresh for the test and better able to recall what you've studied.

STEP 6: TAKE A PRACTICE TEST

Many courses offer sample tests, either online or in the study materials. This is an excellent resource to check whether you have mastered the material, as well as to prepare for the test format and environment.

Check the test format ahead of time: the number of questions, the type (multiple choice, free response, etc.), and the time limit. Then create a plan for working through them. For example, if you have 30 minutes to take a 60-question test, your limit is 30 seconds per question. Spend less time on the questions you know well so that you can take more time on the difficult ones.

If you have time to take several practice tests, take the first one open book, with no time limit. Work through the questions at your own pace and make sure you fully understand them. Gradually work up to taking a test under test conditions: sit at a desk with all study materials put away and set a timer. Pace yourself to make sure you finish the test with time to spare and go back to check your answers if you have time.

After each test, check your answers. On the questions you missed, be sure you understand why you missed them. Did you misread the question (tests can use tricky wording)? Did you forget the information? Or was it something you hadn't learned? Go back and study any shaky areas that the practice tests reveal.

Taking these tests not only helps with your grade, but also aids in combating test anxiety. If you're already used to the test conditions, you're less likely to worry about it, and working through tests until you're scoring well gives you a confidence boost. Go through the practice tests until you feel comfortable, and then you can go into the test knowing that you're ready for it.

Test Tips

On test day, you should be confident, knowing that you've prepared well and are ready to answer the questions. But aside from preparation, there are several test day strategies you can employ to maximize your performance.

First, as stated before, get a good night's sleep the night before the test (and for several nights before that, if possible). Go into the test with a fresh, alert mind rather than staying up late to study.

Try not to change too much about your normal routine on the day of the test. It's important to eat a nutritious breakfast, but if you normally don't eat breakfast at all, consider eating just a protein bar. If you're a coffee drinker, go ahead and have your normal coffee. Just make sure you time it so that the caffeine doesn't wear off right in the middle of your test. Avoid sugary beverages, and drink enough water to stay hydrated but not so much that you need a restroom break 10 minutes into the test. If your test isn't first thing in the morning, consider going for a walk or doing a light workout before the test to get your blood flowing.

Allow yourself enough time to get ready, and leave for the test with plenty of time to spare so you won't have the anxiety of scrambling to arrive in time. Another reason to be early is to select a good seat. It's helpful to sit away from doors and windows, which can be distracting. Find a good seat, get out your supplies, and settle your mind before the test begins.

When the test begins, start by going over the instructions carefully, even if you already know what to expect. Make sure you avoid any careless mistakes by following the directions.

Then begin working through the questions, pacing yourself as you've practiced. If you're not sure on an answer, don't spend too much time on it, and don't let it shake your confidence. Either skip it and come back later, or eliminate as many wrong answers as possible and guess among the remaining ones. Don't dwell on these questions as you continue—put them out of your mind and focus on what lies ahead.

Be sure to read all of the answer choices, even if you're sure the first one is the right answer. Sometimes you'll find a better one if you keep reading. But don't second-guess yourself if you do immediately know the answer. Your gut instinct is usually right. Don't let test anxiety rob you of the information you know.

If you have time at the end of the test (and if the test format allows), go back and review your answers. Be cautious about changing any, since your first instinct tends to be correct, but make sure you didn't misread any of the questions or accidentally mark the wrong answer choice. Look over any you skipped and make an educated guess.

At the end, leave the test feeling confident. You've done your best, so don't waste time worrying about your performance or wishing you could change anything. Instead, celebrate the successful

Copyright © Mometrix Media. You have been licensed one copy of this document for personal use only. Any other reproduction or redistribution is strictly prohibited. All rights reserved.
This content is provided for test preparation purposes only and does not imply an endorsement by Mometrix of any particular political, scientific, or religious point of view.

completion of this test. And finally, use this test to learn how to deal with anxiety even better next time.

Important Qualification

Not all anxiety is created equal. If your test anxiety is causing major issues in your life beyond the classroom or testing center, or if you are experiencing troubling physical symptoms related to your anxiety, it may be a sign of a serious physiological or psychological condition. If this sounds like your situation, we strongly encourage you to seek professional help.

How to Overcome Your Fear of Math

Not again. You're sitting in math class, look down at your test, and immediately start to panic. Your stomach is in knots, your heart is racing, and you break out in a cold sweat. You're staring at the paper, but everything looks like it's written in a foreign language. Even though you studied, you're blanking out on how to begin solving these problems.

Does this sound familiar? If so, then you're not alone! You may be like millions of other people who experience math anxiety. Anxiety about performing well in math is a common experience for students of all ages. In this article, we'll discuss what math anxiety is, common misconceptions about learning math, and tips and strategies for overcoming math anxiety.

What Is Math Anxiety?

Psychologist Mark H. Ashcraft explains math anxiety as a feeling of tension, apprehension, or fear that interferes with math performance. Having math anxiety negatively impacts people's beliefs about themselves and what they can achieve. It hinders achievement within the math classroom and affects the successful application of mathematics in the real world.

SYMPTOMS AND SIGNS OF MATH ANXIETY

To overcome math anxiety, you must recognize its symptoms. Becoming aware of the signs of math anxiety is the first step in addressing and resolving these fears.

NEGATIVE SELF-TALK

If you have math anxiety, you've most likely said at least one of these statements to yourself:

- "I hate math."
- "I'm not good at math."
- "I'm not a math person."

The way we speak to ourselves and think about ourselves matters. Our thoughts become our words, our words become our actions, and our actions become our habits. Thinking negatively about math creates a self-fulfilling prophecy. In other words, if you take an idea as a fact, then it will come true because your behaviors will align to match it.

AVOIDANCE

Some people who are fearful or anxious about math will tend to avoid it altogether. Avoidance can manifest in the following ways:

- Lack of engagement with math content
- Not completing homework and other assignments
- Not asking for help when needed
- Skipping class
- Avoiding math-related courses and activities

Avoidance is one of the most harmful impacts of math anxiety. If you steer clear of math at all costs, then you can't set yourself up for the success you deserve.

LACK OF MOTIVATION

Students with math anxiety may experience a lack of motivation. They may struggle to find the incentive to get engaged with what they view as a frightening subject. These students are often overwhelmed, making it difficult for them to complete or even start math assignments.

PROCRASTINATION

Another symptom of math anxiety is procrastination. Students may voluntarily delay or postpone their classwork and assignments, even if they know there will be a negative consequence for doing so. Additionally, they may choose to wait until the last minute to start projects and homework, even when they know they need more time to put forth their best effort.

PHYSIOLOGICAL REACTIONS

Many people with a fear of math experience physiological side effects. These may include an increase in heart rate, sweatiness, shakiness, nausea, and irregular breathing. These symptoms make it difficult to focus on the math content, causing the student even more stress and fear.

STRONG EMOTIONAL RESPONSES

Math anxiety also affects people on an emotional level. Responding to math content with strong emotions such as panic, anger, or despair can be a sign of math anxiety.

LOW TEST SCORES AND PERFORMANCE

Low achievement can be both a symptom and a cause of math anxiety. When someone does not take the steps needed to perform well on tests and assessments, they are less likely to pass. The more they perform poorly, the more they accept this poor performance as a fact that can't be changed.

FEELING ALONE

People who experience math anxiety feel like they are the only ones struggling, even if the math they are working on is challenging to many people. Feeling isolated in what they perceive as failure can trigger tension or nervousness.

FEELING OF PERMANENCY

Math anxiety can feel very permanent. You may assume that you are naturally bad at math and always will be. Viewing math as a natural ability rather than a skill that can be learned causes people to believe that nothing will help them improve. They take their current math abilities as fact and assume that they can't be changed. As a result, they give up, stop trying to improve, and avoid engaging with math altogether.

LACK OF CONFIDENCE

People with low self-confidence in math tend to feel awkward and incompetent when asked to solve a math problem. They don't feel comfortable taking chances or risks when problem-solving because they second-guess themselves and assume they are incorrect. They don't trust in their ability to learn the content and solve problems correctly.

PANIC

A general sense of unexplained panic is also a sign of math anxiety. You may feel a sudden sense of fear that triggers physical reactions, even when there is no apparent reason for such a response.

CAUSES OF MATH ANXIETY

Math anxiety can start at a young age and may have one or more underlying causes. Common causes of math anxiety include the following:

THE ATTITUDE OF PARENTS OR GUARDIANS

Parents often put pressure on their children to perform well in school. Although their intentions are usually good, this pressure can lead to anxiety, especially if the student is struggling with a subject or class.

Perhaps your parents or others in your life hold negative predispositions about math based on their own experiences. For instance, if your mother once claimed she was not good at math, then you might have incorrectly interpreted this as a predisposed trait that was passed down to you.

TEACHER INFLUENCE

Students often pick up on their teachers' attitudes about the content being taught. If a teacher is happy and excited about math, students are more likely to mirror these emotions. However, if a teacher lacks enthusiasm or genuine interest, then students are more inclined to disengage.

Teachers have a responsibility to cultivate a welcoming classroom culture that is accepting of mistakes. When teachers blame students for not understanding a concept, they create a hostile classroom environment where mistakes are not tolerated. This tension increases student stress and anxiety, creating conditions that are not conducive to inquiry and learning. Instead, when teachers normalize mistakes as a natural part of the problem-solving process, they give their students the freedom to explore and grapple with the math content. In such an environment, students feel comfortable taking chances because they are not afraid of being wrong.

Students need teachers that can help when they're having problems understanding difficult concepts. In doing so, educators may need to change how they teach the content. Since different people have unique learning styles, it's the job of the teacher to adapt to the needs of each student. Additionally, teachers should encourage students to explore alternate problem-solving strategies, even if it's not the preferred method of the educator.

FEAR OF BEING WRONG

Embarrassing situations can be traumatic, especially for young children and adolescents. These experiences can stay with people through their adult lives. Those with math anxiety may experience a fear of being wrong, especially in front of a group of peers. This fear can be paralyzing, interfering with the student's concentration and ability to focus on the problem at hand.

TIMED ASSESSMENTS

Timed assessments can help improve math fluency, but they often create unnecessary pressure for students to complete an unrealistic number of problems within a specified timeframe. Many studies have shown that timed assessments often result in increased levels of anxiety, reducing a student's overall competence and ability to problem-solve.

Debunking Math Myths

There are lots of myths about math that are related to the causes and development of math-related anxiety. Although these myths have been proven to be false, many people take them as fact. Let's go over a few of the most common myths about learning math.

MYTH: MEN ARE BETTER AT MATH THAN WOMEN

Math has a reputation for being a male-dominant subject, but this doesn't mean that men are inherently better at math than women. Many famous mathematical discoveries have been made by women. Katherine Johnson, Dame Mary Lucy Cartwright, and Marjorie Lee Brown are just a few of the many famous women mathematicians. Expecting to be good or bad at math because of your gender sets you up for stress and confusion. Math is a skill that can be learned, just like cooking or riding a bike.

MYTH: THERE IS ONLY ONE GOOD WAY TO SOLVE MATH PROBLEMS

There are many ways to get the correct answer when it comes to math. No two people have the same brain, so everyone takes a slightly different approach to problem-solving. Moreover, there isn't one way of problem-solving that's superior to another. Your way of working through a problem might differ from someone else's, and that is okay. Math can be a highly individualized process, so the best method for you should be the one that makes you feel the most comfortable and makes the most sense to you.

MYTH: MATH REQUIRES A GOOD MEMORY

For many years, mathematics was taught through memorization. However, learning in such a way hinders the development of critical thinking and conceptual understanding. These skill sets are much more valuable than basic memorization. For instance, you might be great at memorizing mathematical formulas, but if you don't understand what they mean, then you can't apply them to different scenarios in the real world. When a student is working from memory, they are limited in the strategies available to them to problem-solve. In other words, they assume there is only one correct way to do the math, which is the method they memorized. Having a variety of problem-solving options can help students figure out which method works best for them. Additionally, it provides students with a better understanding of how and why certain mathematical strategies work. While memorization can be helpful in some instances, it is not an absolute requirement for mathematicians.

MYTH: MATH IS NOT CREATIVE

Math requires imagination and intuition. Contrary to popular belief, it is a highly creative field. Mathematical creativity can help in developing new ways to think about and solve problems. Many people incorrectly assume that all things are either creative or analytical. However, this black-and-white view is limiting because the field of mathematics involves both creativity and logic.

MYTH: MATH ISN'T SUPPOSED TO BE FUN

Whoever told you that math isn't supposed to be fun is a liar. There are tons of math-based activities and games that foster friendly competition and engagement. Math is often best learned through play, and lots of mobile apps and computer games exemplify this.

Additionally, math can be an exceptionally collaborative and social experience. Studying or working through problems with a friend often makes the process a lot more fun. The excitement and satisfaction of solving a difficult problem with others is quite rewarding. Math can be fun if you look for ways to make it more collaborative and enjoyable.

Myth: Not Everyone Is Capable of Learning Math

There's no such thing as a "math person." Although many people think that you're either good at math or you're not, this is simply not true. Everyone is capable of learning and applying mathematics. However, not everyone learns the same way. Since each person has a different learning style, the trick is to find the strategies and learning tools that work best for you. Some people learn best through hands-on experiences, and others find success through the use of visual aids. Others are auditory learners and learn best by hearing and listening. When people are overwhelmed or feel that math is too hard, it's often because they haven't found the learning strategy that works best for them.

Myth: Good Mathematicians Work Quickly and Never Make Mistakes

There is no prize for finishing first in math. It's not a race, and speed isn't a measure of your ability. Good mathematicians take their time to ensure their work is accurate. As you gain more experience and practice, you will naturally become faster and more confident.

Additionally, everyone makes mistakes, including good mathematicians. Mistakes are a normal part of the problem-solving process, and they're not a bad thing. The important thing is that we take the time to learn from our mistakes, understand where our misconceptions are, and move forward.

Myth: You Don't Need Math in the Real World

Our day-to-day lives are so infused with mathematical concepts that we often don't even realize when we're using math in the real world. In fact, most people tend to underestimate how much we do math in our everyday lives. It's involved in an enormous variety of daily activities such as shopping, baking, finances, and gardening, as well as in many careers, including architecture, nursing, design, and sales.

Tips and Strategies for Overcoming Math Anxiety

If your anxiety is getting in the way of your level of mathematical engagement, then there are lots of steps you can take. Check out the strategies below to start building confidence in math today.

Focus on Understanding, Not Memorization

Don't drive yourself crazy trying to memorize every single formula or mathematical process. Instead, shift your attention to understanding concepts. Those who prioritize memorization over conceptual understanding tend to have lower achievement levels in math. Students who memorize may be able to complete some math, but they don't understand the process well enough to apply it to different situations. Memorization comes with time and practice, but it won't help alleviate math anxiety. On the other hand, conceptual understanding will give you the building blocks of knowledge you need to build up your confidence.

REPLACE NEGATIVE SELF-TALK WITH POSITIVE SELF-TALK

Start to notice how you think about yourself. Whenever you catch yourself thinking something negative, try replacing that thought with a positive affirmation. Instead of continuing the negative thought, pause to reframe the situation. For ideas on how to get started, take a look at the table below:

Instead of thinking...	Try thinking...
"I can't do this math." "I'm not a math person."	"I'm up for the challenge, and I'm training my brain in math."
"This problem is too hard."	"This problem is hard, so this might take some time and effort. I know I can do this."
"I give up."	"What strategies can help me solve this problem?"
"I made a mistake, so I'm not good at this."	"Everyone makes mistakes. Mistakes help me to grow and understand."
"I'll never be smart enough."	"I can figure this out, and I am smart enough."

PRACTICE MINDFULNESS

Practicing mindfulness and focusing on your breathing can help alleviate some of the physical symptoms of math anxiety. By taking deep breaths, you can remind your nervous system that you are not in immediate danger. Doing so will reduce your heart rate and help with any irregular breathing or shakiness. Taking the edge off of the physiological effects of anxiety will clear your mind, allowing your brain to focus its energy on problem-solving.

DO SOME MATH EVERY DAY

Think about learning math as if you were learning a foreign language. If you don't use it, you lose it. If you don't practice your math skills regularly, you'll have a harder time achieving comprehension and fluency. Set some amount of time aside each day, even if it's just for a few minutes, to practice. It might take some discipline to build a habit around this, but doing so will help increase your mathematical self-assurance.

USE ALL OF YOUR RESOURCES

Everyone has a different learning style, and there are plenty of resources out there to support all learners. When you get stuck on a math problem, think about the tools you have access to, and use them when applicable. Such resources may include flashcards, graphic organizers, study guides, interactive notebooks, and peer study groups. All of these are great tools to accommodate your individual learning style. Finding the tools and resources that work for your learning style will give you the confidence you need to succeed.

REALIZE THAT YOU AREN'T ALONE

Remind yourself that lots of other people struggle with math anxiety, including teachers, nurses, and even successful mathematicians. You aren't the only one who panics when faced with a new or challenging problem. It's probably much more common than you think. Realizing that you aren't alone in your experience can help put some distance between yourself and the emotions you feel about math. It also helps to normalize the anxiety and shift your perspective.

ASK QUESTIONS

If there's a concept you don't understand and you've tried everything you can, then it's okay to ask for help! You can always ask your teacher or professor for help. If you're not learning math in a traditional classroom, you may want to join a study group, work with a tutor, or talk to your friends. More often than not, you aren't the only one of your peers who needs clarity on a mathematical concept. Seeking understanding is a great way to increase self-confidence in math.

REMEMBER THAT THERE'S MORE THAN ONE WAY TO SOLVE A PROBLEM

Since everyone learns differently, it's best to focus on understanding a math problem with an approach that makes sense to you. If the way it's being taught is confusing to you, don't give up. Instead, work to understand the problem using a different technique. There's almost always more than one problem-solving method when it comes to math. Don't get stressed if one of them doesn't make sense to you. Instead, shift your focus to what does make sense. Chances are high that you know more than you think you do.

VISUALIZATION

Visualization is the process of creating images in your mind's eye. Picture yourself as a successful, confident mathematician. Think about how you would feel and how you would behave. What would your work area look like? How would you organize your belongings? The more you focus on something, the more likely you are to achieve it. Visualizing teaches your brain that you can achieve whatever it is that you want. Thinking about success in mathematics will lead to acting like a successful mathematician. This, in turn, leads to actual success.

FOCUS ON THE EASIEST PROBLEMS FIRST

To increase your confidence when working on a math test or assignment, try solving the easiest problems first. Doing so will remind you that you are successful in math and that you do have what it takes. This process will increase your belief in yourself, giving you the confidence you need to tackle more complex problems.

FIND A SUPPORT GROUP

A study buddy, tutor, or peer group can go a long way in decreasing math-related anxiety. Such support systems offer lots of benefits, including a safe place to ask questions, additional practice with mathematical concepts, and an understanding of other problem-solving explanations that may work better for you. Equipping yourself with a support group is one of the fastest ways to eliminate math anxiety.

REWARD YOURSELF FOR WORKING HARD

Recognize the amount of effort you're putting in to overcome your math anxiety. It's not an easy task, so you deserve acknowledgement. Surround yourself with people who will provide you with the positive reinforcement you deserve.

Remember, You Can Do This!

Conquering a fear of math can be challenging, but there are lots of strategies that can help you out. Your own beliefs about your mathematical capabilities can limit your potential. Working toward a growth mindset can have a tremendous impact on decreasing math-related anxiety and building confidence. By knowing the symptoms of math anxiety and recognizing common misconceptions about learning math, you can develop a plan to address your fear of math. Utilizing the strategies discussed can help you overcome this anxiety and build the confidence you need to succeed.

Tell Us Your Story

We at Mometrix would like to extend our heartfelt thanks to you for letting us be a part of your journey. It is an honor to serve people from all walks of life, people like you, who are committed to building the best future they can for themselves.

We know that each person's situation is unique. But we also know that, whether you are a young student or a mother of four, you care about working to make your own life and the lives of those around you better.

That's why we want to hear your story.

We want to know why you're taking this test. We want to know about the trials you've gone through to get here. And we want to know about the successes you've experienced after taking and passing your test.

In addition to your story, which can be an inspiration both to us and to others, we value your feedback. We want to know both what you loved about our book and what you think we can improve on.

The team at Mometrix would be absolutely thrilled to hear from you! So please, send us an email at tellusyourstory@mometrix.com or visit us at mometrix.com/tellusyourstory.php and let's stay in touch.

294

Additional Bonus Material

Due to our efforts to try to keep this book to a manageable length, we've created a link that will give you access to all of your additional bonus material:

mometrix.com/bonus948/ssatupper